Christianity

A Biblical, Historical, and Theological Guide for Students

MERCER
UNIVERSITY PRESS

Endowed by
TOM WATSON BROWN
and
THE WATSON-BROWN FOUNDATION, INC.

Christianity

A Biblical, Historical, and Theological Guide for Students

by
Kathryn Muller Lopez
Donald N. Penny
W. Glenn Jonas,
and
Adam C. English

MERCER UNIVERSITY PRESS
MACON, GEORGIA USA
2010

Christianity.
A Biblical, Historical, and Theological Guide for Students
Copyright ©2010
Mercer University Press
All rights reserved
Printed in the United States of America
First edition

Mercer University Press is a member of Green Press Initiative <greenpress initiative.org>, a nonprofit organization working to help publishers and printers increase their use of recycled paper and decrease their use of fiber derived from endangered forests. This book is printed on recycled paper and meets the minimum requirements of American National Standard for Information Sciences—Permanence of Paper for Printed Library Materials, ANSI Z39.48-1984.

Maps are from *The Mercer Dictionary of the Bible*, ed. Watson E. Mills et al. (Macon GA: Mercer University Press, 1990ff.) as created by Margaret Jordan Brown, and are used by permission. Permissions for other illustrations are noted at points of insert (see the list on p. 6).

Library of Congress Cataloging-in-Publication Data

Isbn 978-0-88146-204-3

[CIP is available from the Library of Congress]

Contents

List of Maps, Charts, Texts

Foreword and Acknowledgments

Pick a church house. Most any church house. And go inside. Certain things immediately stand out. More than likely, you will find a pulpit, a choir loft, a "baptistry" (especially in Baptist and other like-minded church houses)—that is, a small enclosed pool of water used to submerge and baptize new converts into the fellowship and family of God, a communion or Lord's Supper table, various crosses, and musical instruments—usually a piano and/or organ. With little effort, you will also find multiple copies of the Bible scattered throughout the congregation pews or chairs and on the pulpit and in other parts of the building.

What is the meaning of all this?

Church buildings are wonderful amalgamations of religious conviction, social and historical setting, artistic yearning, and spiritual reverence. Whether in Atlanta's Ebenezer Baptist Church, the home church of Martin Luther King, Jr., with its strong ties to the Civil Rights movement; or in the Basilica of Santa Maria in Trastevere, one of the oldest churches in Rome, with its colorful apse mosaic featuring Jesus enthroned, his arm lovingly draped over his mother's shoulder; or in one of the eleven stunning Lalibela churches in central Ethiopia, each one chiseled out of a single mass of subterranean rock sometime in the thirteenth century and entered only by way of manmade underground tunnels—you find both diversity and commonality, some things you would recognize from other church houses and some things that are unique.

In this book we want to highlight the commonality—those beliefs, practices, ideas, symbols, and events that link together Christians from around the globe and throughout the ages. What is it that identifies Christians as Christians, whether in Ethiopia or California, whether in the first century or the twenty-first?

We want to answer that question in a way that is both basic and broad. We want to offer a short introduction to Christianity that can be read by those who grew up in church and those who have never set foot inside a church. For those who were baptized as infants and reared in the shadow of the steeple, this is a chance to put together in one complete picture many of the different puzzle pieces of your faith. For those unfamiliar with the Christian faith, this is a chance to learn about the religious tradition embraced by nearly two billion people today—by far the largest and most influential religion the world has ever known.

But where should we begin? The most obvious place to begin might be with the question, "What do Christians believe?" or "What do Christians do?" We naturally and rightly want to know what are the core beliefs and practices of this faith. However, these initial and important questions must wait. In order to answer questions about what Christians believe and do we must first consider the main source and fount of all Christian belief and practice: the Bible. Everything that Christians say and do, from the practice of baptism to the belief in Jesus, originates in this book. If we get the Bible right, everything else will fall into place; if we overlook the Bible, then the rest of it will probably not make sense.

Kathryn Lopez will guide us through the twists and turns of the Old Testament story, beginning with the creation account and working through the histories of the patriarchs, Israel, and the prophets. Attention will be given to the various themes and trends that emerge in the overall story, as well as the different genres of writing that also emerge. Donald Penny will introduce the New Testament, focusing on the four gospels, the life of Jesus and rise of the early church, the letters of Paul, and the other writings.

Taken together, roughly half of this introduction to Christianity will be devoted to unpacking the Bible, its themes, events, and personalities. Christians are "people of the Book" after all. Once we have explored this central witness and source of revelation, will we then be ready to give a full description of Christian belief and practice? Not yet. We cannot jump from the Bible to present-day Christianity. To do so would be to ignore the fact that almost two thousand years have elapsed between the end of the New Testament and our present-day situation. Christians today are not the same as they were in the days of Peter and Paul. We have printed Bibles, Bibles in multiple languages, hymnals, theology manuals, sizeable church buildings, seminaries for training ministers, denominations, and even more denominations. How did all this come about? How did Christianity ever spread beyond the borders of Galilee and Palestine? How did it become such a major world force? Why are there so many different kinds of churches today?

Glenn Jonas will answer all these questions and more as he surveys the history of the church and the Christian faith. Emphasis will be given to the major movements and personalities in an attempt to show how we got from there to here, from Jesus' world to ours.

Finally we will be in a position to entertain our initial questions, "What do Christians believe? What do Christians do?" Only then will we be in a position to fully understand Christian practices and beliefs. Adam English will address Christian worship and the major tenets of belief, beginning with the Trinity and ending with resurrection.

Our journey will take us across biblical, historical, and theological terrain. There will be surprises, challenges, and delights along the way. As we go, let's remember the words of the Lord calling Joshua to cross the Jordan River, "Be strong and courageous. Do not be terrified; do not be discouraged, for the LORD your God will be with you wherever you go" (Joshua 1:9).

Acknowledgments

The authors acknowledge with gratitude Phebie Smith, Jenny Lee, Mark Batten, Cody McCain, Amanda Eckelkamp, Nell Grimm, Wayne Ballard, Dean Martin, Marc Jolley, the editors of Mercer University Press, and our colleagues at Campbell University.

Books of the Old Testament/Hebrew Bible[1]

Old Testament
  (The Pentateuch/Law)
    Genesis
    Exodus
    Leviticus
    Numbers
    Deuteronomy
  (The Historical Books)
    Joshua
    Judges
    Ruth
    1, 2 Samuel
    1, 2 Kings
    1, 2 Chronicles
    Ezra
    Nehemiah
    Esther
  (The Poetical and Wisdom Books)
    Job
    Psalms
    Proverbs
    Ecclesiastes
    Song of Songs/Solomon
  (The Prophetic Books)

Isaiah	Hosea
Jeremiah	Joel
Lamentations	Amos
Ezekiel	Obadiah
Daniel	Jonah
	Micah
	Nahum
	Habakkuk
	Zephaniah
	Haggai
	Zechariah
	Malachi

Hebrew Bible
  (Torah, The Five Books of Moses)
    Genesis
    Exodus
    Leviticus
    Numbers
    Deuteronomy
  (Nevi'im, The Prophets)
    Joshua
    Judges
    (1,2) Samuel
    (1,2) Kings
    Isaiah
    Jeremiah
    Ezekiel
    (Book of the Twelve)

Hosea	Nahum
Joel	Habakkuk
Amos	Zephaniah
Obadiah	Haggai
Jonah	Zechariah
Micah	Malachi

  (Ketuvim, The Writings)
    Psalms
    Proverbs
    Job
    Song of Songs
    Ruth
    Lamentations
    Ecclesiastes
    Esther
    Daniel
    Ezra/Nehemiah
    (1,2) Chronicles

---

[1]The names of the individual books and their order follows that of Protestant Bibles for the Old Testament and that of *TaNaKh—The Holy Scriptures. The New JPS Translation according to the Traditional Hebrew Text* (1962–1985) for the Hebrew Bible. Section descriptions (Law, History, Prophets, etc.) of course are arbitrary and (may) differ from one tradition to another.

Apocrypha/Deuterocanonicals[2]

Tobit
Judith
Additions to Esther (Greek)
Wisdom of Solomon
Sirach (Ecclesiasticus)
Baruch
Letter of Jeremiah
Additions to Daniel
    Prayer of Azariah and the
       Song of the Three Jews
    Susanna
    Bel and the Dragon
1, 2 Maccabees
(In some Orthodox Bibles, not RCC)
1 Esdras
Prayer of Manasseh
Psalm 151
3 Maccabees
(In Slavonic Bibles
and the Vulgate appendix)
2 Esdras
(Appended to some Greek Bibles)
4 Maccabees

New Testament

(Gospels)
    Matthew
    Mark
    Luke
    John
(History)
    Acts of the Apostles
(Letters)
    ("Pauline" Letters)
    Romans
    1, 2 Corinthians
    Galatians
    Ephesians
    Philippians
    Colossians
    1, 2 Thessalonians
    1, 2 Timothy
    Titus
    Philemon
    (General Epistles)
    Hebrews
    James
    1, 2 Peter
    1, 2, 3 John
    Jude
(Apocalypse)
    Revelation

---

[2]In general, the names and order of the apocryphal/deuterocanonical books follow the so-called "ecumenical" editions of Protestant Bibles, e.g., the RSV/NRSV, NEB/REB, and the TEV/CEV. Older Protestant Bibles—e.g., the Geneva Bible and KJV/ERV—have only fourteen or fifteen apocryphal books (depending on whether one counts Baruch and the Letter of Jeremiah as one book or two), and they appear in the more traditional order, that is, beginning with 1, 2 Esdras. Beginning with later editions of the KJV and then the ASV, some—especially Protestant, "Evangelical" Bibles—eschew the Apocrypha/Deuterocanonicals and omit those writings altogether.

Part one

The Old Testament

• 1 •

Reading the Old Testament

What is Christianity? There are many different ways to address this question. This book will begin with the Bible. Christians believe the Bible is the basis for our understanding of God and God's work in our world. Christians trace all their religious beliefs and practices to the Bible in some way. To understand the Bible, therefore, is to understand the foundation of the Christian faith. Through the Bible we find there are many different ways of knowing God and many different things to know about God, culminating in the life, death, and resurrection of Jesus Christ. The study of Scripture is important to the Christian faith, but it should not be approached lightly or casually. It takes work to read and understand the Bible well.

Some Basics

The Christian Bible has two parts: the Old Testament and the New Testament. Another word for testament is covenant. While we call it a covenant or testament, a better word might be relationship. In both the Old and New Testament the choice to live in relationship is God's. In the Old Testament God's choice of the people of Israel begins with Abraham and culminates in the making of a covenant based on God's revelation to Moses and the people at Mt. Sinai. The New Testament or covenant represents the work of God through the person of Jesus Christ.

Some of you may have never read the Bible, and some of you may have read it cover to cover. Do you know how to find a reference in the Bible? Every book of the Bible is divided into chapters and verses.[1] If your assignment is to read Genesis 1:3, you would go to the third verse of the first chapter of the book of Genesis. If you do not know where Genesis is, just look it up in the table of contents! All the books of the Bible are listed in order at the beginning of the Bible. If you are asked to read Genesis 1–2, you would read the first two chapters of the book of Genesis. One more example: If you were asked to read Genesis 1:1–2:4, you would begin

---

[1] While useful for finding a text, the chapter and verse divisions are not original. They were added in the medieval period.

reading at the first verse of Genesis chapter one and continue reading through the fourth verse of the second chapter.

[N.B. Except where indicated, all dates are BCE, Before the Common Era.]

The Early History

2000–1550 . . . . The Patriarchs
1550–1200 . . . . Oppression in Egypt, The Exodus, Wilderness Wanderings
1200–1000 . . . . Period of the Judges

The Monarchy

1000–922 . . . . The United Monarchy (David and Solomon)
922–587 . . . . The Divided Monarchy:
                    Northern Kingdom—Israel; Southern Kingdom–Judah

The Assyrian Period

Eighth Century . . . . Beginning of Prophetic Activity in Israel/Judah
722 . . . . The Fall of the Southern Kingdom to the Assyrians

The Babylonian Period

640–609 . . . . The Reforms of King Josiah of Judah
597 . . . . Fall of Jerusalem to the Babylonians
587 . . . Destruction of the Temple by the Babylonians and the Exile in Babylon
539 . . . . Fall of Babylon to Cyrus
538(?) . . . . The Return of the Exiles and Temple Objects to Judah
520–515 . . . . The Rebuilding of the Temple

The Hellenistic Period

332 . . . . Alexander the Great Conquers Palestine
175–164 . . . . The Reign of Antiochus IV Epiphanes
167 . . . . Rededication of the Temple
143–63 . . . . Hasmonean Control of Palestine

The Roman Period

63 . . . . Takeover of Jerusalem by the Romans
70 CE . . . . The Destruction of the Temple by the Romans

Canon

Did the people who wrote the Bible sit down one day and say to themselves, "Today I am going to write a book of the Bible"? Probably not. Parts of the Old Testament may have been written as long ago as 1000 BCE and some as late as the 160s BCE.[2] In other words, the Old Testament took more than 800 years to write. Many people were involved in the writing and transmission of the words that both Judaism and Christianity now consider to be sacred. As they were written and collected, these writings became more and more standardized and more and more authoritative until they reached the form in which we have them today. Can we add or take away a book from the Bible? The answer is no, we cannot. This is because the Bible is now what we would call a closed canon. "Canon" is a word meaning reed, measuring stick, or standard. The Bible is a standard, an authority in matters of faith and practice; and it is a closed canon, meaning we can neither add to it nor take away from it.

The process of canonization of the Old Testament began after the return from the exile in 539 BCE and continued well into the first century CE (see the history chart above). One of the major motivations for the final canonization of the Old Testament was the destruction of the temple in 70 CE, when Judaism lost its physical and spiritual center. At the time of the fall of Jerusalem, a group of Rabbis (Jewish teachers and religious leaders) went to a town on the coast of Israel called Jamnia and began to rethink what it meant to be Jewish. It is from these men that Judaism as we know it developed, including the basic canon of Scripture Christians call the Old Testament.

But is the Old Testament/Hebrew Bible the same for all Christians and Jews? Look at the chart on page 10. The Protestant Old Testament and the Hebrew Bible are in a different order, but the books are the same. However, there are differences among what various Christian groups agree is contained in the Old Testament. The Roman Catholic Old Testament is much longer than the Protestant Old Testament. It contains books and additions to books that are not in the Protestant and Jewish Bibles. Look at the list of books on page 10 again. The writings contained in the Roman Catholic Bible but not the Protestant and Jewish Bibles are collectively known as the

---

[2]BCE = Before the Common Era; CE = the Common Era. These more neutral terms correspond to BC and AD.

Apocrypha or Deuterocanonical writings. The Apocrypha was part of all Christian Bibles until the Reformation, when the Protestant reformers rejected it as authoritative and began to remove it from further editions of the Protestant Old Testament. The Roman Catholic Church continues to use the Apocrypha as authoritative for the Roman Catholic faith.

A final note before we move on: Historically, the Old Testament came together in three parts. We know this from many sources, including Jesus who refers to the Law, the Prophets, and the Psalms (Luke 24:44). Modern scholars call this threefold division of the Old Testament the *TaNaKh*, an acronym derived from the Hebrew names for these three sections.

---

*T*orah—Law (Most Christians refer to this section as the Pentateuch.)
a
*N*ebi'im—Prophets
a
*Kh*etubim—Writings

Dating the sections of the Tanakh is difficult. Generally, scholars believe the Torah began to come together during the period of the exile and immediately afterwards. At the other end, the contents of the Khetubim, particularly the book of Psalms, remained somewhat fluid until the first century BCE or even the first century CE. The presentation of the Old Testament in this book will be organized according the ordering of the books found in the Tanakh.

Translating the Hebrew Bible

The Old Testament was originally written in Hebrew and Aramaic, so what we read in English is a translation of the original language. This leads us to another question: What did the people who produced our modern translations base their translation on? Obviously, we would want to use the most ancient and accurate copies of the Bible available to us; but there are many ancient copies of the Bible, and they do not always agree. This does not mean, however, that there is no hope for providing a reliable translation of the Bible.

We have many ancient copies of parts or the whole of the Old Testament that can be divided into basically two traditions based on language: Hebrew and Greek. The Hebrew tradition is known as the

Masoretic Text, but the oldest complete copy of the Masoretic Text dates to about 1000 CE. Why are there no older complete copies than this? It was the practice in ancient synagogues (Jewish houses of worship) to burn any damaged or worn copies of Scripture. This was a matter of respect, just as today we "retire" American flags and burn them when they are damaged or worn. Because of this, very few ancient copies of the Hebrew survived. The Masoretic Text is named after a group of men known as the Masoretes, whose job was to produce reliable copies of the Old Testament as the older copies wore out. They operated much like an ancient guild, passing from one generation to the next the sacred task of accurately preserving the text of the Old Testament.

Beginning in the late 1940s, archeologists discovered a large cache of Hebrew documents in the area surrounding the Dead Sea, in the southern part of modern Israel, some of which date to as early as the third century BCE. Among these documents were found at least a partial copy of every book of the Old Testament except Esther. These ancient copies of the Scripture, written in Hebrew, are known as the Dead Sea Scrolls. While incomplete, these ancient documents have been a great help to modern scholars, and they have confirmed that the Masoretic Text is a highly accurate transmission of the ancient Hebrew. The Masoretes were very good at their craft, and today almost all translations of the Old Testament are based on the Masoretic Text.

The second tradition, known as the Septuagint, comes from ancient Greek translations of the older Hebrew. In the centuries before Christ, Jews began to spread throughout the Greco-Roman world. For example, there was a large Jewish community in Alexandria in Egypt. We call this migration of Jews throughout the world the Diaspora. Many of these Jews could no longer speak or read Hebrew, but they still wanted to read their sacred Scripture. Beginning in the third century BCE, Greek translations of the Old Testament began to appear. While a translation, the Septuagint tradition represents the oldest, complete copies of the Old Testament that we now have. Although our Bibles are not based on the Septuagint, it was the version of the Old Testament used by the early church and so it has had a powerful influence on Christianity.

The World of the Bible: Geography

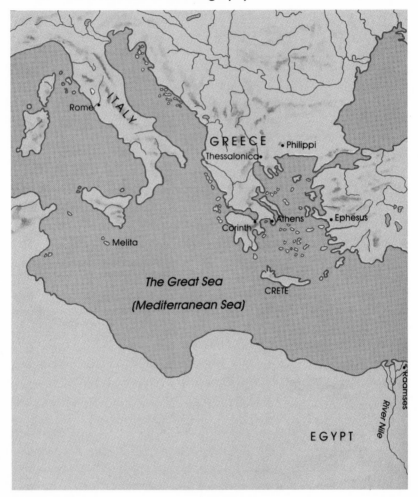

Nobody lives in a vacuum. We are all influenced by the world around us: our family and friends, where we live, what period of history we live in. This is also true for the writers of the Bible, both Old and New Testament. Look at map 1 (two parts—pages 18 and 19). This is the geographical world of the Old Testament, otherwise known as the ancient Near East. Notice that the place we call Israel stands between two of the most ancient civilizations ever discovered: Egypt and Mesopotamia. Even in ancient times cultures

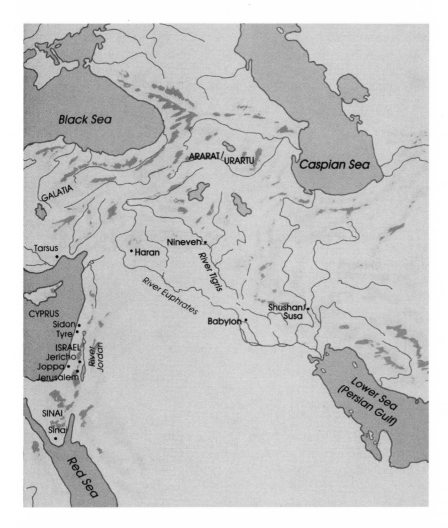

traded with each other, and if you are going to try to get goods from one place to another you want to do it in the most efficient way possible. South of the River Euphrates (and Babylon) is desert. North of the Euphrates are almost impassable mountains. Sandwiched in between is a fertile region of land shaped like a crescent. Therefore, this stretch of land connecting Meso-potamia and Egypt is called the Fertile Crescent. Look at the map again. Where is Israel located along this crescent? It is located at the point where the crescent approaches Egypt and where it is at its narrowest.

There are two important things for you to know. First, from very early on the people of the Bible were in contact with the wider world. Caravans from throughout the known world traveled through Israel. The people of the Bible did not live in a vacuum untouched by the world around them. The second point has to do with power and economics. To control the trade route is to control the economy, and to control the economy is to have power. Have you ever wondered why there are so many wars mentioned in the Bible, and why so much of the Old Testament uses the language of war? Very simply, the people of the Bible were almost constantly under threat from or under the control of their more powerful neighbors. In this political, economic, and geographic reality there arose a people whose writings, preserved in the Bible, are a testimony to their encounters with God.

The World of the Bible: Ancient Near Eastern Culture

While unique in many ways, the writings of the Old Testament show us that the people who wrote the Old Testament were not just aware of, but were influenced by the civilizations that surrounded them. Abraham was originally from the region of Mesopotamia, for example, and was called by God to migrate west toward the land God promised him. Moses was born and raised in Egypt before God called him to bring the people out of slavery into the promised land. Today, we are fortunate to have many writings from the ancient Near East that give us insight into how these cultures understood their world.

Egypt. In general, Egyptian culture did not have much influence on Israel, although several important biblical stories are set in Egypt. According to Genesis, Joseph was sold into slavery in Egypt where he eventually rose to second in command of all Egypt. More important than the Joseph narratives are the stories of Moses and the exodus from Egypt. We will look more closely at these stories in chapter two. The most significant Egyptian influence on Old Testament writing is found in the Wisdom literature of the Bible, in books such as Proverbs. Wisdom literature will be discussed in chapter four.

Mesopotamia. The rediscovery of writings from Mesopotamia has greatly affected our understanding of the Old Testament. The relationship between Mesopotamian and biblical culture can best be described using a modern analogy. Because of American TV, movies, music, and even Coke, American culture has spread throughout the world. Very few places in our world are untouched by or unaware of American culture. Mesopotamian culture operated in much the same way in the influence it had over the ancient Near East. What the writings from Mesopotamia have shown to us is how the ancient people understood their reality; in other words, the cosmology of the ancient Near East. Cosmology means a theory of the beginnings, development, and structure of reality. Mesopotamian cosmology described the world as created out of a watery chaos, an idea we find reflected in passages such as Genesis 1:1-2 and Psalm 74:12-17, for example. Ancient Mesopotamian religion was polytheistic, meaning that people worshiped more than one god. There was a high god surrounded by other gods who inhabited the heavens in a complex structure similar to that of a very dysfunctional family. The most significant parallel between Mesopotamian writings and the Old Testament is the story of a man named Utnapishtim whose story resembles that of Noah and the flood (Gen 6–9).

Ugarit. Ugarit is the name of an ancient city found at a place called Ras Shamra, located near the coastline of the modern nation of Syria. Ugarit flourished during the second millennium BCE due in large part to maritime trade. Lost to history at the end of the second millennium, the city was rediscovered in 1928. Excavations began at the site in 1929 soon after which a large cache of documents was discovered. People who study the ancient world are always excited about finding writings because they give us so much more insight into the way people lived and thought than other kinds of archeological remains (ruined buildings, statues, jewelry, cooking utensils, etc.). Ugarit has been especially significant for studying the Old Testament because we believe that Ugarit was a Canaanite city. The Canaanites were the people who lived in the promised land before the Hebrews entered around 1200 BCE. The Bible itself indicates how influential the Canaanites were on the Israelite people, but before the discoveries at Ugarit we knew very little about them.

There are two discoveries from Ugarit that have influenced our interpretation of the Old Testament. One is the language. Very similar to ancient Hebrew, Ugaritic has helped us better translate some of the more difficult words in the Old Testament. A second has to do with cosmology. The high god of the Ugaritic pantheon was called El, and his consort's name was Asherah. They had four "children," three males and a female named Baal, Yam, Mot, and Anat. All but one, the female deity Anat, are found in the Old Testament in some way.

Yam is the Hebrew word for "sea," and *mot* is the Hebrew word for "death." While death is not deified in the Old Testament, the sea is often spoken of in godlike terms. Read Psalm 74 again. In verses 12-15 God is described as conquering the sea monster, understood throughout the Old Testament as the force of chaos, in order to create the world. Asherah is also mentioned in the Old Testament, although the word is sometimes translated as "sacred pole." Roundly condemned by the writers of the Old Testament, now we know that this sacred pole likely represented some kind of goddess worship. (See 2 Kings 21:3 and 23:4.)

More important in the context of the Old Testament are El and Baal. In the Old Testament El, or Elohim, is a name reserved for God. Baal, meaning "lord or master," is a storm or fertility god who seems to have been a major rival to the god of the Old Testament. The book of Hosea, for example, is basically a condemnation of the people for their worship of Baal. How can this be? While the Israelite people were not polytheists, the Old Testament shows us that for much of their history they were not true monotheists either, meaning they believed that only one god existed. They were henotheists. Henotheism is the belief that only one god is worthy of worship, but other gods were still believed to exist. Worshiping the gods of the Canaanites must have been a powerful temptation to the Israelite people, if the stories are any indication. But, despite the temptation to worship other gods, the Israelite people returned again and again to the affirmation that their God was the only god worth worshiping. Finally they reached the point where they could affirm that their God was the only god, thus arriving at true monotheism. What does the Old Testament tell us about this God whose encounters with the people of Israel are recorded in the Old Testament?

Who Is God in the Old Testament?

Have you ever tried to describe God? It is not an easy thing to do, is it? What words would you use to describe God? Loving, forgiving, judge, holy, parent? The list could go on and on. Now, ask a friend. Is their description of God the same as yours? The answer is likely yes and no. There are two points to be made here. First, we all experience God in different ways, which is not to say that God is different for each of us but that each of us is different. This leads to the second point. God is God, and we are not. This seems like a fairly obvious statement: God is God, and we are humans. By definition, there is an insurmountable difference between God and humans. Can any of us fully know God, know the mind of God? By definition being human means that we cannot know all that there is to know about God. God is ultimately beyond human understanding except where and when God chooses to reveal Godself to us. The fancy words for these concepts are transcendence and immanence. When we say God is transcendent we are saying that God is completely outside of creation and human understanding, and therefore unknowable. On the other hand, Christianity (and Judaism) affirms that God has chosen to be knowable, that God has entered into creation and human reality so that we can know something, but not everything, about God. This is what we mean by the term immanence, that God has chosen to reveal to humans something of the nature of God.

What does this have to do with the Old Testament? The Bible is all about God's choice to be known; but, just like you and your friend, different people have different experiences of God. What are some of the ways of knowing God that we find in the Old Testament? Any list is only partial, but here are some of the more important ways of understanding God in the Old Testament.

God is creator. The first thing the Bible says about God is that God is the creator of the world. "In the beginning God created the heavens and the earth" (Genesis 1:1). God conquers the forces of chaos, often described as the sea or a sea monster, in order to create. If God is the creator, then God is outside the creation (so we are back to the idea of God as transcendent); and the Bible tells us very clearly that God's initial creation, and God's intention for creation, was good. More than just the first thing the Bible says about God, it is one of the most fundamental assertions about God. If God is the creator, then all things are created and are under God's power and authority.

God is holy. What does the word "holy" mean? One of the definitions for "holy" in the dictionary is "divine." What does "divine" mean? "Divine" means "of or related to God." To say God is holy, therefore, is to say that God is God. Does that not sound somewhat circular? Yes and no. To say God is holy is to say that God is wholly different from humanity. The holiness of God and the holiness of the people of God are important concepts in the Old Testament. The people of the Old Testament thought they were God's chosen people; they were set apart. To be God's chosen people was to participate somehow in the holiness of God, but people are not by nature holy. This is where the covenant at Sinai and the giving of the law come into play. The Hebrew people believed that when God chose to make a covenant with them they were set apart from other people and that the laws of the Torah were given to them in order to maintain their relationship with a holy God. The laws were not a burden, therefore, but a gift that made it possible for impure people to draw near to God and live in relation\ship with God.

On the other hand, the prophets came in order to remind the people of their obligations to God when the people failed to live up to the standards of holiness God expected of them. What is the standard of holy behavior emphasized by the prophets? Here is the simple answer: to love God alone, unmixed with the worship of other gods, and to love and treat all people with respect and mercy (Micah 6:8). The people of God in the Old Testament are particularly called to treat the powerless and the stranger with justice, to act as God's agents in order to protect those for whom there is no other protector.

God is king and judge. The Old Testament clearly describes God as a king surrounded by a heavenly council, a group of divine beings we might today call angels (2 Kings 22, Isaiah 6). As a king on a throne, God receives constant praise and adoration from the heavenly beings. Also from the council, God proclaims judgment on the heavens and the earth. Not only does God proclaim judgment, God also enforces judgment. One of the most powerful images of God in the Old Testament is God as divine warrior coming to judge the earth. Called a theophany, a visible manifestation of God, God's appearance as the divine warrior is described in terms of natural disturbances: wind, rain, clouds, and earthquakes (Psalm 29).

God is loving husband/parent. God as judge is not the whole story in the Old Testament. The Old Testament uses a variety of metaphors to talk about God and God's love. In several places in the Old Testament, God is described using the metaphor of family relationships. God is like a loving parent who raises and cares for a child, disciplines the child when necessary, mourns when the child is disobedient, but always loves the child. On the other hand, if God is the husband, then Israel is an unfaithful wife who has gone after other lovers, a metaphor for worshiping other gods. How much love does it take to welcome back a spouse who has been unfaithful? All of us live out these family relationships every day. The metaphors of family in the Old Testament are so powerful for us precisely because of this. We love others, and are hurt by others; sometimes we can heal our broken relationships, but sometimes not. The point is, as Hosea 11:9 says, "I am God and no mortal." God's love is not bound by human imagination or capacity.

Meeting God in History

Another way to talk about God in the Bible deserves special attention: God and history, which takes us back to the idea of God's immanence. How does God become known to us? Each one of us is born in a specific time and place. We are affected by when we live and where we live. We are historical beings. The Bible affirms that God becomes known to us as we are, which is to say God comes to us where we are in specific moments in time. The writers of the Old Testament believed that God was revealed in the events of history, was in control of those events, and historical figures were instruments of God in carrying out God's intentions in history.

Have you ever thought about how much of the Old Testament resembles a history book? Skim through 1–2 Kings or 1–2 Chronicles. Historical events are central to the prophetic books as well, although it may not initially seem as obvious in the prophets as it does in some other books of the Old Testament. What is the point of all this history? Should we read these books just like we would read a textbook in a history class? The answer is no. History in the Bible, while it may tell us something about the actual history of the people of the Bible, has a very different purpose. History is theology. To put it another way, history is a way of learning about and knowing God. If God is in control of history then we can know God in history. History is theology—the people of the Bible met God and learned about God in the historical moment.

Since so much of the theology of the Old Testament is communicated through the presentation of history or references to historical events, it is important to know something of the history reflected in the Old Testament. On page 14 above is a chart of biblical history. Notice that some of the events are given very specific dates and some more general dates. Particularly as we go further back in time, the dates are more difficult to know exactly. It is generally believed that the earliest writings of the Old Testament date from the period of the reign of David and Solomon, and the last parts of the Old Testament to be written date from the Hellenistic period. The Old Testament represents a lot of time! Being familiar with the history of the Old Testament, and referring to this chart as you read will help make much of the Old Testament clearer to read and understand.

Reading the Bible: Preliminary Comments

The Bible is very old. This should hardly be a surprise, but have you ever thought about what that means for how we read it? It is easy to fall into the trap of reading the Old Testament—or the New Testament—as if it were a modern book, but it is not. It is not even a book, but rather a collection of books. The Bible as a whole is very complex. It is made up of a lot of different kinds of material that come from a wide variety of times, and was therefore written by a lot of different people. In many ways, the Old Testament is like a beautiful and complex tapestry, woven together across time and place, creating a work of art that has been meaningful for people of faith across time and space. But, just as with any piece of truly great art, it can only be fully appreciated if we take the time to pay attention to it and accept it on its own terms. You cannot force the Bible to be something it is not without doing damage to it—or your reading of it.

We are all experts at reading the literature of our own culture. We know when we are reading fiction or nonfiction. We can tell the difference between poetry and prose. We accept that a novel can be set in a different time period than when it was written, and that we can find truth even in stories that never literally happened. We are (usually) able to tell when a writer is being earnest or sarcastic, sincere or ironic, serious or funny. We are all experts in our own culture and the ways our culture communicates information. But with over two thousand years between us and the Old Testament, can we be so sure that we can easily read the Old Testament?

Just like today, there are many different types of literature in the Old Testament: history, hymns, short stories, prophetic oracles, narratives, poetry, etc.; and just like today, it is important to figure out what kind of literature a text is before beginning to read and interpret it. Once the macro issues of genre are resolved, there are still many micro issues that are even harder for the modern reader to easily identify and interpret. For example, are we supposed to take seriously the passage in Jonah when the king of Nineveh decrees that, "Human being *and animals* shall be covered in sackcloth, and they shall cry mightily to God. All shall turn from their evil ways and from the violence that is in their hands" (Jonah 3:8)? Or are we perhaps reading a bit of ancient exaggeration and humor?

Also, the Old Testament is full of word plays that would have been clear to the original hearer/readers of the text. Look at Jeremiah 1:11-12. What does an almond branch have to do with God "watching over my word"? The Hebrew word for almond is *shaqed* and the Hebrew word for watching is *shoqed*. The same thing occurs in one of the visions of Amos 8:1-3. The prophet sees a basket of summer fruit, *qayits,* and is told that the end, *qets*, is near. See how the prophet ties the word play into the meaning of the vision. The vision ends with a reference to dead bodies, perhaps killed in war, that are left out to rot. Just as summer fruit will rot once picked, so will the people when the end comes.

Another example of how important it is to be sensitive to the details of reading the text is found in Job 7:17-19.

> What are human beings that you make so much of them,
>   that you set your mind on them,
> visit them every morning,
>   test them every moment?
> Will you not look away from me for a while,
>   let me alone until I swallow my spittle?

Compare this passage with Psalm 8:4-5.

> [W]hat are human beings that you are mindful of them,
>   mortals that you care for them?
> Yet you have made them a little lower than God,
>   and crowned them with glory and honor.

It is generally believed that the author of Job is referring to the passage in Psalm 8, but for what purpose? Likely the author of Job was using the psalm ironically to express how different his life experience and his relationship with God was from that of the psalmist. The psalmist expresses amazement that God would pay so much attention to a mere mortal. On the other hand, the suffering that Job endured caused him to question whether or not it is a good thing to have God's attention.

Moving beyond issues of genre, both large and small, there are also issues of content. There are huge cultural differences between the modern reader and the ancient writer. Today we value monogamy in marriage, but in Genesis every one of the patriarchs had at least one wife, as well as a concubine or two. Jacob had thirteen children by four women! Moreover, slavery was a legal institution in the ancient world regulated by laws given in the Old Testament (Exodus 21:1-21). What do we as modern readers do with these texts? Numbers are also problematic when reading the Bible. Can a number have a symbolic meaning, and therefore need not be read as literal? Further, if at least some of the material of the Old Testament was transmitted orally before being written down, how sure can we be of its accuracy? The long term accuracy of oral literature, numbers in particular, is questionable. On a larger scale, the cosmology of the writers of the Bible was very different from ours. For example, we do not believe that God created the world out of a watery chaos or that hail and snow are kept in storehouses in the heavens (Job 38:22). If this is the case, then how seriously should we read the Bible as an accurate reflection of scientific knowledge? There are no easy answers to any of these questions, which is why it takes work to read the Bible well.

Anyone who reads the Bible will take some parts of it literally and some metaphorically. For example, "The LORD is my rock, my fortress, and my deliverer, my God, my rock in whom I take refuge, my shield, and the horn of my salvation, my stronghold" (Psalm 18:2). Rock, fortress, and shield are all metaphors used by the psalmist to talk about God's strength and protection. God is not really a rock, but Christians do affirm the truth that stands behind the metaphor: God is strong and God will protect God's people. The issue is not whether or not we take the Bible literally, because no one takes the Bible literally in its entirety. A more helpful way of dealing with this issue is to speak of literal truth versus theological truth. Even if the Bible is not literally true in all of its details, it can still carry within it theological truth. The Bible should never be made to stand or fall on the literal truth of any one part of it. Truth can be expressed in many ways, and finding the truths of the Bible is in part dependent on being an educated reader of the Bible. The chapters that follow in this section will focus on giving a basic overview of the Old Testament, both placing the books in their own historical period, and where appropriate looking forward to how the writings of the Old Testament were used by later Christian interpreters as they sought to understand their faith through the words of the Old Testament.

• 2 •

The Torah

The first five books of the Old Testament are known as the *Torah*, meaning "law, instruction," or the *Pentateuch*, meaning "five books." These books form the heart of the Old Testament and are central to understanding both the rest of the Old Testament, as well as much of the New Testament. They contain some great stories: Adam and Eve, Noah and the flood, Joseph and the coat of many colors, Moses and the exodus from Egypt. There are also other kinds of material in the Torah: laws, sermons, genealogies, and so forth. A true tapestry, full of variety, the Torah can be a complicated section of the Bible to read, but some basic information and attitudes in reading can go a long way to help.

The fact that the Torah is complex does not mean there are no unifying themes or organization found in it.[1] Broadly, the Torah can be outlined as follows.

> Genesis 1–11 — The Primeval History
> Genesis 12–50 — The Patriarchal History
> Exodus–Deuteronomy — The Exodus from Egypt
>   and the Wilderness Wanderings

Even though this material is quite diverse, some basic themes can be discerned. The primeval history, Genesis 1–11, stands separate from the rest of the Torah and has its own thematic structure: Creation, uncreation, recreation. The rest of the Torah, beginning with Genesis 12 and running through the end of Deuteronomy, is defined by the three promises given to Abraham in Genesis 12: land, descendants, and blessing.

Formation of the Pentateuch

Before looking more specifically at individual sections of the Torah, something should be said about how this diverse material came together to

---

[1]For my discussion of the themes and structures of the Torah, I am indebted to David Clines, *The Themes of the Pentateuch*, 2nd ed. (Sheffield UK: Sheffield Press, 1997).

form the Torah as a whole. Beginning in the Enlightenment, careful readers noticed details in the Torah that could best be explained by the fact that individual elements of the Torah originated in different time periods and places, derived from the hands of different collectors and writers, illustrated different concerns, and in many cases were written a great distance in time from when the stories took place. Although not a very scholarly term, these details are sometimes referred to as "bumps" in the text. They are the places where, if you are reading carefully, you will notice that the Torah is not as seamless as it might seem at first glance.

Here are a couple of simple examples. Places change names over time, or are known by different names in different traditions. Genesis 23:2 reads, "And Sarah died at Kiriath-arba (that is, Hebron) in the land of Canaan." Why might the writer have found it necessary to add the parenthetical statement? It is likely that, by the time the story was written down, the readers would not have known where Kiriath-arba was. The writer is, therefore, trying to help the reader by indicating the current name of the city. Another example is the name of the mountain where Moses led the people after fleeing from slavery in Egypt. Is it Sinai (Ex 19:1) or Horeb (Ex 3:1)? It is clear from the context that the same place is meant. Since the stories of the exodus were passed down orally, it is likely that they were preserved in slightly different ways among different groups of Israelites.

Many scholars have put their energy into explaining these "bumps," some of which are not as easily explained as the above two examples. By the end of the nineteenth century a working theory known as the Documentary Hypothesis arose. The Documentary Hypothesis, in its classic form, states that there are four basic documents or sources that were used to form the Torah, which later editors took and wove together to form a single text. The following chart illustrates the Documentary Hypothesis in its classic form.

Source Name	Date/Place	Characteristics
J (Yahweh)	Oldest: Southern Kingdom, reign of David and Solomon	Yahweh is the most common name for God; unsophisticated language and descriptions; anthropomorphic descriptions of God

E (Elohim)	Divided Monarchy, from the Northern Kingdom	Elohim is the most common name used for God; more sophisticated language and descriptions; less anthropomorphic in its descriptions of God; heavenly mediators speak for God to the people
D (Deuteronomy)	Reign of Josiah and the Exile (2 Kings 22)	Emphasizes the Mosaic Covenant; represents a reform movement in Israelite faith; black and white language of blessing and curse
P (Priestly)	Exilic and postexilic period	Displays priestly concerns; worship and ritual practices; group that brought together the Torah in its final form

Recently the Documentary Hypothesis has come under a great deal of fire. The history of the Torah is much more complex than the chart would indicate, and the Documentary Hypothesis has been modified in so many ways that some would now argue that we need to throw it out and start again. Wherever scholarship on this topic might lead in the next few decades, the Documentary Hypothesis is still a useful way of explaining—in broad outline—how the Torah reached its final form.

Reading the Torah

Genesis 1–11. Genesis begins with the story of *creation*, which God declares to be very good. It is followed by the story of Adam and Eve, and the murder of Abel by his brother Cain. Next, because people have become corrupt, God sends a flood that covers all the earth. This flood is understood as a form of *uncreation*—God returns the world to the watery chaos out of which God originally created the world (see Genesis 1:1). But God warns Noah, who then builds an ark and is saved from the flood. In this way life is not completely destroyed. The world is then *recreated,* but the second creation is clearly not as good as the original. Genesis 11 ends the primeval history with the story of the tower of Babel and the confusion of language.

To begin, there are actually two creation stories in Genesis: the seven day creation found in Genesis 1:1–2:4a and the story of Adam and Eve, found in 2:4b–3:24. According to Genesis 1:1–2:4a, creation takes place in six days, and on the seventh day God rested. There are certain numbers in the Bible that are generally understood as symbolic, and seven is one of them. Why seven? There are seven days in a week, but why is the number of days in the week so important? In the Old Testament, and in Judaism and Christianity today, the most important day of the week is the Sabbath, the day set aside for resting and worshiping God. Seven, therefore, represents wholeness in life and in worship, completeness, a whole and holy unit of time.[2] God does not need to rest, but God gives us a day to rest and worship. In other words, when God rests, God is giving to the people the gift of time to rest and worship, which Jews and Christians practice every seven days.

What does Genesis 1 tell us about God and creation? Read the chapter paying attention to the repetitions and the order of creation. Again and again creation is declared good! The importance of this affirmation cannot be overstated: God created the world good, so whatever the world is like now—and it does not take much observation to realize the world is not always good anymore—the pain and suffering of this world is not God's intention for creation nor does it reflect creation in its original state. Further, humans hold a unique place in creation. We are created last, on the sixth day, and we are created in the image of God. What does it mean to be created in God's image? To be created in the image of God means humans are capable of living in some form of special relationship with God essentially different from the relationship the rest of creation shares with God. Many would also see in this the root of the human capacity to be rational and moral. Further, verses 28-30 indicate that humans are given dominion over God's creation. In this sense, too, we are taking on part of the nature of God. One more thing, pay attention to verse 27. Notice that humanity is created from the beginning as gendered: God created us "male and female" (verse 26).

Genesis 2–3 contain the story of Adam and Eve. As opposed to Genesis

---

[2]Multiples of seven are also used symbolically. The number four, forty, and multiples of four or forty, should also be understood as symbolic. The number four also represents a sense of completeness, and its symbolism most likely derives from the four points of the compass.

1, here *adam* is created first and everything else follows. *Adam* is placed in a garden between the Tigris and Euphrates Rivers and is given the task of keeping the garden. God decides that *adam* should not be alone. A series of creatures are brought forth from the ground but all prove to be inadequate. Thus woman is created.

Before looking more specifically at the creation of woman, something should be said about the meaning of the names of the *adam* and *eve*. The name *adam* is closely related to the word meaning "ground" or "earth," and the name *eve* most likely comes from the word meaning "to live." We could say that the story is about earth-man and life-woman. Nowhere else in the Old Testament outside Genesis 1–11 are these words used as proper names. This is especially true for the word *adam,* which everywhere else refers to humanity in general. While the story is told about two people, these two people are representative of us all.

Returning to the story, the woman is made from *adam* to be a helper. The Hebrew word used here does not imply subordination. Rather, when used in other places in the Old Testament, the word refers to God as a helper to humanity (Psalm 146:5). *Adam* and *eve* are to live in a relationship of mutual respect and aid. When *adam* awakes from his god-induced sleep, he sees *eve* and declares, "This at last is bone of my bones and flesh of my flesh." He clearly understands the depth of mutuality and connection he shares with *eve*, and it is here that the generic Hebrew words for male and female are first used in what is almost a wordplay, but one that reinforces the reciprocal nature of their relationship. "This one shall be called *ishshah* (woman) for out of *ish* (man) this one was taken" (2:23).

While the story of Genesis 2 speaks of creation, as we have it now the point of the story is something quite different. If God made creation good, then how did it get to be like it is today? The story of *adam* and *eve* gives us the answer: *adam* and *eve* disobeyed God and ate of the tree of the knowledge of good and evil. Why was this tree alone forbidden? The tree does not represent knowledge in general; it is better understood as knowledge belonging to God. By eating the fruit of the forbidden tree, Adam and Eve were saying to God, "We want to be like you. We want to be gods." Out of their pride in themselves, they misunderstand what it means to be made in the image of God and because of this they are punished.

The punishment is not random, but rather is directly related to who they are, their very essence. Read Genesis 3:16-19. *Eve's* curse is to have pain in childbirth. She is alienated from her very being as a life giver. Now, to be *eve* is to experience pain in giving birth. She is also denied a relationship of mutuality with her husband. Read Genesis 3:19. *Adam's* curse is that his work with the earth will be hard. He is alienated from the earth, his very self. To be *adam* is now hard and unproductive. Finally, they are removed from the garden, representing alienation from God. We must always keep in mind that what we read in Genesis 3:16-19 is punishment. Never should we read this as how the world should be but rather what it has become because of human pride.

The primeval history continues with the story of Cain and Abel. Out of jealousy, Cain murders his own brother. Themes of alienation are obvious in this story, but another theme is also carried over from the story of *adam* and *eve*: the desire to be like God. In what way is murder connected with the human desire to be like God? It has to do with the sacredness of life. God gives life and only God can take life. For a human to do so is to presume to be God.

In the story of the flood that follows, God decides to cleanse the earth because of the violence and corruption of humanity. While water purifies, it also symbolizes the return of the world to its precreation state. However, God makes provisions for recreation by saving Noah, his family, and the animals. When the flood is over, God makes a covenant (contract) with Noah never to flood the earth again. But read Genesis 9:1-3. These verses repeat the language found in Genesis 1:28-30, but now all creation will live in "fear and dread" of humanity. Humans are also given permission to eat meat, although certain restrictions are put in place concerning how to do this (Genesis 9:4-6). The creation is thus restored, but it is still corrupted. God recreates, but there is the acknowledgment that the world cannot return to its original state.

The last story in Genesis 1–11 continues the themes we have already encountered. Despite the increasing alienation of humanity from God, from the earth, and from each other, humanity still has one unifying element— language. In Genesis 11, people decide to build a tower with its "top in the heavens." By doing so, they will "make a name" for themselves. What does this mean? To reach into the heavens is to challenge God, to enter the space that is reserved for God. This is human pride, pure and simple. As a result, God "confuses" their language, and one more level of alienation is reached. Beginning with perfect creation, humans are alienated from God, from their own natures, from each other on a personal level, and from each other on the level of language and culture.

Genesis 12–50. In Genesis 12–50, we read about the history of one family; but not just a family, a family that eventually becomes a nation. The writers of the Hebrew Bible believed these stories were not just about long dead ancestors, but they also said something fundamental about themselves. The fancy word for this is eponymous: meaning a person in a story represents not just a single person but also an entire group.

Genesis 12 begins with God calling Abraham to leave his home and go where God tells him to. As a reward for this act of faith, Abraham is promised three things: his *descendants* will be numerous, they will be given their own *land*, and they will be *blessed* by God. Abraham is married to a woman named Sarah. Abraham and Sarah are very old and Sarah is unable to have children. In the ancient world having children was important because children, specifically boys, would take care of you in your old age and inherit all your belongings. Even more important than this, God has promised Abraham lots of descendants. How can this happen if Sarah is barren?

Sarah decides to give her servant Hagar to Abraham so Hagar can bear him a child. Here is a place where we are confronted with how different the world of the Bible can be from our modern world! First of all, this is presented as perfectly acceptable; and second, every indication is the child would legally be Abraham *and* Sarah's child. The name of Hagar's child is Ishmael, and as far as Abraham is concerned Ishmael is his legal heir. Problem solved, right? But God comes to Abraham again and tells him he will have a child by Sarah, and it is this son who will inherit the promises of God given to Abraham (Genesis 17:15-22). In Genesis 18:9-15, Sarah overhears and laughs at this promise. How ridiculous is it that an old, barren woman should have a child? Miraculously, Sarah does become pregnant and bears a son named Isaac, which means laughter. Despite this early threat to the fulfillment of the promise to Abraham, with God's intervention the promise is successfully carried into the next generation.

Isaac grows up and marries a woman named Rebekah. Rebekah is also unable to have children, but in her desperation she prays to God. Again God intervenes, and she becomes pregnant with twins. Esau is born first, followed by Jacob, who is described as actually holding on to his brother's heel as he comes out of the womb. The accounts of Esau and Jacob are some of the most emotionally charged stories of the Old Testament, and both brothers display questionable behavior. (Genesis 25:27-34 and 27:1-29.) Even before the birth of the two boys, however, Rebekah learns that Jacob will inherit the promises of God. "Two nations are in your womb, and two people born of you shall be divided; the one shall be stronger than the other, the elder shall serve the younger" (Genesis 25:23). When Isaac grows old and blind, he announces his intention to pass his blessing on to his eldest son, Esau. Jacob and his mother, however, take it upon themselves to fulfill the prophecy given before the boys were born by tricking Isaac into blessing Jacob (giving him the birthright normally reserved for the eldest son). In one of the most poignant moments of the Old Testament, when Esau learns that his father has blessed Jacob instead of him, Esau cries, "Bless me, me also, father!" But, the deed is done, the blessing has been passed to Jacob, and when Isaac does give Esau a blessing it is a meager one. (Compare the blessing given to Jacob in Genesis 27:28-29 with the one given to Esau in Genesis 27:39-40.)

Fearing for his life because he finds out that Esau is planning to kill him, Jacob flees from his brother to live with his uncle Laban. Jacob wants to marry Rachel, Laban's younger daughter, but is tricked by his father-in-law into marrying her older sister Leah first. The trickster is tricked! Only after Jacob marries Leah does Laban allow Jacob to marry Rachel, "and he loved Rachel more than Leah" (29:30). Leah has lots of children, but Rachel is unable to conceive. God "remembered" Rachel (Genesis 30:22), however, and she bears two children: Joseph and Benjamin. Ultimately, Jacob has a total of twelve sons. This is significant because the nation of Israel was divided into twelve tribes, each of which saw themselves as descending from one of the twelve sons of Jacob. This connection is reinforced by the fact that twice in Genesis God renames Jacob: Israel (Genesis 32:22-32 and 35:9-15). Again we are reminded that these stories represent more than just the history of a single family; they also tell us something important about how Israel understood itself as a nation and as the people of God.

The stories now focus on Joseph. Joseph is Jacob's favorite, the "son of his old age," and he also has the ability to interpret dreams. In one of his dreams he sees all his brothers bowing down and serving him. The brothers did not take Joseph's boasting and their father's favoritism well. In the end, the brothers sell him into slavery in Egypt—although they never confess to their father their role in Joseph's disappearance!

Joseph is sold to a man named Potiphar, and Joseph is such a good worker Potiphar places him in charge of all his estate. However, besides being hardworking and smart, Joseph is also good looking. Potiphar's wife tries to seduce Joseph, but when Joseph refuses she accuses him of attempted rape. Because of this false accusation, Joseph is thrown in jail. While in jail, Joseph's ability to interpret dreams becomes known to people in the court of the pharaoh, so when the pharaoh has some particularly troubling dreams, Joseph is brought from jail to interpret them. Joseph interprets the dreams to mean that Egypt would have seven years of plenty and seven years of famine. Pharaoh immediately puts Joseph in charge of the nation's resources. A wise administrator, Joseph stockpiles enough food during the years of plenty to make sure Egypt survives the seven years of famine.

Now the story returns to Jacob and his sons, who are barely surviving the famine outside Egypt. Jacob sends an envoy to buy grain in Egypt, and, unknown to the other sons of Jacob, they are taken before their brother Joseph whom they do not recognize. After a somewhat dramatic family reunion, Jacob and all his children move to Egypt where they enjoy the favor of one of the most powerful men in the land: Joseph, their brother. This is where the narratives of Genesis end.

The two most prominent themes of these stories are that of the barren woman and the fact that the eldest son never inherits the promise. The first theme indicates that the promises of God are moved to the next generation through God's miraculous intervention. The second theme is more subtle. Why would God pick the younger son? It has to do with the surprising nature of God's blessing to this family and Israel as a whole. Surrounded by bigger and more powerful nations, God chooses little Israel to bless!

Exodus–Deuteronomy. Exodus begins with two pieces of information: the children of Jacob have become numerous and there arose over Egypt a pharaoh who did not know Joseph; in other words, one who had no sympathy toward Joseph's descendants, the Hebrews. Fearing their numbers, the pharaoh enslaves them. However, they keep growing, so pharaoh decides to have all the male Hebrew babies killed. Here enters Moses, one of the most important figures in the entire Old Testament. Moses' mother is determined to save him, and in a somewhat desperate but calculated way, she places Moses in a basket and floats him downriver toward where the royal females came to bathe. Just as Moses' mother hoped, the princess takes pity on the baby and brings him into the royal household. Meanwhile, Moses' older sister follows him downriver and offers Moses' own mother as a nursemaid for the baby!

Moses' life is divided into three forty year periods. The first is his childhood and young adulthood. He is a child caught between two worlds:

the enslaved Hebrews and the enslavers, the Egyptians. As a young adult he sees an Egyptian taskmaster abusing a Hebrew, kills the Egyptian, and buries his body in the sand. Moses soon realizes this action has placed him in jeopardy with the pharaoh, so he flees into the Sinai desert. There he meets a "priest of Midian," marries his daughter, and settles into the life of a herdsman. Thus begins the second period of Moses' life.

Exodus 3 contains one of the most important stories in the Old Testament, Moses' encounter with God in the burning bush. Turning aside to see this bush that is burning and yet not consumed, Moses hears God's voice. God gives Moses two important pieces of information. One, this is the same god who blessed Abraham, Isaac, and Jacob, the God of Moses' ancestors. Second, and significantly, God has "observed the misery of my people." The promises given to Abraham have reached a new stage in their fulfillment, and Moses is chosen to lead the people out of slavery into the promised land. Moses then asks the voice a question:

> "If I come to the Israelites and say to them, 'The God of your ancestors has sent me to you,' and they ask me, 'What is his name?' what shall I say to them?" God [answers], "I AM WHO I AM. . . . Thus you shall say to the Israelites . . . 'the LORD,' . . . has sent me to you."   (Exodus 3:14-15)

Indicated in translation by the use of LORD in all caps, Yahweh (I am) is God's proper name, and its revelation represents the beginning of a new relationship between God and the people. The meaning of the name is significant. In a polytheistic world, the expected answer would be, "I am the god of . . ," and never just "I am."

Moses returns to Egypt with his brother Aaron, and in a series of encounters with pharaoh (the plagues), the LORD proves superior to all whom the Egyptians called gods: pharaoh, the sun, the Nile. The final plague is the most important: the death of the eldest son. (Note the parallel with pharaoh's attempt to kill all the Hebrew babies in Exodus 3.) To protect the Hebrew children, God commands each family to slaughter a lamb and place the blood on the lintel of the doorposts. The angel of the Lord would thus pass over the houses of the Hebrews. This story is the origin of Passover, a celebration of the saving of the people from death and their release from slavery, and one of the most important festivals in the Jewish calendar. It is no accident that it is during the Passover that Jesus was arrested and crucified. One of the oldest titles for Jesus is the lamb of God, and the early church clearly saw the Passover event as a paradigm for understanding Jesus' death.

The people escape from Egypt under the leadership of God through Moses, who leads them to Mt. Sinai (also called Mt. Horeb in some of the texts). The people spend only a year at Mt. Sinai, but about one-third of the material in the Torah comes from this time. At Mt. Sinai the people form a covenant with God. The covenant functions much like a contract with responsibilities on both sides. In essence, God promises to live in relationship with them, to care for them and be their God, and the people promise to fulfill the law (instructions) of God revealed to Moses on the mountain. To follow the covenant brings blessings, to break or ignore the covenant brings curses. These curses include famine, infertility, and war, as well as God's withdrawal from relationship. (See Deuteronomy 28.)

Many of the laws that appear in the Torah seem odd and obscure to us, but they are the foundation of the covenant with God. What are they all about? A complicated question with no clear answer, it is easy to dismiss the laws of the Torah as irrelevant to Christianity; but even if Christianity rejected the practice of Old Testament law it is important to remember the reason why the law was given. The people were called to be "set apart" in their lives in order to be able to draw near to God, and that is what the law helped them to do. First, there are laws that helped create and govern an orderly society. Second, there are laws that dealt with the practice of their religion. In other words, there are laws pertaining to their relationships with each and laws pertaining to their relationship to God. The Old Testament does not make this distinction, however, because treating other people with justice and mercy was understood as a way to honor God, just as the proper practice of worship honored God. Living in relationship with God was something that impacted every element of life, and was not something to be taken lightly. The people of Israel always understood that their life in God was based on God's choice and God's mercy, and not on their actions except in accepting and choosing to obey the laws of the covenant.

For Christians the most famous of all the biblical laws are the Ten Commandments or the Decalogue ("ten words"), and even in the Old Testament the Decalogue was understood to summarize all biblical law. The Decalogue can be found in two different places in the Torah, Exodus 20:1-17 and Deuteronomy 5:6-21. While they are not exactly alike, the only significant difference between the two is the reason given for the command to observe the Sabbath.

"I am the LORD your God, who brought you out of the land of Egypt, out of the house of slavery; you shall have no other gods before me." The

first commandment is a call for exclusivity in worship and allegiance. The LORD is their god because God rescued them and made them God's people through the formation of the covenant.

"You shall not make for yourself an idol." All other religions of the ancient Near East made statues of their gods and worshiped them. They believed that the gods dwelled inside the statue in some way, so making of idols is more than just worshiping something made by humans and therefore false. To make an idol implies the belief that God can be contained in one space and controlled by human beings. God tells the people that the creator of all things cannot be contained by that which is fashioned by humans!

"You shall not make wrongful use of the name of the LORD your God." This commandment relates to the swearing of false oaths or pledges in God's name. An individual who is willing to swear falsely in God's name does not appropriately fear and honor God. It also prohibits the use of God's name in a curse, not in the sense of using a swear word, but rather calling on God to bring evil on someone. God cannot be manipulated by the improper use of God's name.

"Remember the Sabbath day, and keep it holy." Keeping the Sabbath holy means resting or ceasing from labor, but keeping the Sabbath also means allowing others to rest. Exodus appeals to the story of creation to explain this commandment. On the other hand, Deuteronomy appeals to the story of the exodus and God's action in freeing the people from slavery.

"Honor your father and your mother." Despite how this commandment is often used today, this was not originally aimed at children. Rather, the commandment is aimed at adults, and particularly it calls adults to take proper and respectful care of their parents as they age.

"You shall not murder." The Hebrew word refers to the killing of innocent victims and various indirect actions that lead to the death of innocent and unprotected people such as the widow and the orphan. It does not prohibit killing in times of war or capital punishment.

"You shall not commit adultery." In its original context where strict monogamy was not the norm, this command prohibited sexual intercourse between a man and a married or betrothed woman. The marital status of the man was not an issue, and it was acceptable for married men to have sexual intercourse with their female slaves (See Gen 16). In the modern context, where monogamy is the norm, this commandment is understood to prohibit any sexual encounter with someone other than one's spouse.

"You shall not steal." While this commandment may refer to simple

robbery, the word can also mean "kidnap." If this is the case, then the commandment prohibits the stealing of people in order to enslave them or sell them into slavery.

"You shall not bear false witness against your neighbor." This commandment specifically applies to legal situations in which a person would bring false testimony against someone in a court case.

"You shall not covet." The Hebrew word translated as "covet" literally means "to desire, take pleasure in," and it is almost always used in a negative sense. To covet is to desire or take pleasure in something for the wrong reasons or in the wrong way. The commandment is not just about desire; it is about desire that leads to inappropriate or illegal taking of that which belongs to someone else.

After the covenant is made and the law is given, the people leave Sinai heading to the promised land. Along the way, Moses sends spies ahead to scout out the land. All but one of the scouts, Caleb, bring an unfavorable report. Out of their fear, the people call for a leader to take them back to Egypt (Exodus 13–14). Because of their lack of faith in God's promise to give them the land, God curses the entire generation. No adult present that day would be allowed to enter into the promised land. While the Torah understands the wanderings in the wilderness as punishment, the time of wandering is later understood by the prophets as one of special closeness to God. In all their existence as a people, this was the one time they relied completely on God.

The Torah ends with the book of Deuteronomy, a series of sermons that end with the description of the death of Moses on the eastern side of the Jordan. Like the people, he is cursed not to enter the promised land (Numbers 20). The book of Deuteronomy represents a reform movement within Israelite religion associated with the reforms made by King Josiah. Read 2 Kings 22–23. The book that was found in this story is generally believed to be the core of the book of Deuteronomy. Chapter 23 lists a series of reforms made to temple worship and the reinstitution of the celebration of Passover. Above all, Deuteronomy is concerned with the proper observance of the Sinai Covenant and the law given there. The theology of Deuteronomy is very black and white. Follow the covenant, and God will bless you. Do not follow the covenant, and God will curse you. In practical terms this means following the laws given to the people at Sinai. Deuteronomy is particularly concerned with purity of worship, worshiping The LORD alone, and proper treatment of the weaker members of society.

God's call to be holy is lived out in relationship with God, but the writers of Deuteronomy believed that God is also honored through acts of charity and mercy.

By the end of the Torah the descendants of Abraham are now numerous, they have been blessed by God, but the promise of land has not yet been fulfilled. While the promise of land is one of the three basic themes of the Torah, it is not fulfilled within the writings of the Torah itself. The fulfillment of this promise is taken up in the histories that follow, Joshua–2 Kings.

• 3 •

The Prophets

The section of Tanakh known as the prophets contains two different types of material: the so-called Former Prophets, Joshua–2 Kings, and the Latter Prophets, Isaiah–Malachi. The former prophets look a whole lot more like history than prophecy, which is why they are referred to as the historical books in the Christian Bible. The section of the Old Testament known as the latter prophets, Isaiah–Malachi, contains the words of individual prophets and is very different from the material found in the former prophets.

The Former Prophets

The former prophets include the books Joshua–2 Kings, excluding Ruth. Although made up of separate books, they are meant to be read together as a continuous account of the history of Israel, beginning with the conquest of the promised land and ending with the exile from the land to Babylon. It is believed that the writers/compilers of this material were strongly influenced by the theology of the book of Deuteronomy, so these books are often collectively referred to as the Deuteronomistic History. The writers used a variety of sources, but the major concern of these books as we have them now is with the covenant made at Sinai and whether or not the people were living up to its requirements. When the people did, they were blessed; when they did not, they were cursed. Look at the beginning and the end of the narrative. In Joshua, the people enter into the land and God's promises are fulfilled, but by the end of 2 Kings Jerusalem is in ruins and the king and many of the people are taken into exile away from the land. The writers/compilers of this section of the Bible thought that, while there were times when the people had been faithful to God, overall things just kept getting worse, and because of this God punished them. In the end, the people received the ultimate punishment: the destruction of the temple and the possibility that their relationship with God had been permanently severed.

Looking more specifically at the story, Joshua picks up where Deuteronomy ends. Moses is dead, and the people are on the eastern side of the Jordan. Joshua is their new leader, appointed by Moses to lead them into the promised land. In a series of military campaigns, Joshua and the people conquer the land. When this is accomplished, each of the tribes is assigned a portion of land in which to live. The book of Judges shows us a different picture of life in the land. In Judges, the people are living among the Canaanites (the name of the people who lived in the land before the Israelites got there) and are being alternately oppressed by them or tempted to worship their gods. When things got really bad, the people would cry out to God, who would then send them a military leader, called a judge, who would rescue the people. During the lifetime of the judge, the people remained faithful, but when the judge died the people would fall back into their old ways, and the cycle would begin again.

1–2 Samuel follows and is basically the story of how the people went from living as separate tribes to being ruled by a king. God tells Samuel, the last of the judges, to appoint a king. First Samuel appoints Saul, but Saul shows a lack of faith in God by failing to follow all the instructions given him by Samuel, so Saul is rejected by God (1 Samuel 13:7-14). God takes away from Saul the right to be king, and then tells Samuel to anoint David as king. David, a brilliant military leader, unites all twelve tribes under one government and makes Jerusalem his capital. The Old Testament tells us that David was the greatest king ever to rule over Israel. But more than that, we read in 2 Samuel 7 that God promises that the house of David would rule over Israel forever. This is a very important promise.

Before reviewing the rest of the history found in Samuel and Kings, it is necessary to say something more about this promise. David was God's anointed one, and the Hebrew word for "anointed one" is *messiah*. What does it mean to call someone a messiah, an anointed one? Literally, an anointed one is someone who has had oil poured or smeared on him as a part of a ceremony in which a person was given a new role or status. In the Old Testament, anointing was usually reserved for kings and priests. There are, therefore, many messiahs in the Old Testament. In one case even Cyrus the Persian king is called God's messiah (Isaiah 45:1)!

As long as a descendent of David ruled over Jerusalem, the promise of 2 Samuel 7 was a reality, but the Davidic monarchy ended with the Exile. After that, the people were no longer ruled by a king of the line of David but by representatives of the various foreign governments that controlled the region from that time on. But the promises given to David's descendants, and through them to the entire people, were never forgotten. Many people believed that God would fulfill God's promise and someday send a new anointed one, a messiah and descendent of David, who would rule over God's people as David had. This hope for a messiah was very much alive in the years that preceded the coming of Jesus, but clearly their hope for a messiah was "this worldly." In other words, they expected a human king who would overthrow foreign oppression and rule in Jerusalem with wisdom and justice given to him by God. After all, this is what David had done. Even Jesus' disciples expected that Jesus would enter Jerusalem and overthrow the Romans. Read Mark 10:35-45. Based on their request, what kind of messiah do James and John think Jesus will be? An earthly one who would sit on the throne in Jerusalem. It was not until after Jesus' death and resurrection that his followers fully understood who Jesus was. Jesus' death and resurrection redefined what it meant to be the messiah. The early church looked to the Old Testament and specifically those passages related to the promises given to David to understand more fully who Jesus was, but after the death of Jesus they read these passages with a new understanding of what it meant to be the messiah.

Returning to the narrative of Samuel and Kings, when David dies his son Solomon takes over the throne. Solomon is known for several things: his wisdom, his wealth, his harem, and the building of the temple in Jerusalem. While he lived, there was peace in the land. His son was not as wise, however, and when Solomon died Rehoboam, Solomon's heir, was not able to hold all twelve tribes together under one rule. The kingdom split in two: Ten tribes broke off, set up their capital in Samaria, and called themselves Israel. Two tribes remained under the control of the descendants of David who ruled from Jerusalem and called themselves Judah.

The rest of the narrative of Kings tells us the history of these two kingdoms. There were times of great prosperity as well as times of devastating war, as the region was invaded and controlled by external powers. Within the narrative of the divided kingdom we find a series of stories about a prophet named Elijah. Fiery and fearless in his mission, Elijah argued for a strict adherence to the worship of Yahweh unmixed by the worship of others gods, particularly Baal, over against a royal household and nation that had become syncretistic in its religion and culture. Syncretism means the blending of different belief systems and cultures. Elijah was in direct conflict with the leaders of Israel, particularly King Ahab of Israel, his wife Jezebel who was a Phoenician princess, and their son Amaziah.

There are two Elijah stories in particular that illustrate the mission of

Elijah: The confrontation of Elijah with the prophets of Baal on Mount Carmel and the story of Naboth's vineyard. In 1 Kings 18, Elijah asks King Ahab to assemble all the people of Israel on Mount Carmel. There he challenges the prophets of Baal to a contest before the gathered crowds. "How long will you go limping with two different opinions? If the LORD is God then follow him; but if Baal, then follow him" (1 Kings 18:21). The challenge is this: Both Elijah and the prophets of Baal will arrange a bull for sacrifice, but rather than lighting the sacrifice themselves, they will each call upon their god to send fire from heaven to set the sacrifice on fire. The prophets of Baal call upon their god "from morning until noon," but no fire reigns down from heaven. Elijah mocks the prophets of Baal. Has Baal wandered away or fallen asleep? Finally Elijah turns to his own sacrifice, which he prepares by dousing with so much water that it would be impossible to set it afire by any normal means. Calling upon the "LORD, God of Abraham, Isaac, and Israel," Elijah calls down from heaven a fire so intense that it burns up all the water and consumes even the stones on which the offering was placed.

The story of Naboth's vineyard, found in 1 Kings 21, is about the clash between the laws of the Israelite covenant and a king's greed. Naboth owns a vineyard that borders King Ahab's palace. Wanting it for a garden, Ahab asks Naboth for the land, but Naboth responds, "The LORD forbid that I should give you my ancestral inheritance" (1 Kings 21:3). Naboth is appealing to ancient covenant laws that required land to remain within a family. These laws were in place in part to protect small landowners from being pushed off their land by wealthier members of society. Hearing Naboth's response, Ahab basically goes home and pouts. Ahab's wife, the foreign princess Jezebel, however, does not feel constrained by Israel's covenant laws. She concocts a plan of action to take the vineyard away from Naboth. Jezebel sends letters in Ahab's name to the elders of Naboth's town commanding them to bring trumped up charges against Naboth in order that he might be stoned to death. Once Naboth is dead, there is no one to protect his family's property, and Ahab can now claim it for his own. A truly scandalous act, this story illustrates the corruption and wickedness of the royal family of Israel during Elijah's day. In action, if not in word, they had turned their back on God's covenant. Finding Ahab on Naboth's property, Elijah prophesies to Ahab, "In the place where dogs licked up the blood of Naboth, dogs will also lick up your blood" (1 Kings 21:19).

Elijah is not just an interesting figure in the history of the northern kingdom. Elijah continued to play in the imagination of the people of the Bible, both Old and New Testaments. This is because, according to 2 Kings 2, rather than dying, Elijah is taken up into the heavens on a chariot of fire. Because the Old Testament says he did not die, a great deal of hope and expectation arose around Elijah as the figure who would return from heaven to announce the coming of God in judgment. The following quotation from the prophet Malachi illustrates this hope.

> Lo, I will send you the prophet Elijah before the great and terrible day of the LORD comes. He will turn the hearts of parents to their children and the hearts of children to their parents, so that I will not come and strike the land with a curse.   (Malachi 4:5-6)

In the Gospels, some of the people of Jesus' day thought he was Elijah (Mark 8:27-30). However, Jesus identifies John the Baptist with Elijah, as the one who will come first (Mark 9:11-13).

Continuing with the larger narrative, Israel, the ten northern tribes, falls to the Assyrians in 722 BCE. The devastation of this war was complete. The people were brutalized, and many of those who survived were carried into exile never to be heard from again. The Assyrians then repopulated the region with people from other defeated nations. These refugees intermarried with the remaining population of Samaria, and their descendants came to be known as the Samaritans. We know from places like the New Testament that these people were looked down upon because their ancestry was not pure even though they worshiped the same God as the Jews.

From this point on, the narrative focuses solely on the southern kingdom of Judah. Little Judah survived more or less self-ruled for over one hundred years longer than Israel but eventually fell to the Babylonians in 597 BCE. The Babylonians took the royal court and other important people back to Babylon, set up a new king in Jerusalem, and expected Judah to pay yearly tribute to Babylon. However, after several years, Judah refused to pay their annual tribute. In 587, when King Nebuchadnezzar of Babylon again marched on Jerusalem and the surrounding region, he showed no mercy, reducing the city to rubble, tearing down the walls, destroying the temple, and devastating much of the surrounding countryside along the way. When Nebuchadnezzar returned to Babylon he took with him even more of the population of the region, leaving behind only a few survivors who were reduced to living in small settlements surviving on subsistence farming. The book of Kings, and the larger narrative of Joshua–Kings, does not end on a completely negative note, however. The history ends with the report that the exiled king of Judah was released from prison and brought into the court of the Babylonian king.

The Latter Prophets

The latter prophets are books that contain the words of various prophets who spoke to Judah and Israel beginning in the eighth century and continuing through the return from the exile. People sometimes refer to the Major Prophets and the Minor Prophets. The Major Prophets are Isaiah, Jeremiah, Ezekiel, and Daniel (although Daniel is not grouped with the prophets in the Hebrew Bible), and the Minor Prophets are the books beginning with Hosea and ending with Malachi. The only difference between the major and minor prophets is size. Scrolls, and books for that matter, can only be so big before they are impractical to use. Each of the Major Prophets fits on a separate scroll. The twelve Minor Prophets all fit onto a single scroll, which is also called the Book of the Twelve.

What is prophecy in the Old Testament? Often we think of prophecy as telling something about the future, and in some cases, but not all, that is a correct understanding of the word. Divination is a form of prophetic activity that uses some external object or source to learn something about the future. Today we might think of things like tarot cards and tea leaves. Back then it was things like bones and livers. (Yes, livers. When an animal was sacrificed to one of the gods, the priests would save the liver, and its shape, etc. would be read as signs of future events.) Another form of divination we might be familiar with is dream interpretation—not dream interpretation in the modern psychological sense, but dreams understood as messages from God. Joseph and Daniel are the most famous dream interpreters of the Bible.

There are also biblical figures who are called prophets because they participated in ecstatic behavior. Ecstatic behavior is when a person does something to alter the state of their mind/body in order to have an extraordinary experience or encounter with God. Drugs, music, dance, as well as the lack of sleep or food have all been used in various times and places in order to induce one of these experiences. Christianity still considers fasting to be a spiritual discipline of this type.

We also know that in the ancient world there was what we might call a professional class of prophets. They were usually connected with a religious site or the royal court. Read Amos 7:10-17. Why does Amaziah tell Amos to go earn his bread somewhere else? Why does Amos say that he is not a prophet when he so clearly is? Amaziah thinks that Amos is one of these professional prophets while Amos responds that he is not. Rather he is one specifically selected by God to speak God's message. Do you see the reference to David in verse 15? Like David, who was a shepherd but then chosen to lead God's people, Amos was also taken from his life as a farmer/shepherd to perform a specific task in God's name.

While we know very little about the men who stand behind the prophetic books, we can get a clear sense of what they thought they were doing. They saw themselves as speaking for God, but even more, they were the mouthpiece for God to speak to the people. Notice how many times a passage in one of the prophetic books begins or ends with some phrase like, "Thus says the Lord." Also, pay attention to the pronouns used.

> Thus says the LORD:
> For three transgressions of Judah,
>   and for four, I will not revoke the punishment.   (Amos 2:4)

Who is the "I"? It is God, not the prophet.

While the material found in the prophetic books can be quite diverse, three common themes can be found. The first is covenant faithfulness. There were two predominant criticisms of the people in this regard. One was that they were not worshiping Yahweh alone. The worship of other gods was a bigger temptation than you might think. The people that surrounded the Israelites were polytheists, meaning that they worshiped many gods. Eventually we can describe the worship of the people of the Old Testament as monotheistic, the belief that only one god exists and that there are no other gods, but for much of the history of the Old Testament the Israelites are better described as henotheists. Henotheism means that they believed that other gods existed but that only one god, the LORD, was worth worshiping. There was a real temptation to mix worship of Yahweh with that of other gods, particularly Baal, a Canaanite fertility god.

The second criticism aimed at the people of Israel and Judah revolves around the practice of a real, not hollow faith. Someone can go through all the motions of worshiping God—completing all the required rituals and participating in all the proper festivals—but God also requires a way of life larger than just performing religious rituals; God requires justice. "He has told you, O mortal, what is good; and what does the LORD require of you but to do justice and to love kindness, and to walk humbly with your God?" (Micah 6:6-8). This is not an abstract concept in the Old Testament a "feel good" nod to charity that has no affect on a person's day to day life. The expectation was that courts would render just verdicts, that the rights of small landholders would be respected, that there would be a safety net in place for the powerless in society, and that all this would be done *as a part of* their worship of God.

The second theme of the prophetic books is judgment. Think about it: Would God need to send a prophet if everybody was doing exactly what they were supposed to? The role of the prophet is to help correct the people when they have gotten out of sync with God and to announce God's judgment if they do not correct their errors. Jeremiah, the prophet who most directly deals with the problem of true prophecy, indicates that there are three ways that a person can tell true from false prophecy. Read Jeremiah 23:16-22. People who tell you everything is fine, "yes men" we might say, are likely to be leading you in the wrong direction. Second, the reference to standing in the council of God is also very important. Jeremiah is saying, as did Amos in the passage mentioned above, unlike the professional prophets who earned their money giving prophecies, a true prophet has had a unique encounter with the deity. Third, true prophecy will hopefully lead to a change in behavior. In a sense, true prophecy is prophecy that does not come true! While the judgment announced by the prophets may seem absolute, standing behind the mission of the prophets is the hope that the people will change and judgment will be averted.

Finally, an important, though minor, theme of the prophets is hope; but it is more than just a hope that judgment will be averted. The prophetic theme of hope looks toward the future. If the punishment comes, does that mean that God has deserted the people forever? Is there any hope for restoration after the punishment? Is there hope for survival in any form? The historical event of the exile is important here because it was when the temple was destroyed and the people were taken away from the promised land. Read Isaiah 40:1-2 in this context. "Comfort, O comfort my people, says your God. Speak tenderly to Jerusalem, and cry to her that she has served her term, that her penalty is paid, that she has received from the LORD's hand double for all her sins." What amazing words of compassion! On the other side of judgment, God will restore relationship.

The prophetic books of the Old Testament have had a powerful influence on Christianity. For example, Isaiah is the most quoted book of the Old Testament in the New, and Amos has had a clear impact on modern liberation movements, including the civil rights movement in the United States. Hosea uses imagery of marriage and family that is profoundly important for our understanding of God. The book of Revelation has been powerfully influenced by the imagery and symbolism of Ezekiel. Zechariah, while not as well known as other prophetic books was, along with Isaiah, significant in shaping the early church's understanding of Christ. At the same time, each of the prophetic books stands on its own as a testament to God's continuing involvement in the life of God's people, using the prophets to continually call the people back into proper relationship with their God and each other.

Amos is the oldest prophetic book that we have, and its overall theme is social justice. His ministry dates to the early eighth century BCE when the people of the northern kingdom of Israel were enjoying a period of great prosperity. As is often the case during times of prosperity, there are some who do not enjoy that prosperity and the gap between the rich and the poor widens rather than narrows. Clearly, abuse of the poor was rampant in Amos' time. Amos spoke words that challenged the powerful of his day, and his actions and words continue to influence those who would speak out against injustice even in our day. "But let justice roll down like waters, and righteousness like an everflowing stream" (5:24). In a region of the world that does not see much rain, and where almost no rivers run year round, this is a call to the practice of justice that knows no bounds.

Along with his call to justice, Amos speaks of an important Old Testament concept: the Day of the LORD. The Day of the LORD refers to that time when God will come in judgment. The people of Judah and Israel believed that God's judgment would be against other nations who have abused Israel in some way. The radical nature of what Amos says is that God's day of judgment can and will come against God's own people if they do not live up to the level of justice and holiness expected of them. "Alas for you who desire the day of the LORD! Why do you want the day of the LORD? It is darkness not light" (5:18).

Hosea is dated to the second half of the eighth century BCE. He criticizes the people of the northern kingdom for their lack of faithfulness to God in worship; more specifically, he criticizes them for worshiping the fertility god Baal. Hosea is most famous for the family imagery he uses to represent the relationship between God and the people: God as husband and the people as wife and God as the parent and the people as the child. In Hosea 1–3, Hosea is commanded to take Gomer, who is described as a whore, as a wife. While this word implies promiscuity in general, in Hosea it likely has a more specific connotation. We do not know exactly what Baal worship was like, but it is believed that it involved some form of sexual activity. Gomer might have been called a whore because she had participated in some form of Baal ritual. Hosea's life, therefore, becomes a living witness to the people's unfaithfulness to Yahweh. Like Gomer, when the people are unfaithful to God, they are like a wife who commits adultery. In an amazing act of love, God takes back the wife (Israel) even after her unfaithfulness!

In Hosea 11:1-11, God speaks of Israel as a beloved child but when that child turns against the father the child deserves punishment. Again, God responds not with anger but with compassion.

> How can I give you up, Ephraim? . . .
> My heart recoils within me;
>   my compassion grows warm and tender.
> I will not execute my fierce anger;
>   I will not again destroy Ephraim;
> for I am God and no mortal,
>   the Holy One in your midst,
>   and I will not come in wrath.   (Hosea 11:8-9)

God is "no mortal," and God's love transcends human love.

Isaiah is a beautiful and multifaceted book that is worth the effort it takes to fully appreciate its complexity. We now believe the book of Isaiah represents three different historical periods. The first part, chapters 1–39, dates to the eighth century BCE, as identified by the dates of the kings listed at the beginning of the book. Under the threat of Assyrian invasion, the first thirty-nine chapters deal with judgment against the people for their sins. Chapter 40 begins with the announcement that God is doing a new thing with Israel and that the punishment announced in 1–39 is complete and restoration is now possible.

> Comfort, O comfort my people, says your God.
> Speak tenderly to Jerusalem, and cry to her
> that she has served her term,
>   that her penalty is paid,
> that she has received from the LORD's hand
>   double for all her sins.   (Isaiah 40:1-2)

Chapters 40–55 likely date to the end of the exile because the Persian king Cyrus is mentioned in 45:1. Many would also argue that the final chapters (56–66) also form a separate section. They refer to the second temple rebuilt after the return from the exile, so these chapters are usually dated to the years following 510 BCE when we know that construction of the second temple was completed. This section wrestles with what the restored community should look like now that worship in the temple is again possible.

Even if the book comes from three different time periods, this is not to say that the book is not a coherent unity. There are some basic themes woven throughout the three sections of the book that tie Isaiah together. One is the holiness of God. The most often used title for God in Isaiah is "the Holy One of Israel." People who are impure cannot draw near to God, but purity is more than just going through the motions of ritual and worship; it is allegiance to God alone and to doing justice in God's name. However, the writer of Second Isaiah (40–55) believed that the exile had purified the people so that God could begin a new relationship with the people. Third Isaiah's focus on proper temple worship carries this theme into the next generation.

The second major theme of Isaiah is the belief that God has a universal plan for all the people, a plan centered on Jerusalem and the Davidic monarchy. Isaiah clearly articulates what might be called Zion theology. Zion is a poetic term for the temple and sometimes for Jerusalem. Read Isaiah 2:2-4. Zion shall become the center of the world and the God of Israel will be the only source of truth. Second Isaiah carries on this theme in two ways. God is in control of history even to the extent that Cyrus, the great Persian king, is nothing more than an instrument accomplishing God's purposes for the people of Israel (45:1-7). God's restoration of the people will take place in Jerusalem, so the prophet calls the people to begin a new exodus under God's leadership. Third Isaiah continues this theme clearly in its focus on the temple and speaks of the temple as central to all humanity, "For my house shall be called a house of prayer for all peoples" (56:7). Even foreigners and eunuchs, whose presence in the temple was forbidden in Deuteronomy, would be allowed entrance into the temple to worship the Lord there.

Another aspect of Isaiah's message has been central to the Jewish and Christian traditions. It is in Second Isaiah that we read the first clear statement of true monotheism in the Old Testament. Read 44:9-20. How can something a person makes be a god? Not only is God's plan universal, not only is God the one in control of history, there are no other gods at all. In Isaiah 46:1-2 the prophet ridicules the people of Babylon and their "gods."

As refugees flee the city of Babylon ahead of Cyrus's invasion, they strap their gods onto cattle. Not only can the gods of Babylon not protect their people, they cannot even stay on the back of a cow!

Isaiah is most important in the history of Christianity for its messianic passages. In the first section of Isaiah several passages speak of a coming king, the second part of Isaiah contains passages that refer to a mysterious figure called the servant, and in the third section of the book there are some glorious passages referring to God's future work to restore peace to the world and the servant who will aid in bringing that about.

Read Isaiah 9:1-7. Much attention has been focused on this passage, particularly verse 6. "For a child has been born for us, a son given to us; authority rests upon his shoulders; and he is named Wonderful Counselor, Mighty God, Everlasting Father, Prince of Peace." Modern scholarship dates this passage to the birth or ascension to the throne of King Hezekiah who ruled over Jerusalem from 727 to 698 BCE. This was a period of great turmoil and great hope. The prophet speaks of a ruler who will end the terrible wars that plagued this region resulting in the destruction of Israel and the near destruction of Judah. This new ruler would truly represent God, and the language used is familiar to us from the names given to kings throughout the ancient Near East where the king was understood as the adopted son of the god. Therefore, what it likely meant to the people who lived at the same time as Isaiah was that this child was a descendent of David, a human king who would uniquely represent God on earth. But, in the end, this passage transcends any given historical situation. Must this child/king be Hezekiah and no other? Both the Jewish and then the Christian traditions understood that God's work in the life of God's people was ongoing. In Christianity the son is understood as Jesus Christ, while in the Jewish tradition this figure is part of the ongoing hope for God's direct relationship with and protection of God's chosen people.

A related passage is found in Isaiah 10:33–11:9. Jesse was David's father, so we again see the hope that God's spirit would rest in a unique way on a descendent of David who would rule on the throne in Jerusalem; and because of this, true peace and righteousness shall be brought to the earth. Pay attention to 11:1. In the imagery of the passage for a shoot to come out of the stump of Jesse the tree must have been cut down. We again see in this passage the hope for a time after much suffering when God would send the people a ruler who would truly represent God, and the good creation of Genesis 1 will again be real. For the early church, this individual on whom

God's spirit uniquely rested had indeed come in the person of Jesus Christ.
   In the second section of Isaiah there are a series of poems that refer to
the servant. The servant is a mysterious figure in Isaiah, whose identity is
never truly made clear. In Isaiah the servant is likely the people of Israel
who suffer but through their suffering make known to the nations the true
God. The church saw in the suffering servant an explanation for the
suffering of Jesus. The most important of these poems for the Christian
tradition is Isaiah 52:13–53:12.

> But he was wounded for our transgressions,
>   crushed for our iniquities;
> upon him was the punishment that made us whole,
>   and by his bruises we are healed.
> All we like sheep have gone astray; . . .
> [L]ike a lamb that is led to the slaughter,
>   and like a sheep that before its shearers is silent,
>   so he did not open his mouth.   (53:5-7)

   In the final section of Isaiah, the community of people who returned
from the exile struggle with the fact that life in Jerusalem is not as
harmonious as they had thought it would be, nor is there a king of David on
the throne; but the book continues to affirm the truth of God's promises and
looks to the future for their fulfillment. The church picks up on this hope
and applies it to Jesus. In Luke 4:18-19 Jesus quotes from 61:1-2. The story
in Luke indicates that the early church believed that Jesus was the
fulfillment of this prophecy. As Jesus says, "Today this scripture has been
fulfilled in your hearing" (Luke 4:21). Notice that the good news, which is
now placed in the context of the life, death, and resurrection of Jesus, is still
clearly related to the message of the Old Testament prophets: justice and the
proper treatment of the weak of society. Third Isaiah also speaks of the
glorious future when God's promises will all be fulfilled, understood by the
church to mean that time when Christ will come again. See Isaiah 65:17-25.
"For I am about to create new heavens and a new earth; the former things
shall not be remembered or come to mind" (65:17).
   Jeremiah and Ezekiel are both prophets of the exile. Jeremiah lived in
Jerusalem in the years before, during, and after the fall of the city and the
destruction of the temple. Ezekiel was one of the people taken into exile in
597 BCE, so his prophetic activity takes place in Babylon. Jeremiah is often
considered a thoroughly pessimistic book, and the prophet comes across as
a truly unfortunate human being. He is beaten, ridiculed, and put on trial for

his words. There is even a modern word, "jeremiad," coming from Jeremiah, meaning a miserable and gloomy complaint. As a prophet, Jeremiah was heavily influence by deuteronomic theology and he saw the terrible things happening to his nation as judgment against them for their lack of faithfulness to the LORD. Despite all that happened to him, he felt compelled to speak God's word of judgment to the people (Jeremiah 20:7-12); not to condemn them, but to give them a chance to repent. Read Jeremiah 18:7-11. God's judgment is dependent on the people's choice. There were other men in Jerusalem at that time, however, who gave a different message. Appealing to the promise given to David, they believed that God would never completely forsake them; God would never break the promise given to David. Jeremiah was more clearsighted. Could the people continue to disobey God and still expect that God would not punish them? There is hope in God's promises, but there is also truth in God's judgment. As long as the people turned their back on the covenant with God there was only one possible result, judgment; and the longer the people refused to listen and repent, the more thorough judgment would be.

Ezekiel lived during the same time as Jeremiah, but he was taken into exile with the king in 597. The son of a high-ranking priest, he also struggled with how to understand the events leading up to the fall of the city in 597 and the destruction of the temple in 587. The book begins with an elaborate symbolic vision of God on a throne chariot coming to Ezekiel in Babylon. In chapters 8–11, Ezekiel is taken in a vision to the temple in Jerusalem. While Jeremiah and Ezekiel are very different, it is interesting to see how they reinforce each other. This vision of Ezekiel shows us that the leaders of Jerusalem were actually worshiping other gods (8:7-13), while at the same time telling the people that everything was going to be fine. In Jeremiah the leaders of Jerusalem tell the people that God would never forsake the temple: ignore Jeremiah and all his pessimistic words of judgment. In Ezekiel's vision of the temple, however, God gives Ezekiel a glimpse of how truly depraved the leaders of Jerusalem were. At the end of the vision, Ezekiel sees the glory of the LORD depart from the temple representing God's withdrawal of protection from Jerusalem and the people. Soon after, the city falls and the temple is destroyed. According to Ezekiel, the cause of the Temple's destruction is the people's ongoing sin that caused God to withdraw all protections from it.

Does this mean that God has broken the promise made to David? Not according to Ezekiel. True, God has left the temple, the city has fallen, and the temple is destroyed; but God will renew the people. Read Ezekiel 37:1-11. The people of God are like bleached bones in the desert, dead beyond any hope, but God chooses to bring his people back to life. The reenlivened bones are a metaphor, a way of illustrating the promise that God will begin again with the remnant who survived the exile. The experience of the exiles comes to be understood as a punishment that purifies the people rather than destroying them, so that they might return to Jerusalem and begin again the covenant with God in a new temple untainted by the sins of their forebears.

There are several prophetic books that date to the period after the return from the exile. Besides the third section of Isaiah, they include Haggai, Zechariah, Malachi, and Joel. In the period following the return from the exile, the prophets addressed several key issues in the life of the people. Like Ezekiel, they believed that the people who had been taken into exile had been purified by their experiences, and the exiles were the remnant with whom God would begin again (Zechariah 3:2). This new beginning would be centered on the rebuilt temple. When the people delayed construction, prophets like Haggai rebuked the people for ignoring God's intentions. Second, they articulated a theodicy of the exile. In other words, they answered the question why did the people of God have to suffer so great a punishment? While the punishment of Israel was sent by God, the severity of the punishment was not ordained by God, but rather was due to the arrogance and wrongdoing of the other nations (Zechariah 1:15, Joel 3). Because of this, the announcement of God's coming judgment is now turned against the nations. Third, they focused on issues of proper worship in the temple and the responsibility of the leaders to teach and guide the people correctly (Malachi).

The prophets stand alone as some of the greatest writings of the Bible, calling people to practice justice as a part of the worship of God. Christians turned to the messianic passages to express their understanding of Jesus and their own hope in the coming of Christ, but it must not be forgotten that with this understanding and hope comes a call to a lifestyle, not just an assertion of a set of beliefs.

• 4 •

The Writings

The third section of the Tanakh is the Writings, and it is a diverse collection of material. It contains the book of Psalms, one of the most important books of the Bible for both Judaism and Christianity, as well as the book of Job, which has echoed through the centuries as one of the most powerful books ever written because of its themes of undeserved suffering and the nature of true piety. There are also the short stories of Ruth and Esther and the history of Chronicles, for example. The diversity of material in this section means that it cannot be looked at together as one or two units of material with a unifying theme or themes, as with the Torah and the prophets.

The books in the third section of the Tanakh were written and collected in the period following the return from the exile. This period, dating from the rebuilding of the temple to the destruction of the temple by the Romans (520 BCE–70 CE), is known as the Second Temple Period. We know something about the events following the return from the exile from the books of Ezra and Nehemiah. However, we do not have much historical information related to the Bible for the late Persian period and the early Hellenistic period. The book of Daniel reflects the tumultuous events surrounding the Maccabean revolt. See part 2, "The New Testament" for a more specific review of this historical period.

The Psalms

The book of Psalms is a collection of 150 separate poems, most of which were meant to be used in worship, just as the church uses them today. What does Hebrew poetry look like? We all know what a poem is supposed to look like in English; it usually rhymes and/or has some sort of meter or rhythm. Ancient Hebrew poetry is defined by two things: rhythm and parallelism. It is difficult to reconstruct the rhythmic structure of a language that is no longer spoken; however, parallelism is actually a very simple construction that is easily identified in the text. In parallelism, each line of Hebrew poetry is divided in half and the first half and the second half operate in parallel with each other. They can either be synonymous, meaning that the two halves express the same idea; or they can be antithetical, meaning that they express opposite ideas.

Synonymous

> The heavens are telling the glory of God;
>> and the firmament proclaims his handiwork.   (Psalm 19:1)

Antithetical

> [F]or the LORD watches over the way of the righteous,
>> but the way of the wicked will perish.   (Psalm 1:6)

Most of the psalms were used in worship, but there are many different ways that words are used in worship, both now and in the ancient world. Look at a hymnal, for example. Many hymns are classified according to their themes or by what event in the Christian calendar they are associated with (Christmas, Easter, etc). We can classify most of the psalms based on how we believe they were used. Just as in the church today, there are psalms of praise and psalms of thanksgiving, but there are three kinds of psalms that are worth mentioning because they are unique or interesting in some way: psalms of Zion, royal psalms, and laments.

Zion is an important concept in the Old Testament. Mt. Zion is the traditional site of the temple, so the word can refer to the temple, the mountain on which it stood, and sometimes the entire city of Jerusalem where the temple was located. Psalms of Zion talk about the importance of the temple. For example,

> Great is the LORD and greatly to be praised
>> in the city of our God.
> His holy mountain, beautiful in elevation,
>> is the joy of all the earth,
> Mount Zion, in the far north,
>> the city of the great king.   (Psalm 48:1-2)

They also speak of the joy the worshiper feels when approaching the temple.

> How lovely is your dwelling place,
>> O LORD of hosts!
> My soul longs, indeed it faints
>> for the courts of the LORD;
> my heart and my flesh sing for joy
>> to the living God. . . .
> Happy are those whose strength is in you,
>> in whose heart are the highways to Zion.   (Psalm 84:1-2, 5)

While Christians no longer look to the temple as a place of worship, the concept of Zion is still important, as many hymns and spirituals reflect. Broadly, Zion is one of the ways that Christians use to talk about heaven, as well as some future time when God will dwell more immediately with God's people.

In ancient Israel, the king was a central figure in temple worship. Many of the important events in the life of the king took place in the temple. The royal psalms were the words used during some of these ceremonies. Two obvious examples are Psalm 45, a wedding song written for the king, and Psalm 72, a coronation psalm. Notice the emphasis on the justice and good judgment of the king in Psalm 72. In an ancient monarchy people's lives very much depended on the king, so it is no wonder they prayed so sincerely that the king would treat them well! How do Judaism and Christianity use these psalms today? Today these psalms are usually used to speak of the universal king, God.

Some of the royal psalms, in particular Psalms 2 and 110, became an important part of the church's understanding of Jesus. In its original setting, Psalm 2 speaks of the royal house of David and might have been part of a coronation ceremony. For the writers of the New Testament, verse 7 was especially important. "I will tell of the decree of the LORD: He said to me, 'You are my son; today I have begotten you." This verse combines two very important ideas for the New Testament's presentation of Jesus: the idea of the royal messiah of the house of David and the idea of the messiah as the son of God. At Jesus' baptism, the voice from heaven announces, "You are my Son, the Beloved; with you I am well pleased" (Mark 1:11). The church understands Jesus to be God's regent on earth, not just as a ruler but as a son.

Psalm 110 might also have been used as a part of an ancient coronation ceremony. Jesus himself interprets this psalm messianically in Matthew 22:41-45. Psalm 110:1 reads, "The LORD says to my Lord, 'Sit at my right hand until I make your enemies your footstool.' " The church interprets it in light of Jesus' resurrection. Many important creedal statements of the church refer to this verse. For example, the Apostles' Creed says, "On the third day he rose again; he ascended into heaven, *he is seated at the right hand of the Father*, and he will come again to judge the living and the dead."

Finally, there are the laments. In the book of Psalms what type of psalm do you think we would find the most? Praise? Thanksgiving? The answer is neither. There are more laments found in the book of Psalms than any other type. Another word for lament is complaint. What might this imply about worship and the relationship between the people and God? First of all, remember that the psalms are communication from a person or persons to God. The first thing that we can know, then, is that the people who wrote the psalms felt comfortable complaining to God about what was going on in their lives. As an example of a lament, read Psalm 13. The psalm breaks into three parts. The first part is the lament or complaint in verses 1-2. Notice the fourfold repetition of the phrase, "How long?" In verses 3-4 the psalmist makes a request of God, "Consider and answer me." Finally in verses 5-6 there is a note of assurance. "But I trusted in your steadfast love" (verse 5). Whether or not God has yet rescued the psalmist, the writer can know that he/she will indeed be rescued "because he has dealt bountifully with me" (verse 6). The people can complain to God because they know and trust God. They have a history with God, and know that God is trustworthy.

Other Poetic Books

Besides the book of Psalms, there are two other Old Testament books that are pure poetry: Song of Songs and Lamentations. While they may both be books of poetry, they are very different in their subject matter.

Song of Songs. Traditionally known as the Song of Solomon, this is a book of love poetry between a man and a woman. How did a book of love poetry make it into the Bible? Over the centuries, both Judaism and Christianity have interpreted this book to be a love poem between God and God's people. More specifically, Christianity interprets the man and the woman of the poetry to be Christ and the church. Just as a man and woman long for each other, the believer seeks after and longs to be united with God.

Lamentations. The book is made up of five poems, the first four of which are acrostics. An acrostic poem is one in which each successive line or stanza begins with the next letter of the alphabet. There are twenty-two letters in the Hebrew alphabet, so each of the poems, including the fifth one which is technically not an acrostic, has 22 lines or stanzas. For the most part, this book is dated to the months and years immediately following the destruction of Jerusalem in 587 BCE. The poems speak of the horrors of war and its aftermath. Parts of the book are so raw with pain and emotion that it can be hard even for the modern reader to remain unaffected by the agony and suffering of the anonymous authors. Unlike the laments found in the Psalms, there is little if any note of assurance and trust in Lamentations.

While the poets are willing to admit that they have done wrong in the eyes of God, the extent of the devastation is too much to bear.

> My transgressions were bound into a yoke;
>> by his hand they were fastened together;
> they weigh on my neck,
>> sapping my strength;
> the Lord handed me over
>> to those whom I cannot withstand.   (Lamentations 1:14)

Wisdom Literature

Proverbs, Job, and Ecclesiastes are all classified as Wisdom literature. In the Apocrypha, Sirach and Wisdom of Solomon are also books written in the wisdom tradition. If you read these books, though, you will quickly realize that they do not sound much alike. What, then, ties these books together? They all share a common theology or way of understanding the world that we call wisdom. The Hebrew word for wisdom, *hokma,* literally means "to have a skill." For example, in the most basic sense a carpenter would be a wise person. The idea behind wisdom theology is an extension of this idea. To be a wise man is to be skilled at living. To be skilled at living is to learn from the basic order of creation, to observe human nature, and the basic laws of acts and consequences, in order to make good choices. What is the goal of Wisdom theology? It is very simple—to live a good life and to be successful. What did it mean to the wisdom writers to live a good life? Happiness and good fortune, respect from your community, a long life, material success, and finally to be remembered and honored by future generations.

How does Wisdom theology differ from the theology that stands behind the Torah and prophets? The following set of terms might help: special revelation versus general revelation. Covenant theology, the theology that stands behind much of the Torah and prophetic writings, is based on God's ongoing revelation to figures like Abraham and Moses. It is based on the idea that God chooses to be immanent, to be known to humans. We call this special revelation because it is knowledge of God given specially to an individual or group of people and therefore not accessible to everyone. Wisdom theology is based on general revelation. General revelation is most commonly associated with the affirmation that God is the creator and therefore we can know something about God from the creation. Wisdom theology is knowledge of God based on observation of creation and the natural order of God's world and is available to all people. Wisdom writings are found in all the ancient Near Eastern cultures. The book of Proverbs bears a strong resemblance to Egyptian wisdom, and there are writing in both Egyptian and Mesopotamian literature similar to Job and Ecclesiastes.

Proverbs. Proverbs is a clear example of wisdom in its most traditional form. For the most part, the book is full of collections of short statements that teach some kind of lesson or make some observation concerning nature and human reality. These wisdom sayings run the gamut from the philosophical to the practical: Treat those around you with justice, show respect to your elders, work hard, do not drink too much, and do not sleep with another man's wife.

Proverbs 1–9 is an example of traditional wisdom in its more philosophical form. Rather than a collection of short sayings it reads more like an essay. Look at Proverbs 1:8-9. This is a father offering life advice to his son (and given the issues it addresses and the imagery it uses, it really is literature aimed specifically at men). In this section of Proverbs we encounter one of the primary biblical metaphors for wisdom: wisdom as a beautiful woman. Read Proverbs 9:1-6 and 13-18. Following the wise woman leads to happiness and wisdom. Following the foolish woman leads to death.

If Proverbs represents traditional wisdom, in what way are Job and Ecclesiastes wisdom books? Job and Ecclesiastes are often referred to as skeptical wisdom. Both, in different ways, challenge some of the basic assumptions of traditional Wisdom theology. Job asks the question, what are our basic motivations for piety, and can people who do all the right things still suffer? Ecclesiastes addresses issues of meaning, pointing out that attaining wisdom does not always bring the desired results. If being wise does not guarantee results, what is the point of working so hard to be wise?

Job. Job is arguably the most difficult book of the Bible to understand, even though its basic story line is quite simple. Read the first line of the book, "There was once a man in the land of Uz whose name was Job." What does that sound like? It sounds a bit like a folk tale, and what are folk tales supposed to do? Teach us a lesson. Anyone who reads Job thinking that he/she will receive an easy answer, however, will be sadly disappointed. The book is rich and nuanced in its presentation of various views concerning the nature of suffering.

Job is described as the perfect wise man. He is "blameless and upright," pious, and successful both monetarily and personally. One day the heavenly beings come together before the throne of God. One of these divine beings is called *satan*. Before going on with the storyline of the book, some attention needs to be given to this figure. Who is *satan*? The first thing that might come to your mind is Evil personified. That is clear in the New Testament, but is this also true of the Old Testament? The word *satan* comes from the Hebrew meaning "adversary" or "accuser." The word is used nine times in the Old Testament, five times for human beings, and four times for divine beings.[1] When the term is used for a human being it occurs in the context of either a legal accuser or a military adversary.

All but one of the references to *satan* as a divine figure clearly refer to a being who is in God's employ. Numbers 22 is the clearest of these texts, the story of Balaam's donkey. Balaam is hired to curse the Israelites, but along the way he encounters a messenger of God—not that he immediately sees this figure, rather his donkey does. When Balaam repeatedly strikes the donkey, the donkey gets fed up, turns around and begins talking. "What have I done to you?" the donkey asks. Only then does Balaam see the divine being in the road. Verse 22 says that the angel of the LORD stands in the road as a *satan*. (The NRSV says "accuser.") This figure is clearly being directed by God and is actively protecting God's people. What is the point of this brief review of *satan* in the Old Testament? As readers, we run the risk of misinterpreting Job when we automatically assume that *satan* is evil and "out to get" Job. The book cannot be reduced merely to a conflict between the forces of evil and the people of God, in this case Job.

To return to the story, the heavenly council meets in 1:6-12, and God asks them to consider Job. *Satan* responds in verses 9-10, "Does Job fear God for nothing? Have you not put a fence around him and his house and all that he has, on every side?" Who is *satan* accusing? God. What is *satan* accusing God of doing? Fostering piety through what is essentially bribery. Would not any of us be "blameless and upright," if it meant that we would be rich and happy? This is one of the places where the book challenges traditional wisdom. Is there such a thing as disinterested piety? God and *satan* decide upon a way to test Job. First, *satan* takes away all of Job's possessions, including his children, but Job remains faithful. "In all this Job

---

[1]Human references: 1 Samuel 29:4, 2 Samuel 19:16-23, 1 Kings 5:4, 1 Kings 11:14, Psalm 109. Divine references: Numbers 22:22-25, Zechariah 3, Job 1–2, 1 Chronicles 21:1.

did not sin or charge God with wrongdoing" (1:22). Second, *satan* afflicts Job with terrible sores, but again Job remains faithful. "In all this Job did not sin with his lips" (2:10). Job passes the "test," proving that people are capable of loving and being obedient to God even when there is no expectation of rewards.

The book does not stop there, however. Job continues to suffer and mourn his loss. Starting in chapter 3, there follows a series of dialogues between Job and three friends who have come to comfort him. They represent the voice of traditional wisdom. In other words, they repeatedly tell Job that if he would only confess his sins, he would be given back all he has lost. What is the problem with this? We know something that the friends do not. Job has not done anything wrong! Fed up with the friends, he turns to God, asking to receive an audience before the Almighty. Job seems to think that there has been a "glitch" in the system, some bureaucratic error, and if Job could point this out to God, then God would surely make everything right again, or at least Job could die in peace having received some vindication.

Job does get an audience with God, which is recounted in chapters 38:1–42:6. But asking for an audience with God could be classified under, "be careful what you ask for!" Job is given an answer but probably not the one he wanted. On the surface these speeches look like God is bullying Job, and God does make it clear that Job is a mere man who could not possibly understand all creation, much less run it. The God speeches are more complex than that, however. Notice a couple of things. The speeches move from references to the outer edges of reality, represented by God's temple (Job 38:4-7), through chaos and the elements of creation (Job 38:5-21), to what we might call meteorological phenomena: rain, snow, etc. (Job 38:22-38), ending finally with a list of wild animals (Job 38:39–41:34). What is missing? Humans! Nowhere in God's description of creation does God mention humanity. Further, read Job 38:25-27. "Who has cut a channel for the torrents of rain, and a way for the thunderbolt, to bring rain on a land where no one lives, on the desert, which is empty of human life?" Creation does not exist to serve humanity alone , nor is there any simple cause and effect in God's creation that can be mastered by the human mind. Sometimes things just happen that do not make sense to us! God's creation is huge and varied, and God revels in all of it.

Just when the book might start to make sense, the author throws us another curve ball. Read Job 42:7-17. This is the effect of the ending. So far the book has told us that Job does not worship God just for what he can get out of it, he is not suffering because he has done something wrong, he is not suffering because there is a glitch in the system; and in the end, neither Job, nor any of us for that matter, have the ability to figure out why bad things happen to us or the ones we love. So what happens in the end? Job gets everything back double! Is this because he deserves it? Is it because he has passed some test? The book never makes clear to us how to incorporate the ending into the rest of the book. Sometimes good things happen to good people, too!

Ecclesiastes. The Hebrew name for Ecclesiastes is Qoheleth, meaning *teacher.* The book is much like the musings of an experienced teacher reflecting on the reality of existence as he has come to understand it. Ecclesiastes also challenges the relationship between our choices and what happens to us, but its tone is very different from Job. It is not as personal, and many people think it is very pessimistic: "Vanity of vanities! All is vanity" (1:2). The Hebrew word translated as vanity literally means "puff of air." Is life really that meaningless to Qoheleth? If not, what is he trying to say?

Look at the poem that introduces the book, 1:3-11. What do people really gain from all their work? Is creation orderly and beautiful, or orderly and monotonous? What is there new to learn, or is our life as monotonous as creation? Is there any hope that we will be remembered for what we have done or who we are or is everything we do as fleeting as the exhalation of breath? These are the questions that the poem asks. Interestingly, Ecclesiastes uses a lot of the language we would associate with business, language of gain and acquisition. Is being a wise person, making the right choices, nothing more than a cold system of exchange? We do the right thing and God pays us? Pushing the envelop even further, Qoheleth points out that there may be no advantage to making the right decisions at all. What about an intelligent hard-working person who makes lots of money but then dies and his no-good children get to spend it all? Where is the joy in that? While perhaps not the one we want to hear, Ecclesiastes does give an answer. "There is nothing better for mortals than to eat and drink, and find enjoyment in their toil" (2:24). Qoheleth is not telling us to give up but to try our hardest, and enjoy life to the fullest.

The Short Stories

There are two books in this section of the Old Testament that we would call short stories. They are literary gems that tell us the stories of two brave women. Both were written during the period after the return from the exile, although the story of one takes place in the earliest history of Israel and the other in the last period of Old Testament history. Perhaps what they most hold in common is that these two women remain faithful to God and as a result bring life to the people of God.

Ruth. "In the days when the judges ruled, there was a famine in the land, and a certain man of Bethlehem in Judah went to live in the country of Moab, he and his wife and his two sons" (Ruth 1:1). So begins the story of Naomi and her daughter-in-law, Ruth the Moabite. When Naomi and her husband Elimelech move to Moab, their two sons marry Moabite women, Ruth and Orpah. When all three men die, Naomi decides to move back to Bethlehem, her home country. As widows, Ruth and Orpah have two choices: to remain in Moab and return to their fathers' households or go with Naomi to their husbands' land. Orpah remains in Moab, but Ruth chooses to go with Naomi.

> Do not press me to leave you
> 　　or to turn back from following you!
> Where you go, I will go;
> 　　where you lodge, I will lodge,
> your people shall be my people,
> 　　and your God my God.　　　　　　　　　　　(Ruth 1:16)

Not only does Ruth choose loyalty to Naomi, she chooses loyalty to Naomi's god, the LORD! The story begins with famine and the death of a family (with no more adult men, there was no hope for producing children), continues through the creation of a new bond between a mother-in-law and her daughter-in-law, Naomi and Ruth, and ends with a marriage and the birth of a grandson/son. Ruth is loyal and hardworking, obedient to her mother-in-law who manages to "work the system" that existed in the ancient world not only to provide a life for what remains of her family, but actually to begin a new family. From famine and death, the book moves to fertility and new life.

Two interesting facts about ancient Israel will help you understand the story better. The story of Ruth is grounded in two basic commands of the Bible. One, farmers were expected to leave the edges of their fields unharvested and to leave on the ground any produce dropped during harvesting (Leviticus 19:9-10; 23:22; Deuteronomy 24:19-22). This was an ancient method of welfare. The second command revolves around the rules of kinship and land ownership. Family property had to stay within the family. If a man died without having any sons, his closest kin could redeem that land, but there was a catch. With the land also came the man's family. Not only that, the next of kin was expected to take the dead man's wife and have a child with her. If the child were a boy, then the child would legally be the dead man's heir, and the land would revert back to the original family.

From these biblical commands, the story beautifully weaves together a narrative of hope and fulfillment for those who are loyal to each other and to God. A man named Boaz falls in love with Ruth, and when the next of kin refuses the right to redeem the land, Boaz marries her. After their marriage, Ruth conceives a child who is named Obed. The last verse of this little jewel of a book points toward the future, Ruth is the great-grandmother of David.

Esther. Esther was a woman of great beauty. She was so beautiful that when the king of Persia decides to pick out his new wife in some form of an ancient beauty contest, Esther wins. She was also a Jew, but she hides this fact from the king. When one of the king's aides plots to kill all the Jews, Esther's uncle comes and pleads with her to intervene with the king. This was not as simple a task as it might sound to us because even though she was married to the king, she could not enter his presence unasked without risking death. With great prayer on the part of many, Esther gathers the courage to go visit her husband, the king. He must have been in a good mood, because she is allowed to live. Instead of asking for help to stop the plot to kill all the Jews, though, she invites the king and his aide to dinner. Through careful plotting and manipulation of events, Esther reveals the plot to the king.

It is a great story up until this point, but here is where problems arise. The king has already signed an order allowing the Jews to be killed, and he cannot take it back. He decides to send out another order allowing all Jews "to destroy, to kill, and to annihilate any armed forces of any people or province that might attack them, with their children and women, and to plunder their goods" (Esther 8:11). The end of the book tells of great carnage as the Jews carry out this second edict, but at what cost? Esther's courage and devotion to her people are admirable, but the end of the book has troubled many generations of both Jewish and Christian readers.

Daniel

Daniel is a complicated book. There are two basic parts of the book: chapters 1–6, a collection of short stories set in the Babylonian Exile; and chapters 7–12, a series of symbolic visions. The parts of the book have very little in common except the person of Daniel. Daniel is described as a wise man (Daniel 2:12-16) rather than a prophet, who acts with integrity in all he does and remains loyal to God even in the face of persecution and death. He also has the ability to interpret dreams. There are many similarities between Daniel and Joseph. Joseph also lived in a foreign court, was known for his integrity, and had the ability to interpret dreams.

Daniel 1–6. The first section of the book is a series of stories about Daniel and his three friends. Living in the Babylonian court put these young Jewish men under a sometimes greater, sometimes lesser degree of pressure to reject the worship of the LORD and the practice of Judaism. Each story is different in the severity of pressure these men were put under, but the unifying theme is the call to steadfast loyalty to God no matter what the cost. While the stories are set during the period of the exile, they most likely were written down in the form we have them in the mid-second century BCE. During this period there was increasing pressure to conform to the practices of the Greco-Roman world even in Judah. Stories of how respected figures of the past handled these same pressures must have been very comforting to Jews of the second century.

Daniel 7–12. Daniel 7–12 does not contain short stories, but rather these chapters contain a series of highly symbolic visions. No matter how you look at them, they are very strange. The genre of these visions is called apocalyptic. The word means "to reveal, uncover." The book of Revelation in the New Testament is also apocalyptic. Today, scholars date the visions of Daniel to the events surrounding the desecration of the temple by Antiochus Epiphanes in 167 BCE. Antiochus was his given name, and Epiphanes was his throne name, meaning "manifest one." What is he claiming for himself? Basically he is saying that he is a god or godlike. While strange to us, many ancient kings claimed to be divine in some way. Other people who were alive during the same period called him Epimanes. Do you hear the play on the sound of the two words? Epimanes means "crazy"! For reasons that we still cannot completely figure out, Antiochus made the decision to wipe out Judaism altogether. He did this by confiscating and burning copies of the Torah, outlawing Jewish ritual practices, killing mothers who allowed their sons to be circumcised, and forcing priests to make sacrifices to other gods.

The visions are best understood as symbolic. The symbolism might seem strange to us, but it would have been clear to the second-century reader. The visions refer to events of the second century BCE using symbolic language. For example, the "little horn" of chapter 7 is most likely a reference to Antiochus Epiphanes who, through his persecution of God's people, is "speaking arrogantly" before the throne of God. What is the point of these visions? While the details of the symbolism may be difficult to interpret, the intentions are not. First, God is in control of history, so no matter how bad things look at the moment, they are all part of a larger plan of God. If God is in control, then what is required of God's people in times that are this evil? God's people are to remain loyal, even to the point of death, and God will make it right in the end. Not coincidentally, this is also the message of the stories in chapters 1–6. Interestingly, Daniel has the only clear reference to life after death found in the Old Testament (12:1-4). The visions of Daniel argue that it is better to die than to be disobedient or reject God. Martyrdom was okay because God would still reward you in death.

The Histories

Chronicles. The third section of the Tanakh contains several historical books: 1–2 Chronicles and Ezra–Nehemiah. 1–2 Chronicles is a Persian-period rewriting of Israel's history, drawing extensively from books such as Genesis, 1–2 Samuel, and 1–2 Kings. Because it comes from the period after the return from exile, it carries the history past that of 2 Kings, ending with the Edict of Cyrus allowing the Jews to return to Jerusalem. The emphasis of Chronicles turns from covenant theology of the earlier histories to concerns about the temple. This makes sense in a period when Israel was no longer self-ruled, the Davidic monarchy was gone, and the temple and priesthood were the sole survivors of the exile in terms of internal leadership and authority.

Ezra/Nehemiah. These books, which are actually one book in the Hebrew, pick up where Chronicles ends. Also dating from the Persian period, Ezra/Nehemiah deals with the reconstruction of Jerusalem, the temple, and the religious life of the Jewish community. The primary concerns of the book are twofold: the Torah, both in the sense of the books of the Torah and the larger concept of God's instruction lived out in the life of the community, and the problem of assimilation. What is assimilation?

What happens to a small country/culture like Judah when it is taken over by a larger and more powerful country/culture? It is often difficult for the minority culture to preserve its distinctiveness, so the tendency is for the minority culture to be absorbed into the practices and attitudes of the larger culture. It was important to the leaders in Jerusalem that they remain distinct, despite the influence of Persian culture. Figures like Ezra and Nehemiah felt the need to be extra vigilant and strict in holding the line against outside influences. They called for strict obedience to the Torah practice and no "mixed" marriages, marriage with women who were not also Jewish.

Concluding Remarks

The Old Testament is a diverse collection of writings from a number of different time periods. It represents many people's understanding of God and how God works in the lives of believers. It can be difficult for the modern person to read and understand writings that are so old and different from our world. But, at this point, I hope that you have come to appreciate in some small way the beauty and importance of the Old Testament in both Judaism and Christianity.

* * *

Old Testament/Hebrew Bible Suggestions for Further Reading

Beasley, James R., Clyde E. Fant, E. Earl Joiner, Donald W. Musser, and Mitchell G. Reddish. *An Introduction to the Bible*. Nashville: Abingdon Press, 1992.

Blenkinsopp, Joseph. *The Pentateuch: An Introduction to the First Five Books of the Bible*. New York: Doubleday, 1992.

Brown, William P. *Character in Crisis: A Fresh Approach to the Wisdom Literature of the Old Testament*. Grand Rapids MI: Eerdmans, 1996.

_____. *Seeing the Psalms: A Theology of Metaphor*. Louisville: Westminster/John Knox Press, 2002.

Brueggemann, Walter, William C. Placher, and Brian K. Blount. *Struggling with Scripture*. Louisville: Westminster/John Knox Press, 2002.

Clines, David J. A. *The Theme of the Pentateuch*. Second edition. Sheffield UK: Sheffield Academic Press, 1997.

Collins, John J. *The Apocalyptic Imagination: An Introduction to Jewish Apocalyptic Literature*. Second edition. Grand Rapids MI: Eerdmans, 1998.

_____. *Introduction to the Hebrew Bible*. Minneapolis: Fortress Press, 2004.

Crenshaw, James L. *Old Testament Wisdom: An Introduction*. Atlanta: John Knox

Press, 1981.

Dell, Katharine. *Shaking A Fist At God: Insights from the Book of Job*. Liguori MI: Triumph Books, 1995.

Douglas, Mary. *Purity and Danger: An Analysis of Concepts of Pollution and Taboo*. New York: Routledge, 2003.

Flanders, Henry J., Robert W. Crapps, and David A. Smith. *People of the Covenant: An Introduction to the Hebrew Bible*. Fourth edition. New York: Oxford University Press, 1996.

Harris, Stephen L., and Robert L. Platzner. *The Old Testament: An Introduction to the Hebrew Bible*. New York: McGraw-Hill, 2008.

Holladay, William L. *The Psalms through Three Thousand Years: Prayerbook of a Cloud of Witnesses*. Minneapolis: Fortress Press, 1996.

Matthews, Victor H., and James C. Moyer. *The Old Testament: Text and Context*. Peabody MA: Hendrickson Publishers, 1997.

Miller, James M., and John H. Hayes. *A History of Ancient Israel and Judah*. Second edition. Louisville: Westminster/John Knox Press, 2006.

Murphy, Frederick J. *Early Judaism: The Exile to the Time of Jesus*. Peabody MA: Hendrickson Publishers, 2002.

Petersen, David L. *The Prophetic Literature: An Introduction*. Louisville: Westminster/John Knox Press, 2002.

Scholz, Susanna. *Biblical Studies Alternatively: An Introductory Reader*. Upper Saddle River NJ: Pearson Education, 2003.

VanderKam, James C. *An Introduction to Early Judaism*. Grand Rapids MI: Eerdmans, 2001.

Part two

The New Testament

The Gospels

Introduction and Context

As we turn to the New Testament, we will be dealing with the very bedrock of the Christian faith. The New Testament tells the story of Jesus and the rise of the Christian church in response to his life. Moreover, the New Testament was written by Christians for Christians. It contains the earliest Christian writings and has become "sacred" Christian Scripture. Of course, it must not be forgotten that the New Testament presupposes the Old Testament and stands in continuity with it. For Christians, the God supremely revealed in Jesus is the same God already revealed in Moses and the prophets, and the Old Testament rightly remains a part of the Christian Bible. Yet, because the New Testament is explicitly Christian, written in response to the coming of Christ, it has shaped, and continues to shape, the Christian faith even more directly than the Old Testament.

The New Testament is a collection of twenty-seven Christian writings produced during the church's first century of existence. It opens with four "Gospels," accounts of Jesus' ministry, teaching, death, and resurrection. These are followed by the Acts of the Apostles, which describes the rise and growth of the early Christian church. Most of the New Testament books are letters, thirteen letters of Paul and eight "general epistles." The final book is the Revelation of John, an apocalyptic writing calling the church to faithfulness during a time of persecution and giving visions of God's ultimate victory over the powers of evil.

Over the next four chapters, we will use the New Testament to examine the origin and early formation of Christianity. At the same time, we will be surveying the portion of Scripture that Christians call uniquely their own. The purpose of the present chapter is twofold. First, we will discuss the nature of the Gospels as sources for knowledge of Jesus. Then we will set the stage for the New Testament story by exploring the historical setting in which Jesus was born.

The Origin and Character of the Gospels

The founder and central figure of the Christian faith is Jesus Christ, a Palestinian Jew known to his contemporaries as Jesus of Nazareth. Born about 6 BCE, he conducted a brief ministry of teaching and healing and was executed by the Roman governor Pontius Pilate about 30 CE. Afterwards, his disciples came to believe that God had raised him from the dead, that he was the Messiah ("Christ" in Greek) and Son of God, and that in him the long-awaited age of salvation had dawned. For knowledge of the ministry and teaching of Jesus, we are largely dependent on the New Testament Gospels.[1] The word "gospel" means "good news." In secular usage, "gospel" was a term heralding the birth or accession of a new king or a king's victory over his enemies. Christians first used it to refer to their proclamation of the "good news" that Jesus is the long-awaited Messiah who will at last deliver God's people. It was only secondarily that "gospel" came to refer to the written accounts of Jesus' ministry—Matthew, Mark, Luke, and John.

Inquisitive readers of the New Testament may wonder why it includes four Gospels instead of just one. And why do the four Gospels differ from one another in the way they tell the story of Jesus? And which version is "correct"? A brief introduction to the origin and character of the Gospels will shed some light on such questions and enable a more perceptive reading of the Gospels.

Origin of the Gospels. As perplexing as the presence of four Gospels in the New Testament may be, it is equally amazing to ponder the fact that at first the Christian movement got along without any Gospels at all. Since those who knew Jesus were still living and the early Christians believed themselves to be living in the last generation, there seemed to be no need for written Gospels. For some three to four decades after the death of Jesus,

---

[1] There are a number of additional sources, but they do not add substantially to the information found in the Gospels. Several early, non-Christian sources confirm the existence of Jesus as the originator of the Christian movement. Numerous apocryphal (noncanonical) Christian gospels are widely considered too late and legendary to provide useful information, although some scholars believe that the Coptic *Gospel of Thomas* may preserve some sayings of Jesus independently of the canonical Gospels. Apart from the Gospels, the New Testament itself contains scant information about the ministry of Jesus.

the memory of his words and deeds was preserved primarily in oral tradition. For example, a parable or miracle story would be told in the context of a sermon, a saying of Jesus would be repeated in the instruction of new members, or the story of the Last Supper would be retold during a Lord's Supper celebration. This process had a profound impact on the nature of the material in the Gospels.

For one thing, the tradition preserved only those aspects of Jesus' ministry that had continuing significance for the early Christians, leaving huge gaps in what a historian would like to know about Jesus. For instance, what was he doing between age twelve and the time of his baptism? Also, the tradition was often preserved in isolated fragments with the result that often the original sequence of events and the original setting of Jesus' sayings have been lost. The sequence of events and the grouping of sayings provided by the Gospel writers may often be based on thematic considerations rather than purely chronological or historical concerns. It also seems that the traditions were shaped to address the changing needs of the Christian communities in which they were used. For example, a parable created by Jesus to disarm his critics might be retold and applied to Christian conduct in the church.

Eventually, as the Christian movement spread beyond its Palestinian origins and the eyewitness generation began to pass away, the need was felt to have written materials. Possibly there were some earlier written collections of miracle stories or of sayings of Jesus, but most scholars believe that the earliest of our Gospels to be written was Mark. Close comparison of the Gospels reveals that Matthew, Mark, and Luke are quite similar to one another. Hence, scholars call them "Synoptic" (meaning "viewed together"). The Synoptics follow a generally similar outline of Jesus' ministry and contain a large amount of overlapping content with close verbal similarities. The Gospel of John, by contrast, follows a very different chronology and includes very few passages with parallels in the Synoptics, and even the parallels found do not display the degree of verbal similarities seen among the Synoptics. In addition, the content and style of Jesus' teaching in John are quite different from the Synoptics.

The term "Synoptic problem" refers to the scholarly quest to explain why the first three Gospels are so similar while the fourth is so different. Most scholars today account for the similarities among the Synoptics by assuming that Mark, the shortest and least polished of the Gospels, was written first and that it then became a source for Matthew and Luke, both of which include most of Mark's material. As a second source, Matthew and Luke seem also to have incorporated a hypothetical written collection of sayings of Jesus, commonly referred to as "Q" (after German *Quelle*, "source"). In addition, Matthew and Luke each include a significant amount of unique material drawn from each writer's distinctive sources or traditions (often labeled "M" and "L," respectively). This overlapping use of sources by the Synoptic Gospels accounts for the close similarities, as well as the differences, among them. Meanwhile, John appears not to be based on the Synoptics or on their sources but was written out of its own sources and traditions, explaining why John is so different from the Synoptics.

Because all of the Gospels were written anonymously, we do not know for sure the names of any of their authors. The titles now associated with the Gospels are not original but were added in the late second century as the Gospels were being collected. They reflect traditions about authorship which were current at that time. While scholars debate the accuracy of the traditional identifications, honest scholarship must admit less than certainty. Nevertheless, it is customary to refer to the Gospels by their traditional titles even while acknowledging uncertainty about their actual authorship.

In any case, the identity of the Gospel writers is less important than recognition of the nature of their role. They functioned not as individual authors composing their own memoirs but as "redactors" (that is, final editors) editing earlier sources and traditions into final form. The writers worked as skilled theologians who each took the sources and traditions which had come down to them and artistically wove them into a rich tapestry. Their purpose was not to produce objective accounts of precisely what happened but to tell the "good news," that is, to interpret the story of Jesus for the edification of their readers. Each Gospel was written in and for a particular Christian community and was shaped by its author to address the concerns of that community. Each writer selected and arranged the materials to be included, made subtle alterations in wording, and provided an editorial framework—all aimed at producing an account with the distinctive emphases demanded by the situation of the author's readers. The Gospels are not intended to be bare, historical chronicles but rich, theological portraits of Jesus, each bringing out the significance of Jesus for a particular set of readers. This helps explain why we have more than one Gospel and why they tell the story in different ways.

Four Portraits of Jesus. Mark, our earliest and shortest gospel, was written about 65–70 CE. Traditionally attributed to Mark, who was not a disciple of Jesus but a companion of Peter, the book seems to be addressed to Christians facing the possibility of suffering on account of their faith, possibly in connection with Nero's persecution (64–65 CE) or with the Jewish War (66–70 CE). Mark presents a fast-paced narrative with far less teaching material than the other Gospels. After a hurried, itinerant ministry of teaching and healing in Galilee, Jesus journeys to Jerusalem. There the narrative slows and focuses sustained attention on a one-week Jerusalem ministry which climaxes in Jesus' crucifixion and resurrection. Mark strongly emphasizes that Jesus was a suffering Messiah, whose death was "a ransom for many" (10:45), and calls his readers to be willing to take up their own crosses and follow him (8:34-35).

Matthew's Gospel, traditionally attributed to Jesus' disciple of that name who was known as a tax collector, was written about 75–90 CE. Matthew basically follows Mark's narrative, preceding it with a birth narrative (which Mark lacks) and interspersing it with five large blocks of teaching material. The longest and best-known of these five discourses is the Sermon on the Mount (chaps. 5–7). The Sermon opens with a series of Beatitudes conferring the blessing of God's kingdom upon those who depend utterly on God and long for God's justice to prevail. It then challenges Jesus' disciples to be "the light of the world" and "the salt of the earth" by living out a righteousness which transcends the letter of the law and embodies the fullness of God's will as revealed by Jesus. Overall, Matthew was composed with a strong appeal to Jewish readers, emphasizing that Jesus fulfills prophetic expectations and that he did not come to destroy the Torah commandments but to reveal their true intention. The teaching of Jesus is presented as a definitive statement of God's will, obedience to which is of ultimate importance.

The Gospel of Luke and its sequel, the book of Acts, are also dated about 75–90 CE. Both books are traditionally attributed to Luke, a physician and Gentile Christian sometimes found in the company of Paul. The two books are tied together by prefaces (Luke 1:1-4; Acts 1:1-2) which dedicate the two-volume work to an unknown person named Theophilus. Like Matthew, Luke has a birth narrative and generally follows Mark's outline of Jesus' ministry (although omitting nearly half of Mark). Almost half of Luke is material unparalleled elsewhere, most of which is inserted into the journey to Jerusalem (chaps. 9–19). Luke is written with an appeal to Gentile readers and emphasizes the inclusiveness of the gospel. Jesus is good news for the poor, sinners, outcasts, women, Samaritans, and Gentiles. In the book of Acts, it becomes the task of the church to continue Jesus' work by taking the gospel to the whole world.

The Gospel traditionally attributed to the disciple John is the latest of the canonical Gospels, written about 90–100 CE. Transposing the story of Jesus into a higher key, it allows the early Christian theological understanding of Jesus to come through much more explicitly. Whereas the Synoptic Jesus preaches the kingdom of God and avoids attention to his own identity, the Johannine Jesus rarely speaks of the kingdom and focuses entirely on his role as the heavenly Revealer. John's story begins before creation, alluding to the role of the Word of God in creation and maintaining that the same Word of God was incarnated ("enfleshed") in Jesus. As the Son of God, Jesus was sent by the Father to reveal God to the world. His death on the cross embodies and reveals God's love for the world and provides the means by which he returns to the Father. Repeatedly, Jesus invites his listeners to believe in him as the way to eternal life with God (John 3:16).

Not surprisingly, the Gospel of John has long been considered "the spiritual gospel." Clement of Alexandria (about 200 CE) maintained that after the Synoptics had recorded the "bodily facts" about Jesus, John was inspired to write a "spiritual gospel" to interpret their spiritual significance.[2] It would be an oversimplification to say that the Synoptics are purely historical while John is merely theological. All the Gospels contain both historical memory and theological interpretation. Yet it remains true that in John the theological interpretation is more thorough and explicit. It is clear that, on the whole, the historical Jesus lies closer to the surface in the Synoptics than in John. Therefore, the sketch of Jesus' ministry in chapter 6 will be based primarily on the Synoptic Gospels.

The World of Jesus and the New Testament

Before turning to the story of Jesus and the rest of the New Testament, it is necessary to set the stage by taking account of the historical and cultural context of that story. The New Testament did not appear in a vacuum. Jesus was a first-century Jew. Christianity emerged out of Palestinian Judaism and slowly spread around the Mediterranean world, embracing Gentiles imbued with Hellenistic culture. The remainder of this chapter, therefore, will

---

[2]Quoted by George R. Beasley-Murray, in *John*, Word Biblical Commentary 36, ed. David A. Hubbard et al. (Waco TX: Word Books, 1987) lxvii.

discuss some of the more salient aspects of the New Testament world. We will begin by looking at the political and religious situation of Palestinian Judaism; then we will zoom out to bring Diaspora Judaism and the larger Hellenistic world into the picture. This will not only bring the New Testament to life and help us to understand it historically, but it also will enable us to take more seriously the Christian doctrine of the Incarnation, namely, the claim that in Christ, God entered into human history in a definite time and place.

The Political Situation. At the time of Jesus, Palestine, like most of the Mediterranean world, was controlled by Rome. By this time, the Jewish people, with only one brief respite, had already labored under a succession of foreign regimes for nearly six centuries. It was a condition in stark contrast to the promises of the prophets and the hopes of the people. The following survey will provide a sense of the national frustration that developed during those centuries.

Key Dates in the New Testament Context

587–539 BCE . . . . Babylonian period: Jews in Babylonian Exile
539–333 BCE . . . . Persian period: Jewish return and restoration
333–166 BCE . . . . . Hellenistic period: Greek influence and oppression
166–63 BCE . . . . Maccabean Revolt and Hasmonean period:
Jewish independence
63 BCE–135 CE . . . . Roman period: New Testament times
ca. 6 BCE . . . . Birth of Jesus
ca. 30 CE . . . . Death of Jesus
ca. 35–64 CE . . . . Missionary work of Paul
66–70 CE . . . . Jewish War with Rome
70 CE . . . . Fall of Jerusalem; destruction of Temple
132–135 CE . . . . Second Jewish Revolt

Babylonian Period (587–539 BCE). As discussed above in chapter 3, in 587 BCE the Babylonians had conquered the kingdom of Judah (all that then remained of Old Testament Israel), bringing the Davidic dynasty to an end, demolishing the magnificent temple built by Solomon, and taking thousands of Judeans into exile. In spite of this national disaster—which, according to the prophets, had resulted from the peoples' breaking their covenant with God—the Jews survived, reorganized their traditions to form the religion that would now be known as "Judaism," and looked forward to a time of restoration and renewal of the covenant (see Jeremiah 31:31-34).

Persian Period (539–333 BCE). By 539 BCE, the Persians had wrested power from Babylonia and gave the Jews in Babylonian captivity opportunity to return to their homeland. Restoration, however, was painfully slow and partial. Many Jews stayed in Mesopotamia, and those who did return to Palestine found very meager conditions. Eventually, the temple was rebuilt and a Jewish community took root, organized around the recently compiled Torah which was brought by Ezra from Babylon to Jerusalem around 398 BCE. Yet Judah remained a province of the Persian Empire under the authority of Persian appointees.

Hellenistic Period (333–167 BCE). Persian control ended in 333 BCE when Alexander the Great, the conquering general from Macedonia, added Palestine to his vast Hellenistic empire, which ultimately reached to the borders of India. Following Alexander's premature death in 323, Palestine was torn between rival Hellenistic kingdoms, coming first under the control of the Ptolemies (Egypt) and then of the Seleucids (Syria). It had been Alexander's ambition to unify the world through a common Greek language and culture, and indeed, during the centuries after his death, Hellenistic culture permeated the Mediterranean world and Greek became the language of international communication. Greek-speaking Jews in Alexandria translated their Hebrew Scriptures into Greek, producing a translation known as the Septuagint (250–100 BCE). By New Testament times, the Greek language had become so widely known that it served as a ready-made vehicle for the spread of Christianity. Most of the early Christian churches adopted the Septuagint as Scripture, and all of the New Testament books were written in *koine* ("common") Greek, the most commonly recognized language of the time.

Maccabean Revolt and Hasmonean Period (167–67 BCE). Although Alexander intended Hellenism to unify the world, it did not unify the Jews. Through a century and a half of Hellenistic rule Palestine had peacefully absorbed much Hellenistic influence, but by 167 BCE a conservative reaction had set in. A policy of aggressive Hellenization by the Seleucid rulers had found eager acceptance among some aristocratic Jews, but it met stiff resistance among traditional-minded Jews. When the Seleucids retaliated with a harsh persecution, it ignited the Maccabean Revolt, a quarter-century conflict which, against all odds, managed to win total Jewish independence. This story, which can be read in 1 and 2 Maccabees (found in the Apocrypha), forms the context in which the book of Daniel was written as a call for faithful resistance to the oppressive Seleucid regime and an assurance that all such "beastly" regimes are destined to be replaced by the righteous reign of God through a mysterious figure known as the "Son of Man."

The Maccabean family (also known as the Hasmoneans) founded a dynasty which ruled for almost a century over a resurgent Jewish kingdom. The Hasmonean rulers assumed the office of high priest and also claimed the title "king." Their military conquests, including Galilee in the north and Idumaea in the south, where the inhabitants were forcibly converted to Judaism, resulted in a Jewish kingdom nearly as large as that ruled by David and Solomon. In 128 BCE, the Jews destroyed a temple of the Samaritans, a rival religious group which claimed to preserve the religion of Moses more purely than the Jews. This contributed to the bitter animosity which characterized relations between Jews and Samaritans from that time on.

In spite of the resurgence of Jewish power, however, many Jews did not see the Hasmonean kingdom as the arrival of the long-awaited golden age. Some objected that the high priesthood had been usurped by a family not of proper lineage; others were offended by the combination of high priest and warring king in one office. Moreover, the Hasmonean dynasty quickly devolved into a morass of self-aggrandizement, Hellenizing lifestyle, and palace intrigue. It is not surprising that several of the Jewish parties known to us from New Testament times had either their origin or early development in this period, as Jews of various persuasions reacted in different ways to the policies of the Hasmonean rulers.

Roman Period (63 BCE–135 CE and beyond). The last period of Jewish independence until modern times came to an end in 63 BCE when the Roman general Pompey took control of Palestine, adding it to the ever-expanding conquests of Rome. By the first century CE, the Roman Empire embraced most of the Mediterranean world and much of Europe. Because all New Testament events took place within the Roman Empire, we will look a bit more closely at this period.

Roman Administration and Taxes. Rome allowed the Jews a measure of local autonomy. At various times there was a puppet Jewish king or governor appointed by Rome, who was expected to maintain order, tend to Roman interests, and ensure the smooth flow of revenue to Rome. The Sanhedrin, a Jewish ruling council presided over by the high priest, was allowed to administer affairs primarily in Jerusalem on the basis of the

Jewish law. Roman control was felt mainly in the presence of Roman troops and in the burden of Roman taxes. Taxes were high and the system of collecting them was corrupt. Most notorious were the duties levied on goods in transit. The privilege of collecting duties in a given district was awarded to the highest bidder, who paid Rome in advance, then made a profit by collecting the duties plus a commission. The system was easily abused simply by overestimating the value of goods. Tax collectors were despised by the Jews both because they were assumed to be dishonest and because they collaborated with Rome.

The Herods: Roman Puppets. Most prominent among the puppet rulers of Palestine under Roman control were several generations of the Herods, an aristocratic Jewish-Idumaean family who curried favor with Rome and got themselves appointed to various positions of authority. The earliest and foremost of the Herods was Herod the Great, who was given by Rome the title "King of Judea," an office he exercised from 37 to 4 BCE. He was a strong, capable ruler who maintained order and conducted a strong building campaign throughout Palestine. Besides the building of palaces, fortresses, cities, and a harbor (Caesarea Maritima, which became the Roman capital of Judea), he rebuilt the Jerusalem temple into a magnificent structure surrounded by acres of courtyards which were enclosed by colonnaded porticoes. At the same time, Herod was a ruthless ruler, more enamored with Roman culture than with Jewish law. He earned a reputation for readiness to assassinate anyone perceived to threaten his authority—even members of his own family. According to Matthew 2:1-19, Jesus was born

---

The "Date" of Jesus' Birth

The exact date of Jesus' birth is unknown. Confusing as it may seem, the best scholarly estimate is 6 BCE, give or take one or two years. This is based largely on the impression given in Matthew and Luke that the birth of Jesus took place shortly before the death of Herod the Great in 4 BCE. Theoretically, of course, according to our calendar system, Jesus' birth should be dated 1 CE. (There is no year 0 in our calendar system. The traditional notation AD stands for *Anno Domini,* "in the year of the Lord.") The anomaly was introduced in the sixth century when a calendar was first devised based on Jesus' birth; the calendar makers simply miscalculated. Based on more accurate calculations, we now leave the calendar as is and revise the date.

shortly before Herod's death in 4 BCE. Upon learning of it, Herod slaughtered all male infants in Bethlehem in a vain attempt to eliminate this prospective new rival. This episode cannot be confirmed historically, but it graphically illustrates the kind of behavior people had come to expect from their king. Such brutality must have contributed to the perennial longing for a different kind of rule.

At Herod's death, Rome divided Palestine among three of his sons, all of whom were governors, rather than kings. Philip (4 BCE–34 CE) ruled territories to the northeast of the Sea of Galilee, where the population was largely non-Jewish. Herod Antipas (4 BCE–39 CE) ruled Perea, east of the Jordan River, where John the Baptist was active, and Galilee in the north, where Jesus grew up and conducted much of his ministry. It was Antipas who imprisoned and then beheaded John after John had criticized Antipas's illicit marriage to his former sister-in-law. Antipas was also suspicious of implications Jesus' ministry might have for his own rule. Archelaus (4 BCE–6 CE) was made governor of Idumaea, Judea, and Samaria—the heartland of biblical Palestine—with the prospect of becoming king if he ruled well. His brutal tyranny, however, elicited such vehement protests that Rome deposed him and placed his territory under the direct control of a Roman procurator.

The Roman Procurators. Also known as prefects or governors, the procurators were a series of Roman administrators who governed various parts of Palestine beginning in 6 CE. This shift to direct Roman rule was accompanied by a census for purposes of tax assessment, all of which provoked a wave of nationalistic unrest. Judas the Galilean, motivated by devotion to God as the only Lord and King, led an uprising which was met by quick Roman reprisal and the crucifixion of some 2,000 Jewish rebels. Sporadic popular rebellions—sometimes led by figures making prophetic, messianic, or royal claims—met a similar fate, as the Romans responded with quick, brutal retaliation. Pontius Pilate (26–36 CE), the fifth procurator of Judea, was involved in several conflicts with the Jews and attacked a band of Samaritans he mistook for revolutionaries. Pilate is best known, of course, as the procurator who ordered the crucifixion of Jesus (about 30 CE), probably because he feared Jesus was stirring up sedition.

The Jewish War and Its Aftermath. Three decades later, the hostility escalated into a full-scale, open rebellion, the Jewish War with Rome (66–70 CE). The Jewish rebels enjoyed some early success but, in the long

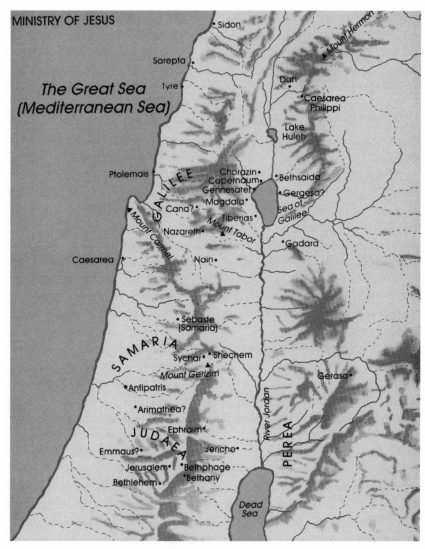

run, were no match for the Roman legions. The Romans first subdued Galilee, then headed south to Judea. After a long siege, Jerusalem fell in 70 CE with a horrific slaughter and the total destruction of Herod's magnificent temple. In many ways, Jewish history had come full cycle since 587 BCE—once again the Jews were a people without a state and without a temple. A second Jewish revolt against Rome (132–135 CE), led by an alleged Messiah (Simon bar Kochba), also failed miserably. Jerusalem was demolished and a Roman colony was established on its site. Meanwhile, near the end of the first century an academy of Jewish scholars in the little town of Jamnia near the Judean coast (sometimes referred to as the "Council of Jamnia") was busy reorganizing Judaism around Scripture, tradition, and synagogue.

The Jewish Religious Situation. With this framework of political events in view, it is necessary also to look at some religious developments in Judaism during this period. Only the most important features can be touched on here.

Synagogues. Jewish synagogues were gathering places for study, instruction, prayer, and worship. The exact origin of the synagogue is obscure. None appear in the Old Testament but they are presupposed in the New. Most likely they emerged during the Babylonian exile, developed among Jews scattered outside the homeland, and eventually became established throughout Palestine as well. Unlike the temple, which was centralized in Jerusalem, synagogues were found wherever Jews were living in sufficient numbers. Synagogues also functioned quite differently than the temple. Whereas temple activity revolved around the priestly function of sacrifice, which was offered twice daily as well as on special occasions, no sacrifices were performed in the synagogues. Synagogue worship rather involved the reading, translation, and interpretation of Scripture along with the recital of prayers. The informality of the synagogues and their openness to nonprofessional participation provided a setting in which the early Christians could present and discuss their gospel. The pattern of synagogue worship also influenced the development of early Christian worship.

Jewish Diversity. Judaism at the time of Jesus was much more diverse than it would come to be in the period after 70 CE. Certainly there were central tenets maintained by all Jews: the one God of creation who chose Israel, entered into covenant with them, and gave them the Torah (the Jewish law) as guidance for living as God's people. Beyond these, there were many issues open to debate: the content and interpretation of the Torah, how to relate to Gentiles and unfaithful Jews, and, not least, the solution to the problem of foreign domination. Within Judaism there emerged many competing groups with differing views and agendas. Among these, the first-century Jewish historian Josephus describes the following three or four as the most important.

Pharisees. The Pharisees were a party of Jewish laymen who had devoted themselves to meticulous observance of the Torah as it was interpreted by the scribes, scholars who studied and interpreted the Scripture. Scribal interpretation sought to take the law seriously by working out the rules by which the commandments could be applied to every aspect of daily life and adapted to changing circumstances. During many generations of scribal activity, there had accumulated a significant body of rulings pertaining to various aspects of Jewish customs and piety, such as Sabbath-observance, tithing, ritual washings, prayers, and fasting. This cumulative body of material came to be called the "tradition of the elders" or the "oral law." Characteristic of the Pharisees was their devotion to both the written Law (Pentateuch) and the oral law. Although numerically small, they had popular influence and were revered as the most exacting interpreters of the Torah. Nevertheless, they were not stick-in-the-mud conservatives but progressive, open to new ideas which are not explicit in Scripture but which can be deduced by interpretation. They accepted such innovative doctrines as the resurrection of the dead, final judgment, and rewards and punishments in the afterlife. They appear to have nurtured the hope for a royal Messiah to redeem and restore Israel. They may also have believed that Israel's subjugation to the pagans resulted from neglect of the law and that the coming of the Messiah depended upon returning to the law. This would account for the Pharisees' contempt for "sinners," flagrant violators of the law, and for the simple, uneducated "people of the land" who had neither time nor resources for studying and applying the meticulous finer points of the law. It also explains why the Pharisees are so prominent in the Gospels as vocal opponents of Jesus. From their perspective, Jesus not only did not keep the law properly but also was engaged in behavior which would delay Israel's redemption.

Sadducees. The Sadducees were drawn from the wealthy ruling families in Jerusalem, including both the priestly and nonpriestly aristocracy. They controlled the temple and dominated the Sanhedrin, which also included a minority of Pharisees. Firmly entrenched in positions of power and privilege, they had a vested interest in cooperating with the Romans to maintain order. They typically urged caution in protesting Roman policies and warned that rebellion could prove disastrous. Theologically, they were conservative, insisting on not going beyond a literal reading of the Torah. On this basis, they rejected not only the oral law as a whole but also the concepts of resurrection, judgment, and the afterlife. The Sadducees viewed Jesus as a potential troublemaker and were instrumental in arresting him and turning him over to the Romans. With the destruction of the temple and the demise of the Jewish government in 70 CE, the Sadducees ceased to function. The rabbinic Judaism reorganized at Jamnia was shaped largely by Pharisaism.

Essenes. The Essenes were a highly sectarian Jewish party, known to us from several ancient accounts. The Dead Sea Scrolls, discovered beginning in 1947 in caves overlooking the western shore of the Dead Sea, are believed by most scholars to have belonged to an Essene group. The ruins at the nearby site called Qumran seem to be the remains of an Essene commune. If these identifications are correct, then the scrolls and the ruins give us a more complete picture of who the Essenes were. They appear to have emerged in the Hasmonean period in protest of the Hasmoneans' control of the temple. They withdrew into the wilderness, where their "Teacher of Righteousness" organized them into a community living in isolation as the "true Israel." Members of the sect surrendered their personal possessions to the group upon entrance and bound themselves together under a hierarchical structure of ranks and a rigid code of discipline. They practiced strict ritual purity, took daily baths of purification, and ate sacred meals. They awaited the appearance of two messiahs, one royal and the other priestly. They expected to participate in a final cosmic war between the "Sons of Light" and the "Sons of Darkness," which would establish them in control not only of Israel and the temple but also of the world. The Essenes are not mentioned by name in the New Testament, but many of their beliefs and practices are comparable to those of the early Christians. Their existence shows just how diverse Judaism was at the time of Jesus.

Zealots. "Zealots" is a term used to refer to the militant freedom fighters who were ready to use violence to defend Judaism against compromise and foreign oppression. It is now considered doubtful that there was a single, continuous Zealot party throughout the period of the Roman procurators. Josephus reserves the term for a faction which appeared soon after the beginning of the Jewish War, refused to allow a negotiated settlement, and fought on to the bitter end. Even apart from the existence of an organized party, however, it is clear that there was a tradition of zeal for God and the Torah which led many to take up arms from time to time. The so-called "fourth philosophy" founded by Judas the Galilean in 6 CE was devoted to the principle that no one but God can be Lord and King, motivating his group's rebellion against the Roman census and tax. There were many royal, prophetic, or messianic pretenders who agitated for violence, apparently hoping that God would honor their efforts by divine intervention. Among the disciples of Jesus was one known as "the Zealot" (Luke 6:15) and two others known as "Sons of Thunder" (Mark 3:17). Among the crowds that followed him there were no doubt many who wished him to lead a zealot-type rebellion (see John 6:15). Jesus steadfastly refused. God's rule would be established in God's own way, without resort to violence.

It should also be pointed out that there were a number of lesser Jewish parties and, above all, that most Jews belonged to none of these parties. In the midst of this diversity, there were soon to appear some new voices announcing a new day and a different agenda for God's people—the voices first of John the Baptist, then of Jesus and the early Christians.

Jewish Future Hopes. It is impossible to understand the New Testament without some awareness of the intense Jewish interest in a decisive future action of God to redeem Israel. The technical term for this concept is "eschatology," literally "the doctrine of last things" or "of the end time." The oppressive conditions of the closing centuries BCE accentuated the development of eschatological hopes. Given the great diversity of Judaism in other regards, it is not surprising to find a variety of future expectations as well. In general, there were two strands of eschatological thought, the messianic hope and apocalypticism, which were often complementary and interwoven.

The Jewish hope for a *Messiah* (from the Hebrew word meaning "anointed one"), as already discussed in chapter 3, grew out of prophetic longings for an ideal king who would fulfill the royal ideology. During the long centuries of Gentile domination after the Exile, these hopes had grown more urgent but also quite diverse. Probably dominant was the nationalistic hope for a royal Messiah, descended from David, who would liberate the Jews from their oppressors, restore the kingdom of Israel, and rule over it. During the New Testament period, a number of messianic claimants appeared with militant aspirations. The Qumran community expected both a royal Messiah and a priestly Messiah. No one was looking for a Messiah whose role would be to suffer and die. (The "suffering Servant" of Isaiah 53, who suffers innocently and vicariously for the sins of others, was typically understood by Jewish readers not as a prediction of the Messiah but as a description of Israel in exile.) Thus, when the New Testament calls Jesus "the Christ" (from the Greek word meaning "anointed one"), it is claiming that he fulfills the messianic hope in spite of his humiliating crucifixion, that he redefines the concept of Messiah and fulfills it in unexpected ways.

Alongside this nationalistic hope, and sometimes intertwined with it, there arose a more radical, cosmic hope which today is called "apocalyptic eschatology." Apocalyptic writings, most of which are nonbiblical, appeared between 200 BCE and 200 CE, usually in response to some intense persecution or upheaval. Purporting to give visions of the heavenly world or of the end time, the apocalyptic seers typically look not for the coming of a Messiah to restore the nation but for the end of the world as we know it. This evil age is destined to be replaced by a glorious new age to come. The present world order is viewed as hopelessly corrupt. Satan is in revolt against God and has temporarily achieved dominance. This accounts for the many evils in the world, above all for the injustices being inflicted upon God's people by the wicked pagans. No improvement is expected in this age; rather, as the end of the age draws near, it must degenerate into a period of terrible tribulation, an intense outbreak of evil. Since the crisis that prompts the writing of the apocalypse marks the beginning of the tribulation, it ironically is a hopeful sign, signaling that the end is near. Soon God will intervene—either directly or through a heavenly "Son of Man" figure who will appear as cosmic Judge—to set things right. This world will meet a cataclysmic end and a new creation will take its place. A resurrection of the dead and final judgment according to deeds will rectify the injustices of this world. In a reversal of fortunes, the wicked, who prospered in this age, will be doomed to eternal punishment or annihilation; the righteous, who suffered in this age, will be rewarded with eternal life in a new age of bliss. Thus, the oppressive pagan kingdoms of the world are doomed to be swallowed up by the coming "Kingdom of God."

The persistence and variety of the Jewish eschatological hopes testify to the deep yearnings of a people who longed for freedom and who looked to their God for redemption. It is important to see the Christian movement against the background of Jewish eschatology not only because the New Testament takes up and presupposes many of its concepts, but also because the early Christians saw Jesus as God's answer to these longings.

Diaspora Judaism. Our background study so far has focused on Judaism in Palestine, for that is the context in which Jesus and the first Christian church appeared. Before turning to that story, however, we must briefly broaden our scope because New Testament Christianity quickly moved out into the larger Mediterranean world where it encountered both Diaspora Jews and Gentiles imbued with Greco-Roman culture.

"Diaspora" means "dispersion" or "scattering," and refers to the many

Jews who had come to live in scattered places outside Palestine. Sometimes through forced displacement, sometimes through voluntary migration, Jews had come to live in Mesopotamia, Egypt, Syria, Asia Minor, Greece, and Italy. Most major cities had at least one synagogue. Though the difference should not be exaggerated, Diaspora Jews tended to absorb more of the Hellenistic culture than Palestinian Jews did. They typically spoke Greek and read Scripture from the Septuagint, the Greek translation produced in Alexandria (250–100 BCE). Some Jews assimilated into the surrounding culture; those who did not assimilate kept the commandments as well as they could, making concessions when necessary.

Although Jews were sometimes ridiculed for their peculiar customs, Judaism also proved attractive to a number of Gentiles, who were drawn to its strict monotheism and high moral standards. Gentiles who actually converted to Judaism—a process involving circumcision, a bath of purification, and sacrifice at the temple—are called "proselytes." Gentiles who loosely attached themselves to the synagogues, supporting Judaism and adopting many of its beliefs but without converting, are called "God-fearers." Both groups appear in the New Testament. The existence of Diaspora Judaism is of tremendous importance to the development of early Christianity. As the Christian missionaries took the gospel around the Roman Empire, the many Jewish synagogues served as natural starting points. The New Testament churches outside Palestine also inherited from the synagogues the Septuagint as their "Bible." The New Testament writers most often quote Scripture from the Septuagint version and its Greek language has profoundly influence the language of the New Testament.

The Larger Greco-Roman World. The Christian mission, of course, was not confined to Jews, but soon embraced not only proselytes and God-fearers but also Gentiles with no previous knowledge of Israel's God. This brought Christianity into ever closer contact with strange new cultures. The Christian faith had to find ways to relate to these cultures and was itself transformed in the process. Many of the New Testament books reflect this process, along with efforts to guard against losing the essence of the gospel as well. Here we can only be suggestive of the bewildering variety of movements which filled the first-century Roman Empire.

The *Pax Romana* ("Roman Peace") established by Augustus (27 BCE–14 CE), the first Roman emperor, brought the Mediterranean world together in an unprecedented way. The great Roman army maintained order throughout the empire. A network of roads, built and maintained to transport the army, facilitated ordinary travel and communication as well. A Roman navy patrolled the Mediterranean, making shipping relatively safe from piracy. For all of this, Augustus was hailed by the Roman poets as a savior, temples were built in his honor, and a cult of emperor worship was inaugurated. Even under Roman rule, the underlying culture continued to be Hellenistic. Greek was still the language of literature and of international discourse—hence, the writing of all the New Testament books in Greek.

The early Roman Empire witnessed a great proliferation of religions. By contrast with the optimistic spirit of classical Greece, it was an age of much pessimism and despair. People felt lost and powerless in a vast, impersonal empire in which they had no meaningful voice. They seemed to be at the mercy of dark, mysterious forces which controlled their destiny. Superstition, magic, the use of amulets and charms, augury, and astrology were prevalent as ways of trying to gain an edge. The old official civic religions were still practiced, of course, and were believed to be a source of Rome's great power, but they were increasingly irrelevant to the personal lives of individuals. Of growing significance was a vast array of religions and philosophies which were oriented more toward the needs and well-being of individual adherents. Many of them were created by "syncretism" (the "blending together" of beliefs or practices from different religions), as religions from the eastern provinces were borrowed, adapted, and combined with Greek elements to provide a virtually endless supply of new religions.

Among the intellectual class, old Greek philosophies such as Platonism, Stoicism, and Cynicism, having been transformed into popularized, semi-religious philosophies of life, enjoyed wide currency. As wandering philosophical teachers would lecture to crowds in the marketplace or in rented halls, they also had a certain mass appeal. Stoicism in particular soared to great heights of ethical challenge.

Even more popular were the so-called mystery religions, which offered the prospect of personal salvation. The many mystery cults were devoted to various gods and goddesses and frequently centered around the myth of a dying and rising deity. Initiation took place through participation in secret rites through which the initiate ritually experienced the death and rebirth of the god. The initiate was thereby assured of security and blessing in this life and of immortal happiness after death. Especially popular and influential were the Eleusinian mysteries, native to Greece; the cult of Isis, from Egypt; and Mithraism, a Persian import which was extremely popular among Roman soldiers and eventually became Christianity's main rival. When it moved into the Hellenistic world, Christianity adopted some patterns similar to those of the mysteries. Baptism, for example, was conceived as dying and rising with Christ and coming to share his new life. Therefore, care had to be taken to distinguish Christianity from the mysteries. In contrast with the mystery religions, Christianity is rooted not in a timeless myth but in a historic person, Jesus Christ, who lays exclusive claim to believers and makes ethical demands unknown in the mysteries.

A final category that deserves mention is Gnosticism (from the Greek word *gnosis*, "knowledge"), a highly syncretistic, philosophically oriented group of religions which sought salvation through knowledge. Rooted in a radical dualism which defined spirit as good and matter as evil, Gnosticism rejected the material world as a cosmic mistake. Human beings are essentially sparks of the divine spirit trapped in evil, material bodies, alienated from and forgetful of their true origin in the realm of spirit. Salvation comes through revealed knowledge, which consists of both the Gnostic myth, explaining the origin of things, and secret formulas by which at death the spirit may escape the physical world and return to God. Gnostic ethics tended either toward ascetic rigorism, designed to subdue the evil flesh, or toward libertine immorality, justified by the irrelevance of the material body. Christianity already interacted with Gnostic ideas in the New Testament period, and their interaction became particularly acute in the second century when fully developed Gnostic systems emerged.

This great proliferation of religions indicates that people were looking for something that could provide security in the midst of all the dangers and uncertainties of life, something that could give purpose and hope to an otherwise mundane or miserable existence. Into this maelstrom of movements came one more—Christianity, from the tiny eastern province of Palestine, proclaiming that in Jesus Christ the one true God of Israel had acted not only to redeem Israel but also to meet the deepest needs and longings of all humanity. To that story we will turn in the next chapter.

• 6 •

The Ministry
and Message of Jesus

But when *the fullness of time* had come, God sent his Son, born of a
woman, . . . so that we might receive adoption as children.

(Galatians 4:4-5)

The previous chapter sought to describe something of "the fullness of time."
The stage is now set for the birth of the Messiah. This chapter will present
a sketch of Jesus' ministry based primarily on the Synoptic Gospels.
Because Mark's account is the earliest and simplest, its outline will be
followed wherever possible.

Before the Public Ministry

Jesus' birth is recounted only in the captivating narratives found in the
opening two chapters of Matthew and Luke, both of which are primarily
concerned to set the story of Jesus in the context of the long history of
God's dealing with Israel and to evoke in their readers a sense that God is
about to act again in a decisive way for the salvation of God's people. The
two accounts develop these themes in rather different ways. Matthew
focuses on the role of Joseph, who declines to dissolve his engagement to
Mary despite her mysterious pregnancy; the visit of "wise men" from the
East bringing gifts worthy of a king; and Herod's brutal slaughter of male
infants in Bethlehem. Luke's story revolves more around Mary and includes
the birth of John the Baptist to Mary's cousin Elisabeth, the journey to
Bethlehem for the census, the birth of Jesus in a stable, and the angelic
announcement of the Savior's birth to lowly shepherds in the field.

In spite of these differences, the two accounts agree on the key points:
Jesus was born to a young Jewish woman named Mary, who was engaged
to a Jewish man named Joseph, though the marriage had not been sexually
consummated; the birth took place in Bethlehem, a little town in Judea just
south of Jerusalem, but Jesus grew up in Nazareth, an obscure village in
Galilee. Both accounts give witness to the "virgin birth" (or "miraculous
conception") of Jesus, which is a way of affirming his special relationship

with God, but which should not be construed to mean that Jesus is less than fully human (as if he were half-god and half-human, as in Greek mythology, for example). Jesus' birth in Bethlehem, King David's hometown, connects him to the hope for a Messiah, a new David (see Micah 5:2). The name "Jesus," a Greek form of the Hebrew name "Joshua," was a common Jewish name of the period. The name means "Yahweh saves" and gives witness to Jewish longings for redemption.

We have scant traditions related to Jesus' childhood and early adulthood. We get the impression he grew up in Nazareth in a devout peasant Jewish family. Luke 2:41-52 tells the story of a family pilgrimage to the Jerusalem temple when Jesus was twelve. He had four brothers and at least two sisters (Mark 6:3). He followed Joseph into the carpentry trade (Matthew 13:55; Mark 6:3). As Nazareth is only about six miles from Sepphoris, a splendid Roman-style city which served as Antipas's capital, Jesus would have had ample opportunity to witness the luxury the powerful were able to enjoy by oppressing the poor. It is even possible that Joseph and/or Jesus were employed in the rebuilding of Sepphoris, which was razed in 4 BCE after an uprising.

All four Gospels connect the beginning of Jesus' ministry with the mission of John the Baptist, a fiery eschatological prophet who warned of impending judgment which was about to visit God's wrath on the ungodly (Mark 1:1-8; Matthew 3:1-12; Luke 3:1-20; John 1:19-28). John urged people to repent (turn from sin) before it was too late, and those who did repent he baptized, immersing them in the Jordan River as a symbol of their repentance. He warned his fellow Jews not to depend upon their descent from Abraham, for what was required was genuine repentance which results in changed living. John viewed his work as preparation for one greater than he, whose coming would bring salvation for the repentant but judgment for the unprepared. Thus, the Gospels depict him as a forerunner of the Messiah. John's message created quite a stir. People were flocking to him for baptism. Perhaps many saw in John a sign that God was about to purify and renew Israel.

Among those who came to John for baptism was a young Jewish man from Nazareth named Jesus. That Jesus was baptized by John is considered historically certain, since the early Christians would never have invented a story that could seem to imply Jesus' subordination to John. Apparently, Jesus submitted to John's baptism because he agreed with the message that Israel must repent. At his baptism Jesus experienced God's call to a prophetic mission of his own and the Spirit of God empowered him for the task (Mark 1:9-11). The voice of God designating him as "my Son, the Beloved" echoes Old Testament texts related to a royal Messiah (Psalm 2) and to a suffering Servant (Isaiah 42), combining these previously distinct roles into one figure.

Immediately after his baptism, Jesus found himself in the barren Judean wilderness for a time of temptation (or testing), where he says "no" to the misuse of his divinely given power for personal benefit, for winning fame, or for gaining political power (Mark 1:12-13; Matthew 4:1-11; Luke 4:1-13). These initial confrontations with Satan seem to foreshadow later pressures on Jesus to be a militant-political Messiah, leading a revolt against the reigning powers and setting up a theocracy (see John 6:15; Mark 8:31-33; 11:9-10; Matthew 26:51-52). That was not to be his mission. The shape his mission *would* take remained to be seen.

The Galilee Ministry

After the imprisonment of John the Baptist, Jesus returned to Galilee and began an itinerant ministry of teaching and healing. The Synoptics do not say how long this lasted. John's Gospel gives the impression of a three-year ministry punctuated by three visits to Jerusalem. No attempt will be made here to trace a sequence of events. Rather, we will summarize key aspects of Jesus' message and activity.

Preaching and teaching. Jesus was known to his contemporaries as a prophet and teacher. He confronted them with a message of redemption and renewal as God's people. That message can be summarized under the following themes.

The central theme in Jesus' preaching was *the arrival of the "kingdom of God."* Mark's Gospel opens its account of Jesus' ministry by summarizing his message as an announcement of the arrival of God's long-awaited kingdom:

> Now after John was arrested, Jesus came to Galilee, proclaiming the good news of God, and saying, "The time is fulfilled, and the kingdom of God has come near; repent, and believe in the good news."   (Mark 1:14-15)

"Kingdom of God"[1] is an eschatological concept, referring to the end-

---

[1]"Kingdom of heaven," which is frequently found in the Gospel of Matthew, is synonymous with "kingdom of God." Matthew frequently uses "kingdom of

time reign of God which will set things right and bring salvation for God's people. It is widely agreed that this was the key theme not only of Jesus' teaching but also of his whole ministry. Although scholars have debated whether for Jesus the kingdom is present or future, there is a sense in which it is both. In essence, and certainly in its fullness, the kingdom still lies in the future, as when Jesus teaches his disciples to pray, "Your kingdom come" (Matthew 6:10; see also Luke 11:2). Yet, on occasion, Jesus dares to speak of the kingdom as already present in his own ministry. "But if it is by the finger of God that I cast out the demons, then the kingdom of God has come to you" (Luke 11:20). The kingdom has drawn so near that its power is already breaking into the present as Jesus announces good news to the desperate and heals the infirm (see Matthew 11:2-6). Thus, Jesus himself embodied the coming kingdom.

In Jesus, God's kingdom has come so near that it shapes the present by demanding a response.[2] Jesus invites people to enter the kingdom by repenting and believing the good news (Mark 1:15). To "repent" means "to turn around." Individually this involves turning away from sin and toward God. Corporately, it involves abandoning the many alternative paths to national restoration, such as legal and ritual purification (Pharisees, Qumran) or armed resistance (Zealots).[3] Such paths are not only futile but unnecessary, for "believing the good news" means trusting God to establish his own reign. Jesus neither charges his listeners to "bring in" the kingdom nor to qualify themselves for entrance—except by repenting and receiving the kingdom and its salvation as a gift in childlike trust (Mark 10:15). "Do not be afraid, little flock," he assures them, "for it is your Father's good pleasure to give you the kingdom" (Luke 12:32). Jesus' whole ministry is focused on the restoration of Israel as God's people who have repented and

---

heaven" in passages where the parallels in Mark or Luke have "kingdom of God." He is simply being sensitive to the concerns of his Jewish readers. Pious Jews, out of reverence, tended to avoid direct reference to God, using circumlocutions instead. Another example is the high priest's question to Jesus in Mark 14:61: "Are you the Messiah, the Son of the Blessed One?"

[2]See Leander Keck, *Who Is Jesus? History in Perfect Tense* (Columbia: University of South Carolina Press, 2000) 79, 81-89.

[3]On this meaning of "repentance," see N. T. Wright, *The Challenge of Jesus: Rediscovering Who Jesus Was and Is* (Downers Grove IL: InterVarsity Press, 1999) 43-44.

received the gift of salvation in the coming kingdom of God.

A second theme in Jesus' message was *the "Good News" of forgiveness and justice*. The arrival of God's kingdom is good news ("gospel") because it brings healing for the sick, forgiveness for sinners, and justice for the poor and oppressed. Jesus turned his ministry toward the lowly, the marginalized, the outcasts—"the lost sheep of the house of Israel" (Matthew 10:6; 15:24). He preached "good news to the poor" (Luke 4:18-19; Matthew 11:5-6), the oppressed, the hungry, the powerless. His ministry embraced the sick, the blind, the lame, the lepers. Above all, he was "a friend of tax collectors and sinners" (Matthew 11:19). "Sinners" was a label designating a category of sinners whose lifestyle or occupation left the possibility of their repentance and forgiveness in serious doubt.

In many ways, the categories of the poor, the sick, and the sinners tended to blur and overlap. It is well known that poverty breeds disease, and *vice versa*. Conventional wisdom taught that poverty and disease were divine punishment for sin. Many illnesses rendered a person ritually unclean. Because the poor had neither the time nor the means to follow the austere purity rules cherished by strict sects such as the Pharisees, they were often shunned as unclean sinners. Jesus' ministry reached out to all of these outcast groups and sought to include them in the renewed Israel which would inherit the coming kingdom of God.

To many of Jesus' contemporaries, this was the most startling and offensive aspect of his ministry. Rather than targeting a righteous remnant for inclusion in the kingdom, he welcomed sinners freely. An unprecedented time of salvation had dawned in which God was restoring Israel not by purging the wicked but by offering forgiveness to any and all, a sort of general amnesty, so to speak. Occasionally, Jesus is reported to have said directly, "Your sins are forgiven" (Mark 2:5; Luke 7:48), meaning "God has forgiven them." More frequently, forgiveness is portrayed in word pictures: rejoicing over finding something that was lost (Luke 15:5-6, 9, 23-24); large or small debts being freely canceled (Matthew 18:27; Luke 7:42); the sinful tax collector being justified rather than the pious Pharisee (Luke 18:14).[4] Jesus told the chief priests and elders, "the tax collectors and the prostitutes are going into the kingdom of God ahead of you" (Matthew 21:31). He told the Pharisees, "I have come to call not the righteous but sin-

---

[4]See Joachim Jeremias, *New Testament Theology: The Proclamation of Jesus*, trans. John Bowden (New York: Scribner's, 1971) 114.

ners" (Mark 2:17). Even more remarkable is the way Jesus not only declared forgiveness verbally but also enacted it in his treatment of people, most notably in his table fellowship with "tax collectors and sinners." Jesus' table fellowship was highly symbolic. On the one hand, it symbolized acceptance and forgiveness of those with whom he ate. On the other, it anticipated the joy of God's coming kingdom by celebrating in advance the "messianic banquet" which was expected at the end time. But as far as Jesus' critics were concerned, he was celebrating the kingdom with precisely the crowd who ought to be excluded (Mark 2:15: Luke 15:1-2).

The demand of the kingdom was a third theme in Jesus' teaching. "Your kingdom come. Your will be done, on earth as it is in heaven" (Matthew 6:10). The parallelism of these lines from the Lord's Prayer shows that the coming of the kingdom is synonymous with the doing of God's will. The kingdom of God, therefore, not only offers unconditional forgiveness but also demands radical obedience to the will of God. Nobody enters the kingdom by qualifying through righteous deeds; entrance is only by accepting God's forgiveness. Nevertheless, belonging to God's kingdom implies submission to his lordship and, accordingly, demands total obedience.

The Lord's Prayer

"Pray then in this way:
Our Father in heaven,
> hallowed be your name.
Your kingdom come.
Your will be done,
> on earth as it is in heaven.
Give us this day our daily bread.
And forgive us our debts,
> as we also have forgiven our debtors.
And do not bring us to the time of trial,
> but rescue us from the evil one."[5]   (Matthew 6:9-13)

---

[5]This version of the Lord's Prayer is from Matthew. A briefer but less-familiar version is found in Luke 11:2-4. The familiar doxology—"For the kingdom and the power and the glory are yours forever. Amen."—is not found in the best Greek manuscripts. It was probably added later based on 1 Chron. 29:11-13 to round out the prayer for liturgical use. Most modern versions print it only in a footnote. The Lord's Prayer most-often prayed in worship follows the version in the *Book of*

Jesus sets his own proclamation of God's will over against the Jewish law. He does not dismiss the Torah as irrelevant but calls for a kind of radical obedience that transcends it. His ethical teaching tends to simplify, intensify, and internalize the commandments. Like other Jewish teachers of his day, he *simplifies* the Torah, quoting two passages from the Old Testament itself to reduce its many provisions to the all-embracing Great Commandment to love God and one's neighbor:

> He said to him, " 'You shall love the Lord your God with all your heart, and with all your soul, and with all your mind.' This is the greatest and first commandment. And a second is like it: 'You shall love your neighbor as yourself.' On these two commandments hang all the law and the prophets."   (Matthew 22:37-40)

For Jesus it is impossible to love God without also loving one's neighbor. Ritual acts of piety directed toward God are not acceptable unless matched by kindness towards others. So important is love of neighbor that Jesus even reduces the whole Torah to the one Golden Rule—"In everything do to others as you would have them do to you" (Matthew 7:12)—which in itself fulfills all the commandments.

Simplifying the law does not mean Jesus was watering down the law to make it easier. Often he *intensifies* the commandments almost unimaginably, for love often demands more than what the law requires. For example, whereas the law requires love of neighbor, Jesus expects love for the enemy as well (Matthew 5:43-47) and even redefines "neighbor" to include the enemy (Luke 10:29-37). Again, whereas the law allows measured retaliation against an offender, Jesus counsels "turning the other cheek" and even urges aid to the offender (Matthew 5:38-42). In an occupied land, where every act of resistance was met with increasingly brutal oppression, Jesus' way was to break the cycle of violence through willingness to return love for hate. Jesus' words would later inspire the nonviolent resistance of, for example, Mahatma Gandhi and Martin Luther King, Jr.

Jesus also *internalizes* the law. It is not only one's actions that count, but also the inward motivation and attitude of the heart. For example, whereas the law prohibits murder and adultery, Jesus is concerned about anger and lust as well (Matthew 5:21-22, 27-28). He deemphasizes the

---

Common Prayer, which follows Tyndale's New Testament and reads "trespasses/trespass" instead of "debts/debtors."

meticulous rules of Sabbath keeping, tithing, ritual purity, and the like to which the Pharisees were devoted and subordinates them to ethical concerns. The purity that counts is not a matter of mere ritual cleansing but of right character and conduct (Mark 7:1-23; Luke 11:38-42).

Jesus insists that his followers must treat others the way God has offered to treat them. To be recipients of God's mercy and forgiveness, they must be willing to forgive others (Mark 11:25). They must renounce the judgmental spirit that so readily condemns in others faults conveniently overlooked in oneself (Matthew 7:1-5). He charges them to live now in ways that correspond to the values of the coming kingdom of God, which will turn worldly values upside down. Thus, he urges them to have a detachment from possessions which enables generosity toward the poor (Matthew 6:24; Luke 12:33-34; Mark 10:21); a spirit of humility which declines to seek status and honor but confers dignity on all alike (Luke 14:7-14); an attitude which finds greatness not in domination and power over others but in service to them (Mark 10:42-44). It is not that by adopting such a lifestyle Jesus' followers can make the kingdom come, but that, because in Jesus it has *already* come, they can enter into it and live now by its standards.

A final theme in Jesus' message is *the "Fatherhood" of God*. Because God's kingdom has not fully come, living by its rules in the midst of this evil age can be dangerous. It makes disciples vulnerable to those who would take advantage of them. Indeed, Jesus frequently warns of suffering and persecution. The disciples' reassurance is Jesus' teaching about the "fatherhood" of God.[6] The God whose kingdom is coming is compared to a loving, benevolent father who knows and cares for his children. Jesus assures that God knows our needs even before we ask; that God is more ready than any earthly father to "give good things to those who ask him;" that the same God who feeds "the birds of the air" and clothes "the lilies of the field" is even more eager to supply our needs (Matthew 6:8; 7:7-11; 6:25-34). Jesus addressed God with the intimate word "Abba" (Mark 14:36), an Aramaic word used by children for their own fathers. It expresses Jesus' sense of

---

[6]It should not be assumed that Jesus is attributing male gender to God. Rather, he is using an image taken from his culture to express the benevolence of God. In Matthew 23:37 and Luke 13:34, Jesus expresses benevolence in feminine imagery, describing his own desire to care for the wayward people of Jerusalem "as a hen gathers her brood under her wings."

special intimacy with God (Matthew 11:25-26), an intimacy he also sought to convey to his disciples, for he taught them to pray with the same intimate form of address (Galatians 4:6; Romans 8:15). It is likely that this Aramaic word lies behind the more formal "our Father" of the Lord's Prayer. In this prayer, Jesus teaches his disciples to pray for the coming of God's kingdom on earth. The prayer petitions God for the forgiveness of sins and for provision of daily needs. At the same time, the prayer acknowledges the petitioner's obligation to do the will of God and to pass on God's forgiveness by forgiving others. Praying for God's kingdom entails a commitment to doing battle with evil and becoming agents of God's love and justice. The assurance of God's fatherly provision for both daily needs and future salvation frees disciples to live in the present according to the values of the coming kingdom.

In some ways, *Jesus' manner of teaching* was as remarkable as its content. Two aspects in particular stand out: parables and authority. Approximately one-third of Jesus' teaching in the Synoptic Gospels is in the form of *parables*, brief scenes or stories drawn from everyday life which function metaphorically. Far from mere teaching illustrations, they are works of art which capture the imagination and compel new insight. Jesus used parables both to give glimpses into the nature of the kingdom and to disarm his critics. Two of the best-loved parables are the Prodigal Son and the Good Samaritan.

The Prodigal Son (Luke 15:11-32) is a two-part parable. The first part describes how the younger of two sons shamefully leaves home, emigrates, squanders his inheritance, then returns begging for mercy. The father's lavish, joyful reception of his wayward son—surprising but also understandable—depicts God's joyful forgiveness of sinners who repent. Part two shows the loyal older son scornfully refusing to join the celebration of his brother's return. His attitude is like that of the Pharisees who scorned Jesus' table fellowship with sinners, suggesting that the parable may have been told for their benefit (see Luke 15:1-2).

The Good Samaritan (Luke 10:29-37) is told in response to the question, "Who is my neighbor?" The story tells of a Jewish traveler, mugged and left dying beside the road. Listeners may be amused as a priest and a Levite, fellow Israelites, pass by without helping, but they are shocked when a Samaritan, a despised enemy, out of deep compassion does everything humanly possible to care for the victim. By identifying with the victim who was rescued by the enemy, the hearer of the parable is led to the remarkable insight that even one's enemy must be considered a neighbor. For those rescued by God's mercy, love of neighbor must not exclude anyone, even those who are outside one's own ethnic, racial, religious, or social group.

A frequent response to the teaching of Jesus is astonishment at the *authority* with which he taught. "They were astounded at his teaching, for he taught them as one having authority, and not as the scribes" (Mark 1:22). With authority he commanded unclean spirits and forgave sins (Mark 1:27; 2:10). He placed his own "but I say to you" over against the word of Scripture (Matthew 5:21-48). His frequent use of the solemn formula, "Truly (Greek, *amen*) I say to you" (for example, Mark 3:28), to claim certainty and finality for his own words was unparalleled. He claimed to speak directly for God, demanded total commitment from his followers, and implied that entrance into God's kingdom depended on acceptance of his mission.

Gathering Disciples. As Jesus went about teaching and healing, great crowds turned out to see him. From among these crowds he singled out a smaller group to be his disciples. A "disciple" is literally a "learner," hence a pupil or follower. The Synoptic Gospels focus special attention on a group of disciples known as "the Twelve." Four of this group were two pairs of brothers—Simon (also known as Peter) and Andrew, James and John—who were fishermen. Jesus called them away from their nets and invited them to "follow me and I will make you fish for people" (Mark 1:16-20). By various accounts, the Twelve also included both a tax collector named Matthew (Matthew 10:3) and a second Simon who was known as "the Zealot" (Luke 6:15). Little is known about most of the Twelve, and even the names of several differ among the various listings (Matthew 10:1-4; Mark 3:16-19; Luke 6:12-16; Acts 1:13). Even so, it is evident that Jesus chose not the educated elite, but the ordinary, the disreputable, and even a few "hotheads." We can also be sure that the number twelve is not accidental but intended to symbolize the twelve tribes of Israel. Jesus' mission is to restore Israel as a renewed people of God. The task of the Twelve is first to spend time with Jesus, learning from him, and then to be sent out to gather others into the kingdom of God (Mark 3:13-15). Hence, the same group came to be known also as "apostles," those who are "sent out" as authorized messengers.

It should also be recognized that Jesus' disciples were not limited to the Twelve. There was a broader group of followers from whom they were chosen. Among these there were some who traveled with Jesus and others who remained behind in their homes. It is especially remarkable that the disciples included a number of women. Luke 8:1-3 mentions by name Mary Magdalene, Joanna, and Susanna, as well as "many others" who traveled with Jesus on a tour through "cities and villages" and "who provided for them out of their resources." On a visit in the home of Mary and Martha, Jesus allowed Mary to sit at his feet as he taught and commended her for doing so (Luke 10:38-42). The inclusion of women among the disciples of a Jewish teacher is highly unusual.

While Jesus does not appear to have organized a "church" in any institutional sense, his band of disciples formed a new community of those who broke ties with the past and devoted themselves wholeheartedly to the kingdom of God. This community later constituted the nucleus of the early Christian movement. Discipleship has also become an important symbol of the Christian life. Being a Christian means more than believing certain things about Jesus. It means following him, living according to his teaching and his example.

Performing Miracles. The Bible speaks not in terms of "miracles" but of "signs, wonders, and mighty deeds," unusual events which point to the power of God at work. Many such deeds are attributed to Jesus in the Gospels. They can be classified as *healings*, such as the cure of a leper (Mark 1:40-45); *exorcisms*, such as the restoration of the Gerasene demoniac (Mark 5:1-20); *resuscitations*, such as that of Jairus's daughter (Mark 5:21-24, 35-43); and *nature wonders*, such as the feeding of the five thousand with five loaves and two fish (Mark 6:30-44). Jesus had great compassion for people whose lives were broken by disease or infirmity. Such conditions were often regarded as a sign of God's disfavor and sometimes, as in the cases of leprosy and physical deformity, resulted in exclusion from society and/or from worship in the temple. Jesus' healings demonstrate that the kingdom of God is concerned not only with "spiritual" needs but with restoration of the wholeness of life in all its dimensions—physical, spiritual, and communal. The exorcisms show Jesus as God's agent routing Satan's demons and breaking Satan's subversive power over God's creation (Mark 3:22-27). Jesus' miracles are signs that in his ministry the kingdom of God is breaking into this world. "But if it is by the finger of God that I cast out the demons, then the kingdom of God has come to you" (Luke 11:20). In Jesus, God was at work, setting right the brokenness of the world.

One should not think of these miracles, however, as unique events which prove the truthfulness of Christian claims about Jesus. For one thing, they are *not* unique. Many Jewish and Hellenistic teachers are said to have performed similar deeds. For another, they do not actually *prove* anything. Jesus' critics witnessed his miracles and could not deny them, yet they accused Jesus of operating by satanic power (Mark 3:22). This is strong evidence that Jesus really performed miracles, for his opponents would have denied them if they could. But it also indicates that miracles in themselves do not settle the matter. More than once Jesus' critics demanded a sign of his authority to teach and act as he did, but he refused (Mark 8:11-12; Luke 11:16, 29-32). To see God at work in Jesus requires an act of faith, and that is what Jesus' critics could not produce because he did not fit their presuppositions.

Engaging in Controversy with Religious Leaders. Jesus' Galilee ministry involved a number of clashes with Jewish religious leaders—especially with a group labeled "the scribes and Pharisees"—over a variety of issues. Jesus and his disciples did not observe the regular, biweekly times of fasting advocated by the Pharisees (although Jesus himself fasted in times of spiritual need and did not condemn the practice when performed out of true motivation). When confronted, he explained that it was not a time for fasting, a sign of mourning, but for rejoicing over what God was doing in his ministry (Mark 2:18-22). On several occasions, Jesus gave a more lenient interpretation of the Sabbath rules than was customary among the Pharisees. He allowed his disciples to harvest and eat grain on the Sabbath, and he performed cures on the Sabbath even when life was not in danger. When challenged, he argued that the need to satisfy hunger and the requirement to perform deeds of mercy took precedence over the prohibition of work on the Sabbath (Mark 2:23–3:6). He took issue with the Pharisees' emphasis on purity rules, for example in the ritual cleansing of utensils and hands before eating, declaring that even the most meticulous observance of such rules amounts to hypocrisy (mere role playing) if not accompanied by purity of heart as expressed in deeds of obedience, justice, and kindness (Mark 7:1-23; Matthew 23:25-26; Luke 11:37-44).[7]

---

[7]The intensity of these scathing attacks on the "hypocrisy" of the Pharisees, especially in Matt. 23, probably reflects church-synagogue hostilities near the end of the century when the Gospels were written. It should not be imagined that Judaism or Pharisaism was a purely sham religion of pretenders, devoid of true

Perhaps the most significant area of dispute involved Jesus' attitude toward sinners. When Jesus pronounced that a paralyzed man's sins were forgiven and demonstrated his authority to do so by curing him, some scribes who were present declared it blasphemous, since only God can forgive sins (Mark 2:3-12). Some scholars believe the real offense here was that Jesus totally bypassed the temple and its rituals, which were designed to mediate God's forgiveness, thus presenting himself as a substitute for the temple. Similarly, Jesus' table fellowship with sinners came under fire from the Pharisees because it was diametrically opposed to their own program, which called for restricting table fellowship to those who were ritually pure. From the Pharisees' point of view, Jesus' open table fellowship was celebrating the joy of the coming kingdom with those who ought to be excluded in order to purify the community. Jesus defended his conduct by comparing his role to that of a physician. Just as a doctor is not needed by the healthy but by the sick, so Jesus came "to call not the righteous but sinners" (Mark 2:15-17).

In the context of Judaism, "the righteous" referred not to people who are perfect but to those who honestly strive to keep the law properly and who make atonement for any failures through the prescribed rituals. As part two of the parable of the Prodigal Son makes clear, God's love seeks to embrace both sinners (the wayward son) and the "righteous" (the dutiful son). But for that to happen the "righteous" must be willing to accept God's merciful inclusion of sinners. Indeed, they must be willing to see their own need for mercy. The parable of the Pharisee and the Tax Collector (Luke 18:10-14) shows that it is not the one who depends on moral superiority to others but the one who says "God be merciful to me, a sinner" who is right with God. Jesus warned those who presumed themselves to be "heirs of the kingdom" that failure to embrace the good news of the kingdom would result in their exclusion from it (Matthew 8:12). At some point, Jesus determined that the challenge of the kingdom must be taken to Jerusalem and laid at the feet of those who regarded themselves as dutiful guardians of access to God.

---

piety. Hypocrisy is a perennial problem for all religions, including Christianity. Christians should read Jesus' denunciations of hypocrisy as directed also at their own pretenses.

The Journey to Jerusalem

We do not know how long Jesus' Galilee ministry lasted and no one should claim to be able to reconstruct an exact sequence of events. Mark 6–8 suggests a period of growing tensions and temporary withdrawals from Galilee. Tension is in the air in two ways: Herod Antipas, the ruler of Galilee, has executed John the Baptist and is suspicious of Jesus' activity (Mark 6:14-29; Luke 13:31); and there is growing public inquisitiveness about who Jesus is (Mark 6:14-15). That Jesus had not explicitly been claiming any special role for himself but had been acting with great authority left his identity tantalizingly ambiguous. People were free to fill in the blanks in their own ways or to try to capitalize on his charismatic power and press him into their own agenda. Thus, on one of the withdrawals, some in the crowd saw messianic implications in the feeding of the five thousand (Mark 6:30-44) and, according to John's account, were "about to come and take him by force to make him king" (John 6:14-15), but he slipped away.

According to Mark's presentation, a critical turning point came during a withdrawal to the northeast, near Caesarea Philippi (Mark 8:27-33). As Jesus is questioning his disciples about his identity, Peter declares, "You are the Messiah" (the Greek text of course has "Christ"). This pronouncement, known as "Peter's confession," seems to be the first open declaration of Jesus' messianic identity. Jesus has not been claiming the title "Messiah," and when Peter blurts it out Jesus commands the disciples to silence about it and quickly changes the subject. Evidently, Jesus did not care about titles, probably because there was no existing title that exactly described his mission. He may have avoided "Messiah" in particular because, for many, it carried political and military implications with which he did not want to be associated. Immediately, now using the highly enigmatic term "Son of Man," he announces his intention to go to Jerusalem, where he expects to be rejected and killed. Peter's reaction (he "rebuked" Jesus) shows why titles are at this point premature. What Peter meant by "Messiah" and how Jesus understood his own role were totally incompatible. Only after Jesus' completed mission has redefined the concept of "Messiah" will this title become appropriate.

On the way to Jerusalem, the Gospels record Jesus predicting his fate two more times (Mark 9:31; 10:33-34), yet each time the disciples respond in ways that show they either fail to comprehend or refuse to accept it. It may be, as many scholars suppose, that Jesus' intimations were not so explicit as the present form of the "passion predictions" sound. It is surely the case that the disciples did not have the benefit of viewing Jesus' ministry from our vantage point on this side of the cross and resurrection. Yet, even if Jesus' predictions have been made more explicit in retrospect—and even disregarding the possibility of divine foreknowledge—there is every reason to believe that he really did reckon with a violent death. If there were sharp conflicts already in Galilee, they could only intensify in Jerusalem. In addition, Israel's rulers had a long history of rejecting and ill-treating God's prophets, of whom Jesus considered himself the last in a long line (Matthew 23:29-39; Luke 13:33-34; Mark 12:1-12). So Jesus set out for the holy city to lay his call for national repentance at the feet of Israel's leaders. He was fully aware of the danger that awaited him, but willing to die for the sake of God's kingdom.

The Final Week in Jerusalem

Although John's Gospel reports extensive activity of Jesus on three visits to Jerusalem, the Synoptics compress his ministry there into the span of one week. This period is highlighted by a number of significant "symbolic actions" of Jesus in the style of the Old Testament prophets, who not only delivered their messages verbally but often acted them out in dramatic actions. Many of the events of the Jerusalem ministry are commemorated by Christians in "Holy Week" observances during the week before Easter.[8]

As Jesus and his followers approached Jerusalem on a Sunday, there was much anticipation in the air. It was the week of Passover, which brought great crowds of Jewish pilgrims to Jerusalem to celebrate the Exodus from Egypt. Hopes always ran high that this might be the year when God will act to liberate Israel again as in the days of Moses. In an event traditionally known as "the triumphal entry into Jerusalem" (Mark 11:1-11), Jesus made arrangements to ride into the city on a donkey in the style of the Old Testament kings (see 1 Kings 1:38), symbolically declaring himself "king." A crowd gives him a royal welcome, spreading their garments and leafy branches in the road, as we might roll out a red carpet, and hailing him as a royal Messiah. John 12:13 specifically mentions "palm branches," such

---

[8]The following account reflects the traditional chronology of the events of "Passion Week." In the Gospel accounts, there are a number of points at which it is unclear on which day an event occurred. There are also a number of discrepancies between accounts.

as had been used in celebrations of the Maccabees' purging of Jerusalem and purification of the temple. If the crowd expects him to stage an overthrow and clean house as the Maccabees did, they will be disappointed. That the "king" rides a donkey, not a warhorse, indicates peaceful intentions, fulfilling the expectation in Zechariah 9:9-10 of a peaceful king who comes not to make war but to end war (Matthew 21:4-5). In Luke 19:42-44, Jesus laments that his nation is failing to recognize "the things which make for peace" and warns that rejection of the way of God's kingdom will put Israel on a disastrous collision course with her enemies. The triumphal entry is commemorated on Christian calendars as Palm Sunday, which comes one week before Easter.

After spending the night with friends in Bethany, a small village just outside Jerusalem, Jesus and the disciples returned to the city on Monday for one of the week's more fateful events, the "cleansing" of the temple (Mark 11:15-19). In the outer courtyard, known as the Court of the Gentiles, Jesus attacked the money changers and pigeon sellers, overturning their tables and driving them out. The money changers were there to exchange Roman coins, with their idolatrous images, for the local coinage, which alone was acceptable to the temple. The pigeon sellers provided unblemished sacrifices for Jewish worshipers. Quoting the prophets, Jesus accused the temple authorities of turning God's "house of prayer for all peoples" (Isaiah 56:7) into "a den of robbers" (Jeremiah 7:11). The action symbolically attacked the temple establishment, but the exact point of the protest is debated. Was it a protest against the commercialization of the temple which detracted from worship? Or was it an attack on the corruption and greed of the temple authorities, who exploited the worship system in order to live in luxury at the expense of the common people? Or was it an assault on the exclusiveness of the temple, which the prophets had promised would one day have a place even for "the outcasts of Israel" and for foreigners (Isaiah 56:1-8)? Some scholars think Jesus was symbolically purging the temple in preparation for the end-time coming of the Gentiles long expected by the prophets (Isaiah 2). Others think Jesus' temple action was not so much a cleansing as an act of judgment against the temple. Within days, Jesus will predict the destruction of the temple (Mark 13:1) and will be accused of threatening to destroy it and build another (Mark 14:57-59; 15:29). Whatever its precise meaning, this temple protest was a provocative action which not only challenged the temple authorities but also threatened to spark an uprising. It is not surprising that this event seriously disturbed the temple authorities and precipitated their decision to arrest Jesus and press for his execution.

On Tuesday, Jesus boldly returned to the temple, denouncing the religious leaders for rejecting his message and engaging in controversy with various delegations (Mark 11:27–12:44). Set just outside the temple is a lengthy "eschatological discourse" (Mark 13) addressed to the disciples. This "little apocalypse" outlines expectations for the future: suffering for the disciples of Jesus, the destruction of the temple and the nation, the cataclysmic end of the age, and finally the glorious coming of the "Son of Man" bringing the fullness of God's kingdom. Apparently Jesus was not arrested in this setting because the authorities feared that his sway over the crowds could be used to start a riot (Mark 14:1-2). They needed an opportunity to take him away quietly.

By Wednesday they had found such an opportunity. Judas Iscariot, one of the Twelve, went to the chief priests and volunteered to betray Jesus to them, apparently by agreeing to inform them whenever Jesus could be found in a vulnerable setting (Mark 14:10-11). Because Judas's motivation for this conspiracy is unstated, it has been the subject of much speculation. One reasonable suggestion is that Judas perceived Jesus as a reluctant military Messiah and thought that betrayal would force him to make a move. If so, it certainly would not be the last time Jesus' cause would be betrayed by those who thought they were supporting him. In the meantime, while dining with friends in Bethany, Jesus was anointed by a woman with an expensive bottle of perfumed oil, an action Jesus interpreted with reference to his impending death (Mark 14:3-9).

On Thursday evening, Jesus and the Twelve gathered in a borrowed upstairs room in Jerusalem to eat the Passover together (Mark 14:12-25). Passover was the annual celebration of Israel's deliverance from bondage in Egypt; Jesus would give it a new significance. As the meal began, Jesus announced that one of the disciples would betray him but did not specify which one. During the meal, he blessed and broke a loaf of bread, saying:

"Take, eat; this is my body."   (Matt 26:26; cf. Mark 14:22)

He then took a cup of wine, gave thanks, and said:

"Drink from it, all of you; for this is my blood of the covenant, which is poured out for many for the forgiveness of sins. I tell you, I will never again drink of this fruit of the vine until that day when I drink it new with you in my Father's kingdom."   (Matt 26:27-29; cf. Mark 14:23-25)

The meal anticipates Jesus' death the next day and interprets it as a sacrifice that will renew the covenant between God and his people. This "Last Supper" is commemorated by Christians whenever Communion (or the Lord's Supper) is observed and especially during Holy Week in Maundy Thursday services, which may include Communion and even a foot-washing ceremony (based on the account in John 13:1-38).

After the meal, Jesus led the disciples out to Gethsemane (Mark 14:32-42), an olive grove on the Mount of Olives overlooking the temple area. There Jesus wanted to spend time in prayer. In a very human moment, he was struggling with what was to happen next. He prays, "Abba, Father, for you all things are possible; remove this cup from me" (Mark 14:36). Jesus could easily have slipped away into the refuge of the Judean wilderness or called upon crowds of followers for defense—not to mention "legions of angels" (Matthew 26:53), as suggested by the devil in Jesus' initial temptation (Matthew 4:6). But either course, even if successful, would have betrayed the cause of the kingdom. Jesus continues: "yet, not what I want, but what you want" (Mark 14:36). In an act of utter trust in God, Jesus chooses the way of the kingdom and embraces his destiny.

Meanwhile, Judas had slipped away and led a detachment of temple police to the garden (Mark 14:43-52). He betrayed Jesus by identifying him with a kiss on the cheek. As Jesus was arrested, one of the disciples drew a sword in defense, but Jesus stopped him. The disciples then abandoned him and scurried for cover (Mark 14:50).

Late Thursday night, Jesus was given a hasty hearing before the Sanhedrin, the Jewish ruling council (Mark 14:53-65). After an initial charge of threatening the temple does not stick because of disagreements among the witnesses, the high priest Caiaphas asks Jesus directly whether he claims to be the Messiah. Matthew 26:64 and Luke 22:67-68 report an evasive answer; only Mark 14:62 recounts an affirmative response. In any case, the high priest declares Jesus guilty of blasphemy (speaking words contemptuous of God), and the council concurs. Although blasphemy was a capital offense under Jewish law, punishable by stoning to death, under Roman administration the Sanhedrin seems to have lacked the authority to execute.

Therefore, on Friday morning the temple authorities bound Jesus over for trial before Pontius Pilate (Mark 15:1-15), the Roman governor, who normally resided in Caesarea but came to Jerusalem during feast days because of the potential for disturbances. Before Pilate, the charge against Jesus is sedition or insurrection. The chief priests accused Jesus of calling himself "the Messiah, a king" or "the King of Israel" (Luke 23:2; Mark 15:32), alleging that he was another of the rebel leaders with whom Rome had to deal periodically. Pilate interrogates Jesus as to whether he claims to be "King of the Jews," but his response is evasive and uncooperative.

Curiously, the governor is painted in the Gospel accounts as unconvinced that Jesus is guilty, yet he allows himself to be pressured into condemning him. He declares Jesus innocent and offers to release him as a good-will gesture, a custom otherwise unknown. The crowd, however, goaded by the chief priests, demands the release of Barabbas instead, an insurrectionist guilty of murder, and the crucifixion of Jesus. All of this is quite curious. Ordinarily, Pilate did not hesitate to deal harshly with suspected agitators and needed no such persuasion. Many scholars have suspected that the evangelists, for their own purposes, have overemphasized the responsibility of the Jewish authorities for Jesus' death and underplayed that of Pilate. Unfortunately, Christians have often used these texts to blame "the Jews" for the death of Jesus and to justify all manner of anti-Jewish atrocities. This is a serious misreading of the Gospels. Historically, it is clear that Jesus was executed by the Roman governor, who alone had power to crucify. The complicity of the chief priests, who after all were Roman collaborators, does not make guilty the Jewish people as a whole. And theologically speaking, Christians believe that Jesus died for the sins of us all—not because of "the Jews" in particular. In any case, reluctantly or not, in the end Pilate orders the crucifixion of Jesus and hands him over to the Roman soldiers.

Crucifixion was a horrifying method of execution inflicted by the Romans upon criminals whom they most wanted to make an example, especially provincial rebels and insubordinate slaves. Victims were typically flogged, sometimes so cruelly that death resulted from this alone. They were then fastened, by ropes or spikes, to a wooden cross and left to die from exposure, exhaustion, and suffocation. The process could be agonizingly slow, sometimes lasting several days. Jesus was flogged, mocked by the soldiers, and crucified between two "thieves" (or "rebel-bandits") at a place outside the city called Golgotha (Mark 15:16-41). His agony was comparatively brief. Placed on the cross about mid-morning, he was dead by mid-afternoon. As Jesus died on the cross, the Twelve were nowhere to be seen, but a group of women who had followed him from Galilee stood watching from a distance.

According to the Gospels, Jesus' death was accompanied by such phenomena as an earthquake, darkness at midday, and the tearing of the temple veil. Whether taken literally or figuratively, these cosmic signs are intended to give eschatological significance to Jesus' seemingly ignominious death. Yet it was only in retrospect that such significance could be seen. At the moment of his death, Mark reports that Jesus himself cried out, "My God, my God, why have you forsaken me?" (Mark 15:34). This is the opening line of Psalm 22, a lament of the righteous sufferer who is tormented unjustly but is confident of vindication by God. Had Jesus been abandoned not only by his disciples but even by the God in whom he had put his trust? Had the sin and injustice of the worldly powers prevailed over the love and justice of God's reign, for the cause of which Jesus had died? On "Good Friday," as it is commemorated on the Christian calendar, the darkness was too thick to tell.

Late Friday afternoon, Jesus' body was secured by a certain Joseph of Arimathea, a wealthy member of the Sanhedrin, and buried in a tomb, that then was sealed with a large, round stone (Mark 15:42-47). Sundown on Friday marked the beginning of the Jewish Sabbath, which was observed by resting through Saturday. Jesus' disciples had fled into hiding, disappointed that their hopes for the appearance of God's kingdom had not materialized and fearful of being implicated in Jesus' alleged crimes.

The closing chapters of all four Gospels, with varying details, report that at the crack of dawn on Sunday morning, some of the women who had been present at the cross went to the tomb, bringing spices to anoint Jesus' body according to the funeral customs. To their surprise, they discovered the tomb had been unsealed and the body was not there. An angel appeared and announced that Jesus had been raised from the dead. Thus, all the Gospels give witness to the discovery of the "empty tomb." There follows a series of appearances of the resurrected Jesus to various disciples in various places. Here the Gospels diverge considerably. In Mark and Matthew, the angel instructs the women to tell the disciples to return to Galilee, where Jesus will appear to them. The authentic text of Mark ends abruptly at this point.[9] Matthew reports that Jesus appeared to the women outside the tomb and later to the disciples on a mountain in Galilee, where he commissions them to take the gospel to all nations (Matthew 28:16-20). Luke 24:13-35

---

[9]The various endings of Mark beyond 16:8 are considered by textual critics to be later scribal additions. It is also possible that Mark had an ending which is now lost.

reports an appearance to two disciples on the road to Emmaus, just outside Jerusalem, and subsequently to the disciples assembled in Jerusalem (Luke 24:36-53). John 20-21 records appearances both in Jerusalem and in Galilee.

It is difficult to arrange these experiences into a plausible chronological sequence. What is clear is that collectively they gave rise to faith in the resurrection of Jesus. This means that the final chapters in the Gospels mark not the end of Jesus' story but a whole new beginning. A new era was dawning in which the powers of sin and death had been broken by a decisive action of God. The resurrection of Jesus is celebrated by Christians on Easter Sunday, the holiest day of the Christian calendar. It is also celebrated every Sunday. Most Christians worship on Sunday (the Lord's Day)—rather than on the Jewish Sabbath (Saturday, the seventh day)—in recognition of Jesus' resurrection on the first day of the week. It was this "Easter faith" which became the decisive starting point for the Christian movement.

Matthew's account closes with a saying of the resurrected Jesus giving his disciples their marching orders for keeping the movement going:

> "Go therefore and make disciples of all nations, baptizing them in the name of the Father and of the Son and of the Holy Spirit, and teaching them to obey everything that I have commanded you. And remember, I am with you always, to the end of the age."
>
> (Matthew 28:19-20; cf. Luke 24:46-48; John 20:21-23; Acts 1:8)

This saying, which has come to be known as the "Great Commission," points forward to the rise and spread of the Christian church, which will be examined in the next chapter.

Rise and Growth of the Christian Church: The Book of Acts

The Christian movement began among a band of Jesus' disciples as a response to his life, death, and resurrection. Christianity was at first essentially a sect of Palestinian Jews who believed Jesus was the Messiah. Soon the movement spread into the Jewish Diaspora and embraced Gentiles as well. Our task in the present chapter is to survey the rise and growth of the Christian church during its formative period, from its beginnings in Jerusalem through the work of the Apostle Paul (about 30–65 CE).

The book of Acts, a sequel to the Gospel of Luke, is our only narrative account of this formative period. Acts paints a picture of the Christian church arising in Jerusalem among Jewish followers of Jesus, moving out into the Greek-speaking world to embrace Gentiles, and finally arriving in Rome, the capital of the inhabited world. A key theme in Acts is that the message of Christ is good news for the whole world. Although written perhaps as late as 90 CE, Luke's account seems to be based on earlier sources and traditions and contains solid information about the earlier period. However, Acts is not an objective, comprehensive historical account in the modern sense but a "theological history," a selective account put together to commend the Christian faith to its readers. It leaves many gaps in what a historian would like to know about the early development of Christianity. Fortunately, Paul's letters, which begin about 50 CE, contain much information that supplements and helps interpret the picture found in Acts. For matters related to Paul, his own letters are, of course, our primary sources.

The Easter Faith as a New Beginning

The Christian church arose on the basis of faith in the resurrection of Jesus. At his arrest and crucifixion Jesus' disciples had fled in fear and disappointment (Mark 14:50). They "had hoped that he was the one to redeem Israel" (Luke 24:21), but now their hopes seemed misplaced. Yet soon those same frightened, disappointed disciples had reassembled in the city where Jesus had met his fate, now with a vibrant new hope and conviction. What made the difference is that they had become convinced that God had raised Jesus from the dead. And what convinced them was not so much the empty tomb, which is not mentioned in the earliest sources and traditions, but the resurrection appearances. They had seen him alive again! If he was no longer dead, then God must have raised him. The historian is not in a position to say what happened inside Jesus' tomb, but the transformation in the lives of his disciples is well documented.

Faith in the resurrection stands at the very heart of the earliest Christian confessions and preaching. One of our very earliest recorded Christian confessions is found in 1 Corinthians 15:3-8—written about 54 CE, earlier than any of the Gospels. Here Paul passes on an early confession of faith which he had received from even earlier believers. This confession, which Paul labels "as of first importance," has a parallel structure:

> Christ died for our sins . . . and . . . was buried,
> he was raised on the third day . . . and . . . he appeared. . . .
>
> (1 Cor 15:3-5)

Just as Jesus' burial confirms the reality of his death, so six appearances of the resurrected Christ to various disciples attest the reality of his resurrection. The sermon summaries found in Acts, which may be based on traditions of the early Christian preaching, also have affirmation of Jesus' resurrection at their core (Acts 2:24, 32; 3:15; 5:30).

Even more important than this bold assertion of the death and resurrection of Jesus is the significance that came to be attached to it, how it was interpreted theologically. It should not be imagined that the full significance of this extraordinary event emerged immediately. Its implications grew and developed over time and were expressed in different ways against the background of various cultures. The following developments can be documented within the formative period and are foundational to the emerging Christian faith.

First, the resurrection meant that God had justified Jesus' mission and message. In spite of the crucifixion, which seemed to say "No" because no one had expected such a redeemer, Jesus was indeed "the one to redeem Israel" after all. The title "Messiah" (Hebrew), or "Christ" (Greek), which Jesus himself had tended to avoid, now became appropriate—albeit with a new meaning. Jesus' mission both fulfilled the hope and transformed the concept. A Messiah who dies, especially on a cross, was a paradox and a stumbling block to believing in Jesus. It took a tremendous act of faith to believe that the Crucified One was in fact God's way of redemption—the same kind of faith with which Jesus had entrusted himself to God in accepting his fate on the cross.

Not only "Messiah" but other honorific titles were applied to Jesus as well, most importantly, "Son of Man," "Son of God," and "Lord." In general, the tendency was in the direction of ever more lofty acclamations. Thus, the one who had preached the salvation of God's kingdom came to the center as the agent of God's salvation.

Titles for Jesus in New Testament Christianity

(Of the many honorific titles applied to Jesus in the New Testament, four are of central significance. These terms are highly complex and tend to take on varying shades of meaning in different contexts. The following discussion is intended to be suggestive.)

Messiah (Hebrew) / *Christ* (Greek)—both meaning "anointed one"— identifies Jesus as the long-awaited new king like David, who would redeem Israel. Jesus was viewed, however, as fulfilling that expectation in unexpected ways, defeating the powers of this age not by force and violence but through sacrificial love and faith in God. Among the earliest Jewish Christians, Messiah was the most significant title. It was the confession "Jesus is Messiah" which set them apart as a distinct group within Judaism. When the term was translated into "Christ" in Hellenistic Christianity, it tended to lose its force as a title and to be thought of as part of Jesus' name, "Jesus Christ" or "Christ Jesus."

Son of Man primarily identified Jesus as the cosmic Judge who would appear at the end time to pronounce final judgment and usher in the kingdom of God. In the Gospels the term is found frequently and only on the lips of Jesus and may have been Jesus' preferred self-designation. Even so, it is not always clear in what sense he meant it. The phrase can mean "a human being" in the generic sense and can be a polite way of saying "I"; Jesus may have used it in that way on occasion. In other contexts, the term refers to the earthly Son of Man who has authority to forgive sins (Mark 2:10), the suffering Son of Man who is to be rejected and killed (Mark 8:31), and the eschatological Son of Man who will come in power (Mark 13:26-27). For Christians, the Son of Man had come and would come again in power at the *Parousia* of Christ.

Son of God depicts Jesus as standing in such close relationship with God that he reveals the character of God. "Son of God" should not be taken to mean that Jesus was physically descended from God (as in Greek mythology) or that he was in any way less than fully human. In Jewish usage, the term need not imply divinity. In the Old Testament, it often refers to mere mortals—such as the nation Israel or the king—chosen by God for a particular task. In Semitic languages, "to be a son of someone" meant to be like that person. In that sense, to call Jesus the Son of God is to say that his manner of life and his sacrificial death are so God-like that they reveal the essence of God's nature. If we want to know what God is like, we should look at Jesus. In the Hellenistic world, "Son of God" might imply a person specially endowed with supernatural powers; there are echoes of that understanding in the Gospel miracle stories. An early confession quoted in Romans 1:4 holds that Jesus was declared Son of God by his resurrection. Mark 1:11 records a voice from heaven at his baptism calling him "my Son." In Luke 1:35, he is Son of God from birth. Both Paul and John think of Christ as the preexistent, heavenly Son sent by God into the world.

Lord acknowledges Jesus as the Master to whom believers are devoted as servants. In general usage, "Lord" referred either to a human master or to God as Master; it could also be a simple title of respect or polite address (compare "Sir"). In Jewish usage, "Lord" was substituted for the divine name "Yahweh" in reading or translating the biblical text and so came to be closely identified with God. In the Hellenistic world, "Lord" was a frequent title for the many deities worshiped in the various cults, including the so-called "divine" emperor. In the New Testament, "Lord" is a very frequent title for Jesus, but it is not always clear in what sense it is meant. When Jesus is addressed as Lord in the Gospels, it is usually a title of respect. The Aramaic prayer *Marana tha* ("Our Lord, come!") recorded in 1 Corinthians 16:22 shows that the earliest Christians called Jesus "Lord," but not necessarily in the sense of equating him with Yahweh. In Hellenistic Christianity, "Jesus is Lord" became the most important confession, affirming Jesus over against the many pagan gods and even the emperor. Here "Lord" clearly takes on connotations of divinity, as when Old Testament texts in which "Lord" originally referred to God are quoted in reference to Jesus.

A second consequence of the Easter faith is that it revealed a positive significance of the crucifixion. There is evidence that the early Christians pondered deeply and searched the Old Testament for light on the paradox of a suffering Messiah. They found sufficient clues to conclude that the death of Jesus was not just a tragic mistake but was "in accordance with the Scriptures" (1 Corinthians 15:3). It was, somehow, a part of God's plan of redemption. Jesus' death was interpreted on analogy with the animal sacrifices in the temple or with the role of the righteous martyr who makes atonement for the nation or with the "Servant" who suffers vicariously for others (Isaiah 53). Christ died "for us" (Rom. 5:8) or "for our sins" (1 Cor. 15:3). Early confessional language speaks of the death of Christ as "a sacrifice of atonement by his blood, effective through faith" (Rom. 3:24-25). This means that Jesus' death is God's way of dealing with sin, wiping it away, and offering forgiveness and a place in the new Israel.

Third, the death and resurrection of Christ signal the eschatological turn of the ages. The early Christians had a strong sense of living in the last days or even in the overlapping of the ages. This evil age, they believed, is hurtling toward a close. The powers of sin and death have been broken. Jesus' resurrection was the "first fruits" (1 Corinthians 15:20) of the expected end-time resurrection of the dead. His resurrection gave believers hope for their own resurrection and eternal life with God. Already the new age of salvation is dawning, and the Holy Spirit is being poured out on God's people. Jesus the Messiah is creating a new Israel of those who repent and receive forgiveness and who live now by the power of the Spirit as they wait for their final redemption.

A fourth implication of the resurrection is the *Parousia* expectation. Jesus has been exalted to the right hand of God as heavenly Lord. From heaven, he has already sent the Holy Spirit as a continuing presence with his people, and soon he will return in power and glory to establish the kingdom of God in its fullness. There was an intense expectation that the *Parousia* (literally, "coming" or "arrival") of Christ was imminent; it could happen at any moment. The New Testament never uses the phrase "second coming" but reserves the term "*Parousia* of Christ" for his future coming. Soon Christ will return from heaven in glory as eschatological Judge. The dead will be raised to face the final judgment, and Christ will gather those who by faith belong to him into the fullness of God's salvation. This gave a sense of urgency to the appeal to fellow Jews to repent and become a part of the new Israel destined for end-time salvation. Soon even non-Israelites (Gentiles) would be invited to join as well.

The Christian Church in Jerusalem

The preceding analysis of theological insights unfolding out of the Easter faith gets us well ahead of the story, for those developments did not happen overnight. Here we come back to the beginning to survey the major stages in the evolution of the New Testament church. Acts 1–5, examined here, describes the rise and growth of a Christian community in Jerusalem. Subsequent sections will explore the emergence of Hellenistic Christianity and its expansion into the Diaspora (Acts 6–12) and Paul's mission to the Gentiles (Acts 13–28).

Birth of the Christian Church. As the book of Acts opens, the disciples are gathered in Jerusalem. Presumably there have already been resurrection appearances in Galilee—though Luke–Acts does not mention them—on the basis of which the disciples have reassembled and returned to the holy city. There, resurrection appearances occur for forty days during which Jesus instructs the disciples concerning their marching orders. In Acts 1:8, he commissions them to be his "apostles," those who are sent out to bear witness to the whole world:

> But you will receive power when the Holy Spirit has come upon you; and you will be my witnesses in Jerusalem, in all Judea and Samaria, and to the ends of the earth.

This thematic verse sets out an agenda which will unfold through the rest of the book. After Jesus' ascension to heaven (Acts 1:9; also reported in Luke 24:50), the apostles and others gather in an upstairs room in Jerusalem, choose Matthias as a replacement for Judas, who has committed suicide, to round out the Twelve, and spend time in prayer as they wait for the promised coming of the Spirit (1:12-26).

Acts 2 tells the story of the Day of Pentecost, a Jewish pilgrimage feast which came fifty days after Passover. As Jerusalem swelled with pilgrims from throughout the Jewish Diaspora, the band of Jesus' disciples experienced a dramatic outpouring of the Holy Spirit, filling them with the ability to speak in "other languages." Generally speaking, "Holy Spirit" in the Bible signifies God's empowering presence. In the Old Testament, the Spirit is said to have come upon individuals temporarily to enable them to perform a given task. The New Testament connects an eschatological coming of the Spirit with the resurrection and exaltation of Jesus. The Spirit is now a permanent endowment of God's people, giving them a foretaste of the coming salvation and endowing them with power for righteous living and for performing the work of the church. Early Christianity was a

charismatic, Spirit-filled movement. Throughout Acts, the author emphasizes that the church was guided and empowered by the Spirit at every important turn. Here the miracle of speaking in foreign languages symbolizes
God's empowering the church to take the gospel to the whole world. Peter's
sermon reported in Acts 2 interprets the outpouring of the Spirit as fulfillment of prophecy and a sign that the promised age of salvation has
arrived.

Empowered by the Spirit, the apostles begin to preach the good news
about Jesus. Acts records a number of sermons preached in the early days
of the church. While these speeches in their present form seem to have been
composed by Luke—a common practice in Hellenistic history writing—
they also seem to be based on early traditions. The recurring themes in the
apostolic preaching can be summarized in six main points.

(1) The long-awaited age of salvation has dawned (Acts 2:12; 3:18, 24).
(2) In his ministry, death, and resurrection, Jesus has fulfilled the
     messianic prophecies (Acts 2:22-23, 30; 3:13-14).
(3) Jesus the Messiah now sits at the right hand of God as head of the
     new Israel (Acts 2:33-36; 4:11; 5:31).
(4) The presence of the Holy Spirit in the church is a sign of Christ's
     power as exalted Lord (Acts 2:17-21; 2:33; 5:32).
(5) Christ will soon return to bring the consummation of the Messianic
     Age (Acts 3:21; 10:42).
(6) Therefore, repent and receive forgiveness, the Holy Spirit, and the
     promise of salvation (Acts 2:38-39; 3:19, 25-26; 4:12).[1]

It is natural that, at first, this appeal was aimed at fellow Jews, inviting them
to become a part of the new Israel.

Response to the Christian preaching was mixed. Some believed and
joined company with the growing Jerusalem church. Acts 2:41-42 and 4:4
mention 3,000 and 5,000 believers, respectively, being added. Some
interpreters have supposed that these numbers are exaggerated. In any case,
they should be kept in perspective. Most Jews certainly did not become
believers but either ignored or rejected the Christian message. Some,
especially the religious authorities, were hostile to the new movement.

---

[1]Based on C. H. Dodd, *The Apostolic Preaching and Its Developments. Three
Lectures with an Appendix on Eschatology and History* (London: Hodder &
Stoughton, 1944, 1956; New York: Harper & Row, 1964) 21-24. See Acts 2:14-39;
3:12-26; 4:8-12; 5:29-32; 10:34-43.

Nevertheless, a vigorous Christian church was growing in Jerusalem.

A Profile of "Palestinian Jewish Christianity." The earliest Christians who constituted the Jerusalem church were Aramaic-speaking Palestinian Jews who confessed that "Jesus is the Messiah." They were, in essence, a sect of Judaism, since they did not have a sense of leaving one religion to form a new one. Basically, they were Jews for whom the Messiah had come. For them, the coming of the Messiah did not mean they should quit being Jews. They continued to participate in Jewish worship in the temple and in the synagogues, to reverence the Jewish Scriptures, and to observe Jewish customs such as Sabbath, circumcision, and the food laws. Their reluctance to break with such observances, which marked the distinction between Jews and Gentiles, made it difficult for them to accept the inclusion of Gentiles once that issue presented itself.

As a special movement within Judaism, these earliest Christians seem to have thought of themselves as the new or renewed Israel (comparable to the Qumran sect's self-designation as "the true Israel"). Paul once uses the similar term "Israel of God" (Galatians 6:16). Acts several times refers to the Christian movement as "the Way" (Acts 9:2; 19:9, 23; 22:4; 24:14, 22). The term which became normative is "church," the usual translation of the Greek word *ekklesia*, which literally means "gathering" or "assembly." In the New Testament, "church" refers not to a building, but to the assembly of believers in Christ wherever they happened to gather. In the New Testament period they met primarily in the homes of believers who had houses large enough to accommodate the group. Church buildings as such were a later development.

While continuing to participate in Jewish worship, the early Christians also developed two distinctively Christian rituals, baptism and the Lord's Supper (or Communion). Baptism was a ritual of initiation into the community of believers performed by immersion in water. Prerequisite for baptism were repentance and confession of faith in Jesus. The ritual symbolized cleansing from sin and was associated with forgiveness and the gift of the Spirit. This symbolism can be seen in the climax of Peter's sermon:

> Peter said to them, "Repent, and be baptized every one of you in the name of Jesus Christ so that your sins may be forgiven; and you will receive the gift of the Holy Spirit."   (Acts 2:38)

A bit later, in Hellenistic Christianity, baptism would come to depict also the believer's dying and rising with Christ, dying to the old sinful life and rising again to new life in Christ, as seen in Romans 6:4:

> Therefore we have been buried with him by baptism into death, so that, just as Christ was raised from the dead by the glory of the Father, so we too might walk in newness of life.

The Lord's Supper was a communal meal in which Jesus' words over the bread and wine ("This is my body. . . . This is my blood.") at the Last Supper were recalled. The meal commemorated the saving death of Christ and anticipated the joy of the coming kingdom, as seen in an early tradition passed on by Paul in 1 Corinthians 11:23-26:[2]

> [T]hat the Lord Jesus on the night when he was betrayed took a loaf of bread, and when he had given thanks, he broke it and said, "This is my body that is for you. Do this in remembrance of me." In the same way he took the cup also, after supper, saying, "This cup is the new covenant in my blood. Do this, as often as you drink it, in remembrance of me." For as often as you eat this bread and drink the cup, you proclaim the Lord's death until he comes.

Acts describes the Jerusalem Christians as developing a remarkably close-knit fellowship. They practiced a community of goods in which the needs of any were met by the resources of all (Acts 2:43-47). Occasionally they encountered harassment from the temple authorities, who likely feared that their claiming a crucified criminal to be the Messiah was dangerously subversive. On several occasions various apostles were temporarily imprisoned and charged not to preach any longer in the name of Jesus (Acts 4:1-22; 5:17-42).

The Emergence of Hellenistic Christianity

Acts 6–12 describes the emergence in Jerusalem of Hellenistic Jewish Christianity, which leads to internal and external conflict, to geographical and ethnic expansion, and ultimately to a Gentile mission.

Diversity and Tension in the Jerusalem Church. At some point there appeared in the Jerusalem church a group of Greek-speaking Jewish Christians. Their origin is not explained, but apparently they had roots in

---

[2]It is unclear whether Acts's references to "breaking bread" (e.g., Acts 2:42, 46) refer to the Lord's Supper or to common meals. In any case, Paul's letters are earlier than Acts and Paul passes on to the Corinthians a tradition that was earlier still.

the Diaspora, where Jews tended to speak Greek. As Greek-speaking Jews, they typically would have absorbed more of the Hellenistic culture and would have been less strict in the Jewish observances and more open to contact with Gentiles than Palestinian Jews were. When they became Christians, they began to interpret the new faith in ways differing from those of the Aramaic-speaking Jewish Christians. They eventually distanced themselves from certain Jewish practices and showed greater openness to the inclusion of Gentiles. Thus, the Jerusalem church now had two factions, with language, cultural, and theological differences between them. It is not surprising that this situation would lead to tensions.

Acts 6:1-6 describes a conflict within the Jerusalem church between the "Hebrews" and the "Hellenists," apparently referring to Aramaic-speaking and Greek-speaking Jewish Christians, respectively. The dispute has to do with discrimination in the charity relief for widows. The Hellenists complain that their widows are being "neglected in the daily distribution of food." The issue is quickly resolved by the selection of seven men to oversee the charity operation, sometimes viewed as the origin of "deacons" in the church. Interestingly, all of "the Seven" have Greek names and probably were leaders of the Hellenists. Stephen, in particular, stands out as a key leader, and the story now focuses on him.

The Martyrdom of Stephen and the Persecution of the Church. As Acts 6 continues, Stephen functions not merely as a coordinator of food distribution but as a powerful preacher of the gospel. His witness to Jesus in the Greek-speaking synagogues stirs up a hornet's nest of opposition among Diaspora Jews living in Jerusalem. Soon he finds himself hauled before the Sanhedrin on charges of speaking blasphemous words against the temple and the Torah and of advocating that Jesus will destroy the temple and change the Jewish customs. The accusation suggests that Stephen was questioning the necessity of certain Jewish rituals now that the Messiah has come. If so, it would readily account for the outrage against Stephen, which surpasses any opposition the Twelve had faced up to this point.

In Acts 7, Stephen makes a lengthy defense that turns into a harsh attack on his accusers. His speech, which rehearses a good bit of Old Testament history, calls into question the presumed Jewish privileges of Torah and temple—declaring that Israel has a long record of disobeying the Torah and that God is not confined to the temple. At this, Stephen's adversaries pounce upon him, drag him outside the city, and stone him to death (Acts 7:54–8:1). Thus, Stephen becomes, as far as we know, the first Christian martyr. Interpreters frequently draw attention to parallels between Stephen's execution and that of Jesus and to the Christ-like manner in which Stephen died with a prayer for the forgiveness of his attackers on his lips. Present and approving of this action is "a young man named Saul," who will become better known as the Apostle Paul. It has often been speculated that Stephen's dying witness made a deep impression on Saul/Paul and played a role in his conversion to the Christian movement.

In the wake of the action against Stephen, an intense persecution broke out against the Jerusalem church, in which Saul/Paul played a leading role (Acts 8:1-3). This attack seems to have targeted in particular the Hellenistic Jewish Christians because of their more progressive stance in questioning Jewish practices and privilege. If they were already advocating freedom in Christ to abandon practices such as circumcision, the food laws, and Sabbath-observance—the very rituals that marked Jews as distinct from Gentiles—they would have appeared quite offensive and threatening to the Jewish religious establishment. They would also have been preparing the way for the eventual inclusion of Gentiles in the church. In any case, the "Hellenists" apparently bore the brunt of the persecution and were scattered into the countryside, while "the apostles," representing the more conservative Palestinian Jewish Christians, remained in Jerusalem.

Geographic and Ethnic Expansion. Ironically, the persecution did not result in suppressing the movement but in forcing it to spread, as "those who were scattered went from place to place, proclaiming the word" (Acts 8:4). The next few chapters in Acts trace out the beginnings of the expansion of the gospel, mainly through the efforts of the Hellenists as they fled back into the Diaspora. Philip, one of the Seven, traveled to Samaria and began a successful mission there (Acts 8:5-25). This represented not only a geographical expansion but the crossing of a significant ethnic boundary, since Jews and Samaritans were distant cousins but bitter enemies. From the story of Paul's conversion near Damascus (Acts 9:1-22), to be examined later, we learn that a church now existed in that Syrian city, likely also planted by Hellenistic Christians fleeing the persecution in Jerusalem.

Meanwhile, Acts interrupts the story of the Hellenists to show that the Aramaic-speaking church in Jerusalem also was taking some tentative steps toward expansion. After a tour through the coastal cities of Palestine (Acts 9:32-43), Peter took the bold step of evangelizing the Gentile Cornelius (Acts 10:1-48). Cornelius, a Roman army officer stationed in Caesarea, was a "God-fearer," a Gentile who revered Israel's God but had not converted to Judaism. As a Palestinian Jew, Peter considered Gentiles to be unclean, godless sinners, with whom he should avoid close contact. The Acts account dramatically describes how a series of visions overcome Peter's prejudice and bring Peter and Cornelius together. In Acts 10:28, 34-35, Peter's new insight is expressed in these words:

> "You yourselves know that it is unlawful for a Jew to associate with or to visit a Gentile; but God has shown me that I should not call anyone profane or unclean. . . . I truly understand that God shows no partiality, but in every nation anyone who fears him and does what is right is acceptable to him."

With this new conviction, Peter travels to Caesarea, enters the house of the Gentile Cornelius, and preaches the gospel. Upon hearing the message of Jesus, Cornelius and his household receive the Holy Spirit, in a kind of "Gentile Pentecost," and Peter baptizes them into the church. Afterwards, the conservative Jerusalem church severely criticizes Peter's action and only reluctantly accepts what he has done (Acts 11:1-18).

The Cornelius story is the first account of a Gentile conversion told in Acts. Luke clearly views it as a major breakthrough. However, there is little evidence that the Jerusalem church took up the cause of a continuing Gentile mission. That cause would be championed, rather, by the Hellenistic Christians as they fled into the Diaspora.

Apparently, the first real, sustained Gentile mission came in Antioch, a large, cosmopolitan city in northern Syria (Acts 11:19-26).[3] Here Acts resumes the account of the progress made by the Hellenistic Jewish Christians as they fled the persecution in Jerusalem. Some of the Hellenists had traveled to places like Samaria, Damascus, Phoenicia, and Cyprus, still preaching to fellow Jews. Now others of them arrived in Antioch and began something new—a deliberate, concerted mission to the Gentiles. And it was successful. The Hellenists' openness to abandoning the rituals that defined Jewish distinctiveness finally issued in the full inclusion of Gentiles. There arose in Antioch a church that freely included Jewish Christians and Gentile Christians together. Gentile converts were not required to be circumcised.

---

[3]Chronologically, it is unclear whether the conversion of Cornelius or the Antioch mission to the Gentiles came first. Luke may have placed the Cornelius story first for thematic purposes. In any case, the Gentile mission in Antioch was the first deliberate, sustained effort.

Jewish and Gentile Christians ate together without regard for the Jewish food laws.

This was something new, and it may not be an accident that "it was in Antioch that the disciples were first called 'Christians' " (Acts 11:26). This new name, meaning "partisans of Christ"—which out of convenience we have already used anachronistically in describing the earlier period—appears to have been coined by outsiders. Found only twice more in the New Testament (Acts 26:28; 1 Peter 4:16), "Christians" was not embraced as a regular self-designation until the second and third centuries.

The Antioch church was the first church situated in a major cosmopolitan city. It quickly became a center of Hellenistic Christianity and the base of a broader Gentile mission. As the Christian movement penetrated the Hellenistic world, it would face the double challenge of fighting for the right to include Gentiles without imposing Jewish customs on them and of finding ways to express the gospel in terms of Hellenistic culture without compromising the essence of the faith in the process. When the Jerusalem Christians learned of the bold developments in Antioch, they sent Barnabas, a Jewish Christian from Cyprus, to work with the new church. He, in turn, recruited Saul/Paul, who by now had become a Christian apostle and perhaps was already engaged in evangelizing Gentiles. It is hard to imagine a better choice for spearheading the work which lay ahead.

Paul's Mission to the Gentiles

Known as "the apostle to the Gentiles," Paul of Tarsus did not initiate the Gentile mission or pursue it single-handedly, but he did promote it and push it forward more vigorously than anybody else. It was Paul who championed the cause of the Gentile mission and who made a theological case for their free inclusion in the church. Apart from Jesus himself, nobody in the New Testament looms larger than the Apostle Paul. About one-third of the New Testament is connected to his name, including thirteen Pauline letters and Acts 13–28, which details his missionary journeys. Paul is the most ambitious and successful missionary and church planter in this period of whom we have record. He is also widely regarded as the most profound theological thinker in the early church, and his letters have served as a major source of Christian theology. The rest of this chapter surveys Paul's background and missionary career as recorded in Acts. The next chapter will examine his letters.

Paul's Background and Conversion. Paul was a Diaspora Jew who moved easily in the cultures of both Judaism and Hellenism. On the one hand, he was a native of Tarsus, a Greek city in southeastern Asia Minor, which was a center of Stoic philosophy and other schools of Greek learning. In many ways, Paul shows familiarity not only with Stoic ethical teaching and Greek rhetoric, but with Hellenistic culture more generally. His first language was Greek; he readily draws illustrations from the military and athletics. He was a Roman citizen, which provided a certain stature and legal rights. On the other hand, Paul was also a devout Jew, deeply enmeshed in the traditions of Judaism. He quotes Jewish Scripture freely. He was a Pharisee and probably more meticulous in observing the Torah than was typical in the Diaspora. According to Acts, he had even studied in Jerusalem under Gamaliel, perhaps the most eminent Jewish teacher at the time. This background in two cultures ideally fitted Paul to become the "apostle to the Gentiles" (Romans 11:13), to bring the God of Israel to the pagan world.

This dual cultural heritage is also reflected in Paul's two names. There is a popular misconception that "Saul" and "Paul" are pre- and post-Christian names, as if Saul changed his name to "Paul" at his conversion. Rather, they are Jewish and Greco-Roman names, respectively, reflecting the two cultures in which Paul moved. Many Hellenistic Jews had such dual names. Acts 13:9, which first introduces the name "Paul" into the narrative, does not say Saul changed his name but that Saul was "also known as Paul," and the context here is not the conversion but more than a decade later on the first missionary journey.

Prior to his becoming a Christian, Paul had been a vehement opponent of the new movement. In Acts, he first appears playing a minor role in the stoning of Stephen (Acts 7:58), then as a leader of the persecution in Jerusalem (Acts 8:3), and finally is seen headed to Damascus looking for Christians there (Acts 9:1-2). In the letters, Paul attributes his persecution of the church to his "zeal" for the Jewish law (Galatians 1:13-14; Philippians 3:5-6). He had judged Christianity to be in conflict with the law, perhaps because Christians proclaimed as Messiah a crucified criminal whom the law declared accursed by God (see Deuteronomy 21:23, quoted in Galatians 3:13). Or perhaps he saw in Christianity the seeds of abandonment of the Jewish customs and openness to Gentiles. In any case, as a zealous Pharisee, he was devoted to destroying the Christian church. As Paul himself would later come to see, such zeal for God does not put a person in the right (Romans 10:2).

According to Acts, Paul's "conversion" came on the road to Damascus as he traveled there with the intention of continuing his persecution (Acts 9:3-22; retold in 22:4-16 and 26:9-18). Just before arriving in Damascus, he was struck down by a blinding light and the voice of Jesus speaking to him:

> "Saul, Saul, why do you persecute me? . . . I am Jesus, whom you are persecuting. But get up and enter the city, and you will be told what you are to do."   (Acts 9:4-6)

Now convinced of the resurrection of Jesus, Paul was received by the Damascus church and baptized into the community of believers. In his letters, Paul describes his encounter with the risen Christ less as a "conversion" from one religion to another than as a "call" to be an apostle, comparable to the calling of the Old Testament prophets. The risen Christ had appeared to him, just as to the other apostles, and had made him an apostle as well, in spite of the fact that he had not been a disciple of Jesus during his earthly ministry (1 Corinthians 15:8-10; Galatians 1:15-17). Paul's conversion also gave him a new perspective on the Jewish law. He now believed that the death and resurrection of Christ provided the basis for a new kind of righteousness unavailable through the law, a righteousness equally open to Jews and Gentiles alike (Philippians 3:2-9). The persecutor of the church had become the "apostle to the Gentiles" (Romans 11:13).

Paul's Missionary Journeys. Following Paul's conversion, he drops out of our sources for more than a decade. We get only vague references to his presence in Arabia and in Syria and Cilicia (Galatians 1:17, 21). Likely, he was already engaged in evangelism, but we have no information about it. When the apostle comes to light again, it is in connection with the Hellenistic church in Antioch, to which he was brought by Barnabas. Paul and Barnabas spent a year teaching in that church, which had already begun a Gentile mission. Under Paul's leadership, the Antioch church then became a base of operation for an even greater missionary endeavor. Paul's missionary activity as reported in Acts can be conveniently arranged in three journeys, each beginning in Antioch, followed by a final journey to Rome.

Paul's *first journey* (Acts 13–14) involved a brief tour with Barnabas through the island of Cyprus and the relatively small cities of south-central Asia Minor. Along the way, a pattern emerged that would be repeated many times on the rest of Paul's journeys. In a given city, Paul typically begins in the synagogue with initial success, especially among the proselytes and

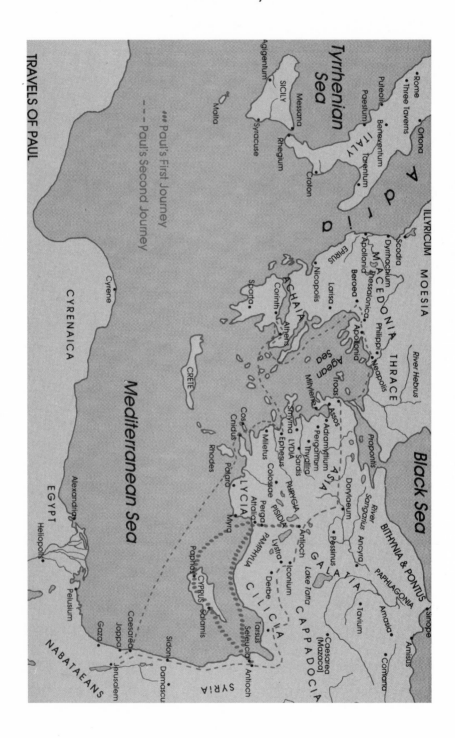

TRAVELS OF PAUL

••• Paul's First Journey

--- Paul's Second Journey

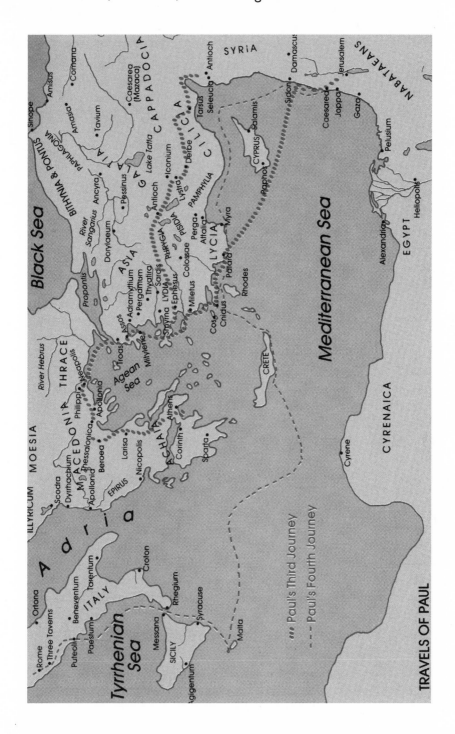

God-fearing Gentiles. Then the unbelieving Jews in jealous anger drive them out, so that Paul turns to the Gentiles apart from the synagogue, among whom he finds acceptance. Repeatedly, he meets rejection and hostility from the Jews. Among many other episodes, once he was stoned nearly to death, and five times he received the synagogue discipline of thirty-nine lashes (Acts 14:19-20; 2 Corinthians 11:24-25). The surprising, and shocking, result was that the churches Paul established were constituted mainly of Gentiles. When news of this "open door" to the Gentiles circulated, it touched off the greatest crisis in first-generation Christianity.

Conservative Jewish Christians from Jerusalem came to Antioch demanding that Gentile Christians be circumcised (Acts 15:1). Circumcision was the key ritual that distinguished Jews as belonging to the covenant people of God (Genesis 17:11) and obligated them to observe the rituals spelled out in the Jewish law. Male Jewish infants were circumcised on the eighth day. Gentiles who converted to Judaism were circumcised as adults. The implication of the demand, therefore, was that Gentiles can become Christians only by first converting to Judaism and subjecting themselves to all of the Jewish rituals and customs. Paul knew that such a requirement would not only hinder his mission but also send the wrong theological message, since he was convinced that salvation is found only by faith in Christ and not by works of the law (Galatians 2:16). As the issue was too serious, and too contentious, to settle in Antioch, the church decided to send representatives to Jerusalem for a high-level conference.

The "Jerusalem Conference" or "Apostolic Council" (Acts 15:1-35; Galatians 2:1-10) was a summit meeting of leaders from the Antioch church (Paul and Barnabas) and the Jerusalem church (Peter, John, and James the brother of Jesus) over the question of the circumcision of Gentile Christians. On the central issue, the Jerusalem apostles agreed with Paul that circumcision must not be imposed on the Gentiles. This decision, dated about 49 CE, is considered one of the most momentous events in earliest Christianity. It meant that the Gentile mission was free to go forward without opposition from the Jerusalem leadership. It also paved the way for the eventual separation of Christianity from Judaism, since, if the demand for circumcision had prevailed, Christianity would have remained a sect of Judaism. In spite of this agreement, tensions over the Gentile issue remained. At some point, the Jerusalem church, following a proposal of James the brother of Jesus, sought to impose on Gentile converts a compromise including certain dietary restrictions (Acts 15:19-21; 21:25; Galatians

2:11-14), which Paul appears not to have accepted.[4] More seriously, a hard-line faction continued to demand circumcision, and Paul had to battle this issue for years to come.

The *second missionary journey* (Acts 15:36–18:22) was much longer than the first, taking Paul ever deeper into the heart of the Gentile world. Accompanied by Silas and Timothy, Paul traveled a vague route through Asia Minor to Troas on the northwest coast. From there, heeding the vision of a beckoning Macedonian man, he crossed into Macedonia, planting churches in Philippi and Thessalonica. Both of these churches—Paul's first in Europe[5]—later received letters from the apostle. Turning southward into Greece, Paul worked briefly in Athens, the city of philosophers and classical Greek culture. There, standing in the Areopagus ("Mars Hill," the city council or court), he preached one of the most famous sermons in Christian history (Acts 17:16-34). Taking a text from an inscription, "To an unknown god," and weaving together themes from Stoic philosophy and biblical theology, Paul announced that the one true god long sought by Greek poets and philosophers is none other than the God of Creation who has now been revealed in the resurrection of Jesus. Results in Athens were meager, and Paul soon left. He then settled in Corinth, where he spent eighteen months establishing a church, his longest stay on the second journey. There Paul met Priscilla (or Prisca) and Aquila, a Jewish Christian couple who, like Paul, were tentmakers. Priscilla is illustrative of Paul's openness to working with women. He commends her warmly as one among "my fellow workers in Christ Jesus" (Romans 16:3 RSV); she participates in giving theological instruction to the learned Christian missionary Apollos (Acts 18:26); four out of six biblical references to the couple list her name first.[6]

---

[4]Acts 15:19-21 depicts this compromise as having been approved by all parties at the Apostolic Council. In Acts 21:25, however, James proposes the same compromise as if it is the first time Paul has heard it. In any case, Paul appears not to agree with it. His own account of the Apostolic Council (Galatians 2:1-10) leaves no room for such a compromise, and his position on idol meat in 1 Cor. 8–10 differs with it.

[5]This is more significant from the perspective of Western history than from Paul's. Paul himself probably did not have a sense of a continental divide running between Asia Minor and Macedonia. In any case, this was not the first incursion of Christianity into Europe, as there were already Christians in Rome by this time.

[6]"Priscilla" in Acts, "Prisca" elsewhere: Acts 18:2, 18, and 26; Romans 16:3;

Near the end of his lengthy stay in Corinth, Paul was brought by Jewish opponents before the proconsul Gallio on charges of sedition, which were summarily dismissed. This appearance is significant because an inscription referring to Gallio allows us to date his term in Corinth. By extension, Paul's arrival in Corinth can be dated to approximately 50 CE. This gives a fixed date from which other Pauline events can be reckoned. Since 1 Thessalonians was written shortly after Paul's arrival in Corinth, Paul's earliest letter and the earliest book of the New Testament can with some confidence be dated about 50 as well.

After a brief return to Antioch, the *third journey* (Acts 18:23–20:38) took Paul back through Asia Minor to Ephesus, an important city on the southwest coast, which became a center of Paul's work for more than two years, his longest stay on any of the journeys. By now, Paul was surrounded by a team of coworkers—including Timothy, Titus, Priscilla and Aquila (now in Ephesus), and others—who shared Paul's ministry and were sent out on missions to establish new congregations and to stay in touch with existing churches. Most of the Corinthian correspondence was written from Ephesus and perhaps several other letters as well. Near the end of his Ephesian stay, Paul's team was the focus of a riot fomented by silversmiths who believed the Christian preaching was cutting into their business of selling miniature replicas of the great temple of Artemis in Ephesus. Based on references in the Corinthian letters, some scholars have theorized that Paul's stay in Ephesus may have involved a period of imprisonment, which could have been the occasion for some of his "prison letters." From Ephesus, Paul paid a final visit to his churches in Macedonia and Greece to complete a collection for the Jerusalem poor that he had been organizing among his churches (Romans 15:25-29). Besides relieving chronic poverty in Jerusalem, Paul hoped this collection, which symbolized the unity of Jewish and Gentile Christians, would help to ease the tensions between them. After delivering the collection to Jerusalem, he planned to go to Rome and from there to Spain.

The last main section of Acts describes Paul's final visit to Jerusalem, his arrest, and his *journey to Rome* (Acts 21:1–28:31). Here Luke recapitulates the overarching theme of the book: from Jerusalem to Rome. Paul's visit to Jerusalem did not go smoothly. His presence in the temple

---

1 Corinthians 16:19; 2 Timothy 4:19.

touched off a riot, instigated by Jewish opponents of Paul's openness to Gentiles. The disturbance was broken up by Roman soldiers, and Paul was arrested. He was jailed briefly in Jerusalem while the Romans tried to sort out what he might be guilty of. When it was discovered that his enemies were plotting to kill him, he was transferred to prison in Caesarea, Roman headquarters for Palestine. There, after languishing in prison for two years without a verdict, he invoked his privilege as a Roman citizen to move the case to Rome for trial before the emperor. On a long, dramatic sea voyage, complete with a shipwreck, Paul was taken as a prisoner to Rome. Under house arrest in Rome for two years while he awaited trial, he was free to receive visitors and preach the gospel. The Acts account abruptly closes at this point without reporting the outcome of the trial or Paul's fate. Why? Some scholars believe Luke ends the story at this point because he wrote Acts before Paul's trial took place. More likely, Luke was writing later and knew that Paul had been executed by Nero (probably 60–65 CE), as later tradition maintains. In that case, Luke concludes his book as he does in order to end on a positive note. Acts, after all, is not a biography of Paul but a story of the triumphant march of the gospel of Christ from Jerusalem to Rome. With Paul in the capital city, "proclaiming the kingdom of God and teaching about the Lord Jesus Christ with all boldness and without hindrance" (Acts 28:31), that story is concluded.

Paul's enduring legacy includes not only the Gentile churches he founded and Luke's stirring account of his heroic mission but also a corpus of thirteen letters, which form a major component of the New Testament. The next chapter will examine these influential writings of Paul along with the General Epistles and Revelation.

• 8 •

The Letters and Revelation

Twenty-one of the twenty-seven New Testament books are classified as letters and two others (Acts and Revelation) contain letters—a reflection of the early Christians' desire to create and maintain community. The term "epistles," which is sometimes used for these books, really just means "letters" but connotes a more formal character which is more appropriate for some of the New Testament letters than for others. For convenience, the letters may be divided into the Pauline Letters (Romans through Philemon), written mostly between 50 and 65 CE, and the General Epistles (Hebrews through Jude), which belong to the post-Pauline period. Revelation, an apocalyptic writing with some letter-like features—it has an epistolary salutation and postscript (Revelation 1:4-5; 22:21) and contains seven letters to the churches of Asia (Revelation 2–3)—also belongs to this later period. This chapter will survey first the Pauline Letters, then the General Epistles and Revelation; it will close with a brief look at the formation of the New Testament canon.

The Pauline Letters

Paul's letters are the earliest Christian writings which have come down to us and, therefore, also the earliest books of the New Testament. They allow us to peer back into the lives of some of the earliest Christian congregations as they were struggling to take shape. This section will discuss the character of Paul's letters and then briefly survey them in rough chronological order.

The Character of Paul's Letters. Paul's letters follow closely the style and form of ordinary Greek letters of his day. Like all Greek letters, they open with a "salutation" naming the sender (Paul) and the recipient (usually a church in a given city) and providing a greeting ("grace and peace"). The salutation is normally followed by a brief "thanksgiving" expressing Paul's appreciation for the recipients and outlining his prayer concerns for them.[1]

---

[1]The only letter without a thanksgiving section is Galatians, which has an "ironic rebuke" instead. Presumably, the Galatian situation is so serious that Paul has nothing for which to give thanks.

The "body" is the main section of the letter, where Paul communicates what is on his mind. Near the end there is usually a section of "parenesis," or general moral admonition. The letter "closing" typically includes a peace wish, final greetings, and a grace benediction. Thus, the letters open with "grace and peace" and close with "peace and grace," perfect "bookends" for Paul's message of grace in between.

It is important to recognize that Paul's letters are "occasional" writings, written in response to real-life situations in his churches. Paul was not a systematic theologian attempting to provide comprehensive coverage of Christian doctrine for all time. Paul believed he was living in the last generation and shows no awareness of writing something that would become Scripture. He was, rather, a pastoral theologian whose thought was hammered out in dealing with real-life issues in his churches. Each letter typically addresses particular problems, questions, or issues that have arisen in one of Paul's young churches and often leaves unmentioned much of Paul's thought which is not at issue. Our understanding of a letter will be enhanced by trying to formulate a picture of its occasion, that is, the situation in the church to which Paul is responding. The survey below will attempt to set the letters in the context of the occasions for which they were written and in selected cases to highlight some aspects of Paul's responses. Although Paul was writing to address particular situations in his first-century churches, his theological insights have proven so helpful to readers in every age that his letters have had a powerful, shaping influence on Christian theology.

Another issue related to Paul's letters is the question of their authenticity. Many scholars believe that some of the Pauline Letters may have been written under Paul's name after his death. Pseudonymity (writing under an assumed name) was common in antiquity and was widely practiced by Christians from the second century on. Several of the New Testament letters attributed to Paul bear varying degrees of difference in style, thought, and setting from his undisputed letters and, therefore, may be pseudonymous. There is a strong consensus that 1 and 2 Timothy and Titus (collectively known as the "Pastoral Epistles") were written around the turn of the century by an admirer of Paul who wanted to speak in Paul's name to a new situation. They will be used alongside the General Epistles to illustrate issues of the post-Pauline period. There are similar concerns, although less consensus, about the authorship of 2 Thessalonians, Colossians, and Ephesians. The remaining seven letters—1 Thessalonians, Galatians, 1 and

2 Corinthians, Philippians, Philemon, and Romans—are undisputed.

1 and 2 Thessalonians: Questions about Eschatology. Written from Corinth about 50 CE to the church in Thessalonica, the capital of Macedonia, shortly after its founding on Paul's second missionary journey, *1 Thessalonians* is probably Paul's earliest letter. Having been driven out of town by Jewish hostility (Acts 17:1-10) and knowing that the Thessalonians were facing similar hostilities, Paul had sent his coworker Timothy back to check on them (1 Thessalonians 2:17–3:6). The letter is a response to Timothy's report. The church has so far remained faithful, but some critical questions about eschatology have arisen in response to the death of some church members. Paul's preaching had emphasized the nearness of the *Parousia*, when Christ would appear in glory to gather his own into the kingdom of God. Subsequently, the deaths that had occurred had raised questions about this hope. What is the fate of those who have died believing in Christ? Will they be left out? When will the *Parousia* come?

In a beautiful passage often read at funerals (1 Thessalonians 4:13-18), Paul instills Christian hope in the face of death by teaching the resurrection of believers. This hope is grounded in the resurrection of Christ: Since Christ *was* raised, those who believe in him *will* be raised. When Christ returns, "the dead in Christ will rise first" (v. 16), so that they will not miss out on anything. "Then we who are alive, who are left, will be caught up in the clouds together with them to meet the Lord in the air; and so we will be with the Lord forever" (v. 17).

On the question of when the *Parousia* will come, however, Paul refuses to set a timetable or to speculate about the details of the end-time scenario (1 Thessalonians 5:1-11). It is enough to know that for believers the coming of Christ will be a day of salvation and that their task in the meantime is the business of faithful Christian living. Paul's purpose throughout is to comfort and encourage his readers (4:18; 5:11).

Second Thessalonians addresses further questions about the *Parousia*. This letter may have been written by Paul shortly after 1 Thessalonians or by a later writer attempting to clarify Paul's teaching. In either case, it combats a false teaching, wrongly attributed to Paul, that the *Parousia* had already come (2 Thessalonians 2:1-2). This notion was shaking up the church and perhaps contributing to a problem of idleness. The letter insists that the *Parousia* has not yet come (2:3-12) and admonishes the idlers to return to work (3:6-13). The command that those who refuse to work should not eat certainly does not intend to discourage helping the needy. It does warn against the kind of fanatical end-time speculation which leads to the neglect of one's Christian duties here and now.

Galatians: Questions about the Law. Addressed to a group of churches located in north- or south-central Asia Minor, Galatians is Paul's feistiest letter. Depending on the exact location of the churches, Galatians could have been written as early as 49 CE or as late as 54 CE. In either case, it addresses a critical situation in which opponents of Paul were preaching "another gospel" and leading the churches astray (Galatians 1:6-9). Paul never says who these people were. Traditionally referred to as "Judaizers," they appear to have been conservative Jewish Christians who were insisting that Gentile Christians must be circumcised, in effect making them Jews subject to the Jewish law (5:2-3; 6:12-13). The situation is quite serious, with the heart of the gospel at stake, and Paul is very emotional, even angry, as he writes (1:8-9; 5:12).

Galatians is Paul's "manifesto of freedom" from the law. The main theme of the letter is justification by faith. The apostle argues "that a person is justified not by the works of the law but through faith in Jesus Christ" (Galatians 2:16). "Justification" depicts salvation under law-court imagery. To be "justified" means to be "declared righteous" before the judgment seat of God. Since the person being judged is actually a sinner, this verdict cannot be based on works of law but only on faith in the saving death of Christ. "Justification by faith," then, amounts to being acquitted, pardoned, or forgiven, and thereby being restored to a right relationship with God on the basis of faith in Christ.

Galatians 3–4 makes intricate arguments for this position. Paul uses Genesis 15:6 to show that Abraham was "reckoned righteous" on the basis of his faith *before* his circumcision and *before* the giving of the law. The true heirs of Abraham, the covenant people of God, are not those who are circumcised and observe the law but those who have faith. The law was never intended to be the basis for righteousness. Its function, rather, was to condemn sin and so to serve as a temporary disciplinarian until the coming of Christ. Now that Christ has come, he has redeemed us from the law. It is not necessary to receive circumcision and place oneself under the law. All who have faith in Christ, Jews and Gentiles alike, are children of God. Indeed, in Christ all human distinctions are erased: "There is no longer Jew or Greek, there is no longer slave or free, there is no longer male and female; for all of you are one in Christ Jesus" (Galatians 3:28).

In Galatians 5–6, Paul emphasizes that freedom from the law does not mean license to sin. Christian living is directed by the guidance of the Holy Spirit and by the commandment to "love your neighbor as yourself," which contains the "whole law" in itself (5:14).

Many interpreters have considered justification by faith to be the central theme in Paul's theology. Others have seen it not as the focal point of his thought as a whole but as an important argument which he uses primarily in combative situations where his law-free gospel to the Gentiles is under challenge. In either case, justification by faith has certainly been an influential theme in Christian theology, especially so in Protestant circles.

1 and 2 Corinthians: Questions about Freedom. Corinth was an industrialized, cosmopolitan, crossroads city in Greece. Famous even among pagans for its wide-open immorality, it was a place where many cultures and religions met and mingled, a phenomenon called "syncretism." Many of the problems which surface in the Corinthian church, established during Paul's long stay on the second journey, were products of this environment. Counting a "previous letter" mentioned in 1 Corinthians 5:9 and a "harsh letter" mentioned in 2 Corinthians 2:3-4 and 7:8 and 12, Paul wrote—mostly from Ephesus about 54–55 CE—at least four letters to this troubled church.

In *1 Corinthians*, Paul tackles a laundry list of problems, many of which were reported to him on a visit by "Chloe's people" (1:11) and in a letter from Corinth (7:1). Among the many problems were quarreling factions with rival claims to superior wisdom (ch. 1-4), toleration of sexual immorality as a mark of spiritual liberation (ch. 5-6), issues related to marriage and divorce (ch. 7), claims of unrestricted freedom to eat meat sacrificed to idols (ch. 8-10), disorder in the Lord's Supper (ch. 11), overemphasis on ecstatic spiritual gifts (ch. 12-14), and misunderstanding of the resurrection of believers (ch. 15). In the letter, Paul takes up these problems one after another and deals with them.

In wrestling with these thorny, local problems, Paul again and again cuts to the heart of what is at stake theologically and articulates enduring principles that have provided guidance in all ages. His treatment of the factions' boasting of spiritual wisdom and power, for example, develops a penetrating "theology of the Cross" that contradicts all human boasting (1 Cor. 1). The sacrificial love demonstrated on the Cross of Jesus appears to the eyes of the world as mere foolishness and weakness. Yet God has chosen the Cross as the instrument of divine power and wisdom. Those who are saved by God's "foolish wisdom" have nothing about which to boast except the Cross of Christ. Again, in dealing with the factions' championing of their spiritual heroes (such as Paul, Apollos, or Cephas), Paul argues that Christian leaders are not rival heroes to be idolized but "servants," all used by God in various ways in building up God's people and all accountable to God for their ministry (1 Cor. 3).

Paul's treatment of sexual immorality, such as incest and prostitution, provides opportunity for clarifying that Christian freedom does not mean license (1 Cor. 5-6). Some Corinthians had the Gnostic-like notion that, because the body is evil, salvation is a matter only of the inner spirit. The body, they believed, is free to do whatever it pleases, and grossly immoral behavior even demonstrates one's spiritual liberation. Their slogan was, "All things are lawful for me" (6:12). Paul quotes and then corrects this slogan (6:12-20). Without putting the Corinthians under a legalistic code, he outlines the principles which must guide genuine Christian freedom: Choose actions which build up the community of faith, actions which do not enslave the doer, actions which are becoming to "the body of Christ" and "the temple of the Spirit," actions which glorify the God who "purchased" us to belong to God.

The long discussion of the idol-meat issue illustrates how far Paul was willing to go in accommodating the Christian faith to Hellenistic culture as well as the limits of such accommodation (1 Cor. 8-10). In a Greek city like Corinth, most meat available for purchase had been slaughtered in a pagan temple and ritually offered to pagan gods. Some Christians (the "weak") strictly avoided this "idol meat," horrified that it would involve them in idol worship. Others, based on their "strong" knowledge that idols are not real gods, ate the meat freely and even pressured the "weak" to do so in violation of their conscience. In principle, Paul agrees with the "strong": Idols are not real gods and idol meat is in itself a matter of indifference. One is free to eat it or not. However, Paul insists that how we treat our Christian brothers and sisters is not a matter of indifference. To pressure the weak to eat in violation of their conscience is wrong. One's freedom must be exercised in a way that is guided by the principle of the love of neighbor. This is not a limitation of freedom but its proper exercise. Paul also insists that overt idol worship must be strictly avoided.

The problem of spiritual gifts and tongue-speaking (1 Cor. 12-14) provides the occasion for the best-known and best-loved passage in Paul's letters, his famous "love hymn" (ch. 13). "Tongue-speaking" (*glossolalia*) is an ecstatic experience in which the worshiper loses control and speaks through the Spirit in an unintelligible language. Those in Corinth who had this gift claimed it as a mark of superiority and practiced it with abandon, dividing the church and disrupting the worship service. Paul begins in

---

Paul's "Love Hymn"

If I speak in the tongues of mortals and of angels, but do not have love, I am only a noisy gong or a clanging cymbal.

If I have prophetic powers and can fathom all mysteries and all knowledge, and if I have a faith that can move mountains, but do not have love, I am nothing.

If I give all I possess to the poor and surrender my body to the flames, but do not have love, I gain nothing.

Love is patient, love is kind. It does not envy, it does not boast, it is not proud.

Love is not rude, it does not insist on its own way, it is not easily provoked, it keeps no record of wrongs.

Love does not delight in evil but rejoices in the truth. It always protects, always trusts, always hopes, always perseveres.

Love never fails. But where there are prophecies, they will cease; where there are tongues, they will be stilled; where there is knowledge, it will pass away.

For we know only in part and we prophesy only in part, but when the complete comes, the partial will come to an end.

When I was a child, I talked like a child, I thought like a child, I reasoned like a child.

When I became an adult, I put childish ways behind me.

Now we see but a poor reflection as in a mirror; the time will come when we shall see face to face.

At present I know the truth only in part; then I will know it as fully as God knows me now.

And now faith, hope, and love abide, these three; and the greatest of these is love.

(1 Corinthians 13:1-13, author's translation.)

---

chap. 12 by showing that tongue-speaking is not the only gift of the Spirit. There are many different gifts, all intended to benefit the whole church. Just as the human body consists of various members with different functions (feet, hands, eyes, ears, etc.), so the church, "the body of Christ," consists of many members with different gifts, all mutually interdependent. The "love hymn" in chapter 13 supports this argument by showing that the one gift for which all Christians should strive is love. Apart from love, all other gifts, no matter how spectacular, are devoid of purpose and value. Paul's word for love here is *agapē*, which he describes as an unconditional, self-giving love, a love which seeks the well-being of another without expecting anything in return. As the kind of love which believers have experienced in Christ, it is the supreme Christian virtue and should become the hallmark of every Christian's life. Then in chapter 14, Paul zeroes in on tongue-speaking, showing that the Corinthians have highly overvalued it and offering guidelines restricting its practice.

Whereas in Galatians Paul fights for freedom from the law, in 1 Corinthians he seeks to rescue an unruly church from an irresponsible overemphasis on freedom. Theirs was a spirituality of individual piety, lacking in the corporate dimension of community spirit and mutual obligation. Paul's final word of advice in 1 Corinthians is, "Let all that you do be done in love" (16:14).

Second Corinthians reveals that 1 Corinthians did not solve the problems in that church. Things actually grew worse. Newly arrived opponents of Paul, whom he sarcastically calls "super-apostles" (2 Corinthians 11:5; 12:11), had turned the church against the apostle. Making a show of their Jewish credentials and of their signs, wonders, and lofty wisdom, they opposed Paul as weak and unimpressive. In the interval, Paul had paid a quick, "painful visit" (2:1) to Corinth to deal with the situation in person, but his efforts were rebuffed. Retreating to Ephesus, Paul wrote an emotional "harsh letter" (mentioned in 2 Corinthians 2:3-4 and 7:8, 12) in an effort to win back his church. Either this letter has been lost or, as many scholars surmise, has been partially preserved in 2 Corinthians 10–13. These chapters exhibit a severe tone not found in the preceding chapters and may represent a separate letter written at the height of the crisis. The stern, threatening tone of this letter seems designed to bring the crisis to a head, one way or the other.

Along with this "harsh letter" Paul also sent his coworker Titus as a personal envoy to Corinth, with instructions to meet him afterwards in Troas with news of the outcome in Corinth. Once Paul got to Troas, however, Titus failed to appear as scheduled. So Paul anxiously crossed over into Macedonia and rendezvoused with him en route. Titus gave him the good news that the Corinthian church was ready to reconcile its relationship with Paul (2 Corinthians 2:12-13; 7:5-16). Overjoyed at this, Paul wrote a "conciliatory letter," found in 2 Corinthians 1–9, in which he breathes a sigh of relief and resumes the task of helping the church to work out its difficulties. A key theme in both sections of 2 Corinthians is Paul's defense of a ministry style of weakness and suffering as consistent with being an apostle of the crucified Christ.

Philippians, Philemon, Colossians, and Ephesians: the Prison Letters. Scholars are divided over the origin of these "prison letters." Traditionally, they are assumed to have come from Paul's final imprisonment in Rome (Acts 28), which puts them late in his career (58–65 CE). Since Philippians and Philemon have close connections with Paul's work in the east, many scholars have argued that they were written during Paul's earlier imprisonment in Caesarea (56–58 CE; Acts 23–26) or during a hypothetical imprisonment in Ephesus (54–55 CE). The authorship of Colossians and Ephesians is often disputed because of differences in style, vocabulary, and theology. Defenders of their authenticity typically date them to the Roman imprisonment, arguing that the later date helps account for the perceived differences in those letters. If they are in fact pseudonymous, then the prison motif is a tribute to what the apostle was forced to endure for the sake of his ministry.

Philippians is a joyful letter to a friendly church with which Paul enjoyed a warm relationship. He writes to thank the church for sending a financial contribution (Philippians 4:15-18), to reassure them about his own well-being in prison (1:12-26), to settle a quarrel in the church (4:2-3), and to warn about a false teaching (3:2-21). A dominant theme in the letter is Paul's paradoxical joy even in prison, facing possible execution. He is confident that if he dies he will "be with Christ," and if he lives he will continue his ministry and see his friends again (1:23-26). He reassures his friends that, even in the midst of trying circumstances, "I can do all things through him who strengthens me" (4:13).

Philemon, Paul's shortest letter, accompanies the return to Philemon of his runaway slave Onesimus. After running away, Onesimus had come to be with Paul, had become a Christian, and had become "useful" in Paul's ministry (v. 11—a pun, since "Onesimus" means "useful"). As Paul is now returning him to his owner, he pleads for clemency on Onesimus's behalf. Since Roman slave law gave the owner of a runaway a free hand for severe punishment, Paul was putting Onesimus in significant jeopardy. Paul, however, asks Philemon to receive Onesimus back not as a slave but as a "beloved brother" in Christ (v. 16) and hints that he would like Philemon to release Onesimus and send him back to Paul. Although Paul's return of a runaway seems to give approval to the institution of slavery, it would be wrong to conclude that Paul's message is to commend the practice of slavery. Slavery was a fact of life in Paul's world—a world he thought was about to end with the return of Christ. Paul gives advice on Christian conduct within the existing structures. In asking that the slave be received as a brother, Paul establishes a Christian principle that ultimately is incompatible with slavery.

Colossians is addressed to a congregation established by Paul's coworker Epaphras (Colossians 1:7), probably as an extension of Paul's Ephesian ministry. Colossians opposes an esoteric Gnostic syncretism which advocated rigorous ascetic practices. Gnostics conceived of certain hostile angelic "principalities and powers" which separate the material world from God. The ascetic practices, apparently, were thought necessary to appease these powers, implying that faith in Christ was not sufficient for salvation. The letter argues that Christ is Lord of all the universe; he is the Creator, the Sustainer, and the Redeemer of "all things" (1:15-20). Whatever rebellious spiritual powers might be at large have been defeated through the cross of Christ (2:8-10, 15). Since the "fullness" of divine power dwells in Christ (1:19; 2:9), faith in him is sufficient for salvation, and the ascetic practices are unnecessary (2:16-23). Authentic Christian discipline is characterized not by ascetic rigor but by appropriate, loving conduct in all of one's relationships (Colossians 3–4).

It is difficult to recognize a concrete occasion behind *Ephesians*, and several early manuscripts even omit reference to a specific location in the salutation (Ephesians 1:1). Possibly, it was a circular letter intended to circulate among churches in a region. The emphasis on the unity of Jews and Gentiles in "one new humanity" (2:15) has suggested to some interpreters that the letter addresses a situation of tension between Jewish and Gentile Christians. Another theory is that it was written pseudonymously by the collector of Paul's letters to serve as an introduction to the published collection. This would account for Ephesians' marked distinctiveness in style, vocabulary, and theology, its lack of personal references, and its apparent heavy borrowing of phrases from the other letters, especially Colossians. In any case, Ephesians 1–3 summarizes Paul's theology, including this memorable statement of his doctrine of salvation by "grace," that is, by God's merciful, undeserved favor:

> For by grace you have been saved through faith, and this is not your own doing; it is the gift of God—not the result of works, so that no one may boast.   (Ephesians 2:8-9)

Ephesians 4–6 gives ethical instruction. Of special note is the "domestic code" (5:21–6:9; cf. Colossians 3:18–4:1), which outlines proper conduct of husbands and wives, of parents and children, and of masters and slaves within the Christian household. Despite the impression often given, it is not the purpose of this text to prescribe a male-dominated patriarchal hierarchy as the proper Christian family pattern. Such a structure was already the prevailing pattern in the Roman world. The text seeks, rather, to modify that pattern by prescribing Christian conduct within it. The whole code is placed under the rubric of mutual submission, and the so-called "dominant" member of each pair is said to have in Christ an obligation to the so-called "subordinate" member. Husbands are to love their wives sacrificially; fathers are not to provoke their children; masters are to treat slaves justly. The presence of this text in the Bible no more establishes male-dominated family structure as the Christian pattern than it makes owning slaves a proper Christian privilege.

Romans: Paul's Gospel. Romans is a letter of introduction to a church Paul did not establish but which he plans to visit. We do not know how Christianity came to Rome. Perhaps it arrived not by an organized mission but informally, as "all roads led to Rome." There is reason to believe the Roman church experienced tensions between Jewish and Gentile Christians. In 49 CE, Emperor Claudius expelled the Jews from Rome, including Jewish Christians, leaving behind a purely Gentile church. After Claudius's death in 54, the return of Jewish Christians likely aroused leadership tensions. As Paul writes from Corinth about 55–56 CE near the end of his third journey, his plans are to take his poverty-relief collection to Jerusalem and then head west, first to Rome and ultimately to a new mission field in Spain (Romans 15:22-33). Paul is introducing himself to the Roman Christians and trying to enlist their support for his new work in Spain. Because his gospel of law-free inclusion of Gentiles was controversial, he outlines, explains, clarifies, and defends his theology in hopes that the Roman church will receive him and help send him to Spain. Paul may also have one eye on tensions in the Roman church and another on the defense of his gospel he will have to make on his impending visit to Jerusalem.[2]

Since the occasion of Romans has as much to do with Paul's own agenda as with problems in the Roman church, the letter turns out to contain the most orderly, systematic presentation of Paul's thought. For that reason, it has also been the most influential letter in the history of Christian theology. Paul's theology in Romans is quite complex and interpretations of it differ at many points. What follows is an attempt to summarize the broad flow of Paul's argument.

In Romans 1:16-17, Paul states his overall theme. Through the power of the gospel, God seeks to save all people who respond in faith, Jews and Gentiles alike. God's own righteousness is demonstrated by making people righteous (that is, putting them in right relationship) on the basis of faith. Throughout Romans, Paul is concerned to show that Jews and Gentiles are on equal footing before God—both are saved only by a faith response to the gospel. This is the text which later captivated Martin Luther and helped shape his doctrine of "justification by faith alone" as the basis for the Protestant Reformation.

The first major section of the letter describes *the sinful human condition* (Romans 1:18–3:20). Sin (*hamartia*) means "missing the mark," rebelling against God's intention that created human beings should live in trusting obedience to the Creator. Paul's concern here is to show that Jews and Gentiles are equally guilty. Gentiles (1:18-32), without the law, committed the fundamental sin of idolatry, worshiping the creation instead of the Creator, and from that sprang all manner of immorality. Jews (2:1–3:8) sinned in spite of the law, since they did not keep it. Paul concludes that Jews and Gentiles alike are under the power of sin (3:9); none are righteous (3:10). All people, therefore, are sinners, rightfully subject to God's wrath. Works of the law cannot restore righteousness, for the law only creates knowledge of sin (3:20).

The next section turns to *God's solution—justification by faith in Christ* (Romans 3:21–4:25). In Christ, God has provided a new way of righteousness, apart from the law—"the righteousness of God through faith in Jesus Christ for all who believe" (3:22). The death of Christ is a "sacrifice of atonement" (3:25) which pays the penalty for sin. This benefit becomes

---

[2]See, e.g., Günther Bornkamm, *Paul*, trans. D. M. G. Stalker (New York: Harper & Row, 1971) 88-96; Karl P. Donfried, ed., *The Romans Debate* (Minneapolis: Augsburg, 1977).

effective when it is received in faith. For Paul, "faith" means not merely believing the gospel message but also trusting God for one's salvation and putting oneself at God's disposal in genuine obedience—just as Jesus did in accepting his fate on the cross. Such faith becomes the basis of a right relationship with God. God "justifies," or "declares righteous," those who have faith, acquitting them of sin and restoring them to a right standing. Since it is precisely undeserving sinners who are justified, justification is an act of God's "grace," that is, God's unmerited favor, God's free gift of salvation. Righteousness, then, comes not by works of the law but through faith in Christ and is equally open to Jews and Gentiles alike. To show that this principle is consistent with Jewish Scripture, chapter 4 develops at length the example of Abraham as one whose faith was "reckoned as righteousness" apart from works.

Paul now goes on to describe *the new life in Christ as a life of freedom* (Romans 5–8). Sinners justified by faith in Christ now have peace with God and *freedom from God's wrath* at the final judgment (ch. 5). From this perspective Paul describes salvation as "reconciliation," the restoration of a broken relationship. Believers also have *freedom from Sin* (ch. 6), *from the Law* (ch. 7), and *from Death* (ch. 8). Here "Sin" is depicted as a cosmic power that enslaves a person to a life of sin. Sin attacks the "flesh" (understood not as material stuff but as human weakness, frailty, and proneness toward sin) and even enlists God's law as an ally, misusing the commandments to incite their violation. The result is "Death," separation from God and the inability to do God's will. Christ redeems believers from such bondage. "Redemption" depicts salvation as liberation from bondage to Sin, just as a slave could be set free by a benefactor who was willing to pay the purchase price. Here Paul makes it clear that justification should not be taken to imply that God pretends that sinners are righteous and leaves them free to go on sinning. Rather, the death and resurrection of Christ have broken the power of Sin and Death. Christ delivers sinners from the tyranny of Sin and gives them the power of the Holy Spirit to do God's will. At the same time, Paul acknowledges that Christians are not automatically zapped into sinless perfection. The new possibility must be actualized by consciously rejecting sin and choosing righteousness, by living according to the Spirit and not according to the flesh. For Paul, salvation is a total transformation of one's life which is not yet complete. Salvation is a past accomplishment in the death and resurrection of Christ but also a continuing process and a future goal of being transformed into the likeness of Christ.

Romans 9–11 discusses *the place of Jews and Gentiles in God's plan of salvation*. Paul wants to make it clear that his successful mission to the Gentiles does not imply that God is being unfaithful to the covenant with Israel. God has not rejected Israel, but most Jews have rejected the righteousness of faith. Paul believes that the Jews' temporary rejection of the gospel is being used by God to allow the Gentiles to be included in the people of God. He is hoping that the Gentiles' inclusion will make the Jews jealous enough to accept the gospel as well so that, in the end, "all Israel" will be saved (11:13-26).

The last major section of Romans is devoted to the *ethical application of the gospel* (Romans 12:1–15:13). Paul is concerned to show that his gospel of grace does not leave Christians free to do as they please but issues in ethical behavior. Paul's "therefore" (12:1) signals an ethic based on the preceding theology. Because of all the "mercies of God," Christians are under obligation to present themselves to God "as a living sacrifice." Christian living should no longer conform to the pattern of "this world," which is passing away, but should be transformed to fit the pattern of the coming age, to which by faith believers already belong (12:2). Paul goes on to give practical advice about Christian living in a variety of settings. Topics include the exercise of spiritual gifts; love for fellow believers and nonbelievers, including one's enemy; obedience to civil authorities; and mutual respect among Christians with differing scruples with regard to diet and holy days. Above all, he again commends the practice of love, for in the end "the one who loves another has fulfilled the law" (13:8-10).

Depending on the origin of the prison letters, Romans may be the latest undisputed letter of Paul. It is surely his last letter written as a free man. Written at a significant turning point in his ministry, it beautifully sums up his career as the "apostle to the Gentiles" and is a noble capstone to the development of Christianity in its formative period. Its influence in the history of Christian theology is unrivaled.

As mentioned earlier, Paul likely died under Nero, 60–65 CE. His most distinctive contribution was to have fought for the law-free inclusion of the Gentiles and in the course of that fight to have hammered out—mostly in Galatians and Romans—his theology of justification by grace through faith. His legacy is thirteen New Testament letters written by him or under the shadow of his influence and the stirring Acts account of his heroic efforts on behalf of the gospel.

The General Epistles and Revelation

For the period after Paul we have no narrative account of the church such as Acts provides for the earlier period. We do have knowledge of some key events shaping this period. Nero's persecution of the church (64-65 CE) foreshadowed growing tensions between church and empire. The fall of Jerusalem and destruction of the temple (70 CE) not only devastated the Jewish community but also uprooted the Jewish Christian church and exacerbated hostility between Jews and Christians, as each blamed the other for the disaster. The Jewish Academy of Jamnia ©. 90 CE) reorganized Judaism along Pharisaic lines and took measures to exclude Jewish Christians from participation in the synagogues. By the end of the first century, Christianity was well established around the Mediterranean and had become a largely Gentile movement. The apostles and others of the eye-witness generation were dying out and giving way to a second and third generation of Christians. In this setting, the church confronted a new set of issues.

The literature of this period includes the Gospels, the General Epistles, Revelation, and any of the Pauline Letters that may be pseudonymous. The Gospels, which we have already examined, were written between 65 and 100 to preserve the Jesus traditions and to meet the needs of diverse Christian communities.[3] This section will briefly examine the remaining New Testament literature against the background of the new issues confronting the church in this later period. Because many of these issues were still unresolved in the New Testament period, this section also looks ahead to the period of early church history.

The General Epistles (Hebrews[4]–Jude) are so called because these letters are not addressed as specifically to particular churches as are Paul's letters. In most cases, the intended readers are either unnamed or very

---

[3]The Gospels clearly reflect the Jewish-Christian tensions of this period. The harsh polemic against the hypocrisy of the Pharisees (as in Matt. 23), the tendency to shift blame for Jesus' death from Pilate to "the Jews" (see chap. 5 above), and the numerous hostile references to "the Jews" in John are all likely colored by the hostile relations between church and synagogue during the period when the Gospels were written. Modern readers should not use such texts to justify anti-Jewish attitudes or actions.

[4]Although Hebrews was for a long time grouped with Paul's letters, it is actually anonymous; today, very few believe it was written by Paul.

loosely defined. In fact, Hebrews and 1 John do not have a salutation at all. Although dating the General Epistles is very difficult and controversial, they appear to belong mostly to the later New Testament period (late first century to early second century). The Pastoral Epistles (1 and 2 Timothy and Titus) are widely believed to have been written pseudonymously in Paul's name around the turn of the century. They differ markedly from the undisputed letters in style, vocabulary, and theology; they are difficult to fit into the circumstances of Paul's career; and they presuppose an advanced level of false teaching and church structure. They will be considered here as illustrating concerns of the post-Pauline period. Revelation is an apocalypse, partially dressed in the form of a letter, probably written about 95 CE.

Christian Complacency: Hebrews and James. As Christianity moved into its second and third generations, there was a natural tendency, at least in times of peace, for complacency and apathy to set in. The Spirit-filled enthusiasm of the earlier period gradually gave way to a more staid emphasis on doctrine. "Faith," understood as a dynamic quality of trusting obedience, yielded to "the faith," understood as sound doctrine. Christians whose parents and grandparents had been Christians before them tended to take the faith for granted. They were Christians but it seemed not to matter much to them. This problem in the church has never gone away. Church history has been punctuated by the need for periodic revival and renewal movements. Two of the General Epistles, Hebrews and James, can be viewed as calls to wake up from such lethargy.

The anonymous "letter" to the *Hebrews* has no epistolary address. It reads much like a sermon designed for a church that has grown cold and complacent. That church is drifting and is in danger of falling away. At some time in the past the church had faced persecution and had remained faithful (Hebrews 10:32-34). But what if persecution should come again? Would these complacent Christians stand the test? The author tries to rouse them from their apathy by demonstrating that Christianity is a "superior" faith worth being excited about. Christ is superior to Moses (3:1-6), to the Israelite priests (7:23-28), and to the sacrifices (10:11-12). Christ offered himself as the perfect sacrifice which takes away sin "once for all" (7:27; 9:25-26) and does not need to be repeated. Surely this is worth holding onto. But the author exhorts the readers to do more. He encourages them neither to go backward, nor to stand still, but to move forward on the journey of faith (12:1-2, 12-13).

The *Letter of James*—whether written by James the brother of Jesus
sometime before his death in 62 CE or in his name or by an unknown James
near the end of the century—is a collection of moral exhortations concerned
to emphasize the importance of moral action in the Christian life. Lip
service and profession of faith are not enough. Words must be translated
into action: "But be doers of the word, and not hearers only" (James 1:22).
True religion is defined not in terms of correct doctrine but of moral action:
"to care for orphans and widows in their distress, and to keep oneself
unstained by the world" (1:7). James is protesting a trend toward resting
content with adherence to sound doctrine as if that were all that matters. In
a text that greatly offended Martin Luther, James' insistence that "a person
is justified by works and not by faith alone" (2:24) sounds as if he might be
taking issue with Paul's doctrine of justification by faith. But the two are
actually not so far apart. For Paul, the "faith" that justifies is an attitude of
trusting obedience which issues in deeds of love (Galatians 5:6). For James,
the "faith alone" which does not justify is a mere intellectual assent to
doctrine which does not result in good works. A religion concerned only
about doctrine and not about caring for the poor and needy is a dead
religion:

> What good is it, my brothers and sisters, if you say you have faith but
> do not have works? Can faith save you? If a brother or sister is naked and
> lacks daily food, and one of you says to them, "Go in peace; keep warm
> and eat your fill," and yet you do not supply their bodily needs, what is the
> good of that? So faith by itself, if it has no works, is dead.
>
> (James 2:14-17)

"Delay" of the Parousia: 2 Peter. Closely related to the problem of
complacency, and probably contributing to it, is the "delay" of the
Parousia. First-generation Christians believed the coming of Christ in glory
was imminent. Paul writes about it as if he fully expects to see it soon,
which gave a sense of urgency to his mission. As decades passed and new
generations arose, that sense of imminence and urgency began to fade.
Slowly the realization dawned that the end was not as near as once believed.
This does not appear to have created a crisis for the church, but the church
did have to adjust to the new reality. It had to find ways of settling down
and learning to live in the midst of this world for a more extended period.
Of course, in times of intense crisis more imminent expectations could be
revived.

The later Gospels all confront this issue in one way or another. Both

Matthew and Luke reckon with an extended period before Jesus' return. John seems to replace the *Parousia* expectation with the coming of the Spirit at Jesus' resurrection. The issue is most directly addressed by *2 Peter*, which refutes false teachers who are scoffing at the *Parousia* expectation and denying that it will ever come (2 Peter 3:3-4). The author insists that "the day of the Lord" *will* come, although not necessarily "soon" from our perspective (3:8-10). God, who has eternity as a frame of reference, measures time a bit differently than we do. The so-called "delay" should be viewed, rather, as an opportunity to repent before the Day of Judgment. Second Peter, incidentally, is widely regarded as a pseudonymous work written in Peter's name in the first half of the second century and may be the latest book in the New Testament.

Development of Organizational Structures: the Pastoral Epistles. In the earlier period, church structure appears to have been relatively free, charismatic, and spontaneous. As time passed and the churches grew and settled into the reality of an indefinite life in this world, it is natural that more definitive organizational structures would emerge. Probably there was not a uniform development throughout all the churches, but different patterns appeared at various times and places. It is possible to see here the beginnings of the hierarchical structure which came to characterize the later patristic church (see chapter 9). The letters of Ignatius of Antioch (died about 110 CE) describe three church offices arranged in a graded hierarchy. At the top stood the *bishop* (literally, "overseer"), who supervised the many congregations in and around a given city. Under his authority, the *presbyters* (literally, "elders")[5] served as pastors of individual congregations. Below the presbyters came the *deacons* (literally, "servants"), who ministered to the sick and needy.

Not many years earlier, the *Pastoral Epistles* mention the same three offices and state qualifications for holding them (1 Timothy 3:1-13; 5:17-19; Titus 1:5-9), although here they do not seem to stand in a hierarchy. It is not even clear that bishops and presbyters are totally separate offices at this point. There are hints that women may have been included among the deacons (1 Timothy 3:11; cf. Romans 16:1). There may also have been an "order" of widows which played some role in the churches (1 Timothy 5:3-16). Unfortunately, we do not have any job descriptions for these offices. One important function of the bishop is teaching the church and safe-

---

[5]*Presbyteros* (Greek) or *presbyter* (Latin) became *priest* in English.

guarding "sound doctrine" against the threat of heresy (1 Timothy 3:2; Titus 1:9), a role that will become increasingly important in the centuries ahead. Presbyters also are said to be involved in teaching and preaching (1 Timothy 5:17). A troubling text is 1 Timothy 2:9-15, which prescribes silence and a narrowly restricted role for women in the church. This seems far from the inclusive spirit of Jesus and the undisputed letters of Paul.[6] Possibly, the author is accommodating the church to prevailing cultural patterns in the interest of respectability. Or he may be treating a local situation in which uninformed women were contributing to the problem of false teaching. In that case, his short-term strategy would be to silence them, while his long-term strategy is to educate them. In any case, such texts should not be made the starting point for Christian teaching on the role of women today.

The Problem of Heresy: 1, 2, and 3 John and Jude. Internally, the greatest challenge the churches faced was heresy, that is, false teaching. Certainly this was not entirely new in the later period. Many, if not most, of Paul's letters confront some sort of false teaching. But by the turn of the century heresy was beginning to reach new proportions. Gnosticism (see chapter 5) in particular was maturing into fully developed systems of thought. Soon it would have teachers, schools, literature, and organizational structure. By the mid-second century Gnosticism would threaten to become the dominant form of Christianity.

The author of the three *Letters of John* twice calls himself "the Elder" but is otherwise anonymous. The letters, probably written around the turn of the century, are closely related in vocabulary and themes to the Gospel of John, whose author is likewise anonymous. In the letters, "the Elder" confronts a Gnostic heresy which has already provoked a division in his church. Two characteristic Gnostic features are evident in the false teaching—Docetism and libertinism. Both are rooted in the Gnostic contempt for the evil fleshly body. Docetism (from Greek *dokeō*, "to seem") taught that the spiritual Christ could not really have come in the flesh but only appeared to do so, thus denying Jesus' true humanity (1 John 4:2-3). This teaching, by questioning the reality of Jesus' death, seriously threatens

---

[6]A striking exception is 1 Cor 14:34-35, which also silences women. This text is so similar to the one in 1 Timothy that it is often suspected of having been inserted into Paul's letter by a later hand. Elsewhere Paul champions the full participation of women (see 1 Corinthians 7; 11; Romans 16).

the doctrine of the atonement. Against this, "the Elder" vigorously denounces the Docetists and reaffirms the true humanity of Jesus and the reality of his saving death. Libertinism, the absence of moral restraint, was justified by Gnostics on their assumption that, since only the spirit is to be saved, the deeds of the body are of no consequence. The Elder's opponents seem to have claimed the freedom to live deliberately in an immoral way and still profess to be without sin (1 John 1:6-10). The author argues that claiming to know God without obeying God's commandments, especially the commandment to love one another, is living a lie (1 John 2:3-11). Knowing God cannot be purely a matter of private piety having no implications for living. Rather, a true relationship with God will turn us in love toward our brothers and sisters, for "God is love" (1 John 4:8). We love others because God first loved us (1 John 4:19). And, "the Elder" insists, love includes using our material resources to help those in need (1 John 3:17).

The little *Letter of Jude*, probably written in the early second century, also denounces some sort of heresy with tendencies toward libertinism. The heretics may have been of Gnostic type, although it is difficult to be sure, since the author does not discuss their theology but only condemns their lifestyle.

The *Pastoral Epistles* confront a Gnostic heresy which advocated ascetic practices such as celibacy and abstinence from certain foods. In countering this teaching, their author appeals to Scripture (2 Timothy 3:16-17) and in particular to the Old Testament doctrine of the goodness of God's creation (1 Timothy 4:1-5). He also advocates the standard of Paul's teaching as it has been handed down through Timothy in a living chain of tradition (2 Timothy 2:1-2). A third safeguard of sound doctrine is church office. The Pastorals' emphasis on church structure and qualifications for office, mentioned above, is largely motivated by the need to have good people in office in order to fight heresy. All three of these safeguards—Scripture, apostolic tradition, and church office—were developed further in the later patristic church (see chapter 9).

The Growing Hostility of the Roman Empire: 1 Peter and Revelation. Externally, the Christians' greatest threat was the growing hostility of the Roman Empire. The earliest period had generally been characterized by benign neglect. Through the time of Paul, hostility was more likely to come from Jewish authorities than Roman. As long as the Christian movement was small and could still be viewed as a sect of Judaism, it was easily ignored. Judaism was an officially "legal religion" and was exempt from the expectation of worshiping the Roman gods and the emperor. In the early period, Christians enjoyed the same privilege. However, in the latter part of the century, as Christianity grew and became more distinct from Judaism, it faced a rising tide of suspicion. The peculiar practices of Christians, especially their refusal to worship the emperor and the Roman gods, made them appear subversive and dangerous. There was constantly the danger that local rulers could use acknowledgment of the gods and the "divine" emperor as tests of loyalty and punish severely those unwilling to comply.

In the New Testament period, persecution is associated with three emperors. The first major conflict occurred under Emperor Nero in 64 CE. In that year, a major fire devastated the city of Rome, and rumors abounded that Nero himself was responsible. Looking for a place to shift the blame, he found a convenient target in the unpopular Christians. He organized a horrible persecution in which many Christians in Rome were tortured and put to death. Relatively early traditions maintain that the apostles Peter and Paul were executed by Nero. By some accounts, persecution broke out again in the mid-90s under Domitian (reigned 81–96 CE) when Christians refused to give the emperor the divine honors he demanded. This is the traditional setting for the book of Revelation. By the time of Trajan (reigned 98–117 CE), it was possible to punish Christians simply for being Christians. When Christians were accused, they were given a chance to renounce the faith and to prove it by offering worship to images of the emperor or of the gods. Otherwise, they were punished. Roman persecution was a continuing threat for Christians until the fourth century and will be discussed in more detail in chapter 9.

Two New Testament books, 1 Peter and Revelation, are set against the background of persecution. Scholars are divided over whether *1 Peter* was written by Peter himself or is pseudonymous, as well as over whether it was written during the reign of Nero, Domitian, or Trajan. In any case, it addresses Christians in Asia Minor who are facing persecution for the faith. The letter encourages the readers to honor and obey the civil authorities in spite of the persecution (1 Peter 2:13-17); to live above reproach and to be ready to defend the faith so that persecution will serve as an opportunity for witness (3:13-17); and not to consider suffering "as a Christian" to be disgraceful, since Christ himself also suffered (4:12-19).

The *Revelation* of John is usually dated about 95 CE near the end of Domitian's reign. The author, a Christian prophet named John—probably not to be identified either with the Apostle John or with the author of the Fourth Gospel—is in exile on the little island of Patmos (Revelation 1:9), just off the coast of Asia Minor near Ephesus. There John received the visions on the basis of which he writes to strengthen and encourage persecuted churches in western Asia Minor. He gives them assurance that "soon" Christ will return to destroy the evil powers oppressing the church.

Revelation is an apocalyptic writing and shares many features of that type of literature. Apocalypses were typically written in times of persecution or crisis and described in fantastic images and symbols an end-time cosmic battle between Good and Evil which results in God's victory. It is the symbolic language of Revelation that has made it seem so impenetrable and given rise to such diverse interpretations. Some Christians tend to avoid Revelation because it is so hard to understand. Others are obsessed with it and try to interpret its imagery as predictions of historical events down to their own time and beyond.

Modern readers of Revelation should recall that the book was originally addressed to persecuted first-century Christians as a word of encouragement to them. It calls them to "endurance" in the midst of trial (Revelation 13:10; 14:12) and promises God's deliverance "soon" (1:1, 3; 22:6, 7, 10, 12). Its apocalyptic symbols, then, were a way of interpreting their circumstances and giving hope in a hopeless situation. To interpret those symbols as referring to events of our day would be to impose on them a meaning from which the first readers would have been excluded, yet the book is addressed to them! This is not to say that Revelation does not have a message for us. It certainly does, but to hear it we must first set it in its original context and try to see how the first readers would have understood it.

The churches addressed in Revelation seem to be facing a persecution related to the issue of emperor worship. In Revelation 13, two beasts appear, one from the sea and one from the earth. The first beast (13:1-10)—with ten horns, seven heads, and ten crowns—represents the Roman Empire with its emperors. The beast receives power from the dragon (Satan) and rules the whole earth without rival, just as Rome did. The "blasphemous words" uttered by the beast and his being worshiped by the whole earth reflect the practice of worshiping the emperors as divine. (Three of the seven cities addressed in Revelation 2–3 had temples to the emperor.) The beast's war on "the saints" (a term for Christians) suggests persecution. The second beast (13:11-18), which compels the whole earth to worship the first beast, represents the imperial cult which enforces emperor worship. Those who refuse to worship the image of the beast are killed. Those who refuse to bear the mark of the beast are denied the right to buy and sell. The mysterious number of the beast, 666, is a *gematria*, a kind of numerical symbolism in which the numerical value of the letters in a word or name was totaled up. Of the countless possibilities, the most likely reference here is to "Neron Caesar" (Nero) who was popularly believed to have returned to life in Domitian.

The context, then, is a crisis in which the mighty Roman Empire is making war on the tiny Christian church—overwhelming odds. Already there have been martyrs (Revelation 2:13; 6:9-11) and John the prophet is under banishment. Of course it did not take a "revelation" to see this much; it was all too evident. What the visions allow John and his readers to "see" is that this conflict is but an earthly manifestation of a larger cosmic battle. Behind Rome stands Satan; behind the church stands God—the timeless conflict of Good and Evil. Revelation takes an extremely harsh view of Rome. It is the embodiment of satanic power. It is "Babylon the great" (17:5), a reincarnation of the wicked city that had conquered God's people and destroyed the temple in Old Testament times. It is the "great whore" (17:1) and is "drunk with the blood of the saints and of the martyrs" (17:6).

The visions also show that God in Christ is in the process of defeating Satan and his human agents. Already the decisive battle has been won by the death and resurrection of Christ (Revelation 12:5, 11), and "soon" Christ will return to consummate the victory. The readers are assured in advance that "Fallen, fallen is Babylon the great" (14:8; 18:2) and the wreckage of the once-great city is surveyed (chaps. 17–18). John then depicts the final victory over Satan (chap. 20) and the coming of "a new heaven and a new earth" (chaps. 21–22). Punctuating the visions are choruses of praise celebrating God's victories: "Hallelujah! For the Lord our God the Almighty reigns" (19:6; cf. 11:15; 19:1-5).

On this basis, John calls the churches to faithful endurance, assuring them that, in spite of appearances, God has things under control and ultimately will be victorious. That message can reassure Christians in all ages, especially in times of crisis. Although Revelation probably is not the latest book of the New Testament, it appropriately stands last in the canon, pointing forward to the day when we can finally rejoice, "The kingdom of the world has become the kingdom of our Lord and of his Messiah, and he will reign forever and ever" (Revelation 11:15).

Formation of the New Testament Canon

Within a century after the death of Jesus, all of the New Testament books had been written, yet even then there was not a "New Testament" as such. First the books had to be sifted out of the many Christian writings which would soon be in circulation and had to be gathered into a recognized collection, a "canon." The word "canon" originally meant "reed" or "measuring stick." The New Testament canon came to be a "standard" by which orthodoxy was measured. The process of gathering and sorting the New Testament books is referred to as "canonization." For the most part, each of the writings was originally intended for a particular church or region and was read only there. Gradually, churches began to share writings, and eventually collections began to form. The formation of the canon was a long, slow, and messy process. The following glance at four stages along the way will give a sense of its course.

By 100 CE, Paul's letters were being collected. Originally addressed to individual communities in scattered places, they were now being read in collected form in places far from their original destinations. Ignatius of Antioch (died about 110 CE) quotes them freely. The author of 2 Peter 3:15-16 is familiar with "all the letters" of Paul and laments that false teachers are able to twist them "as they do the other scriptures" (that is, the Old Testament).

The earliest New Testament canon on record is one created about 140 CE by a Christian teacher named Marcion on the basis of views that the church in Rome found to be heretical. Marcion believed that the God of the Old Testament was a God of law and punishment, while the Father of Jesus Christ was a God of love and grace. For Marcion, these were two different Gods. He further maintained that, of all the apostles, only Paul had properly grasped the gospel of grace which does away with Jewish legalism. On these grounds, Marcion rejected the Old Testament and established a Christian canon consisting of Luke's Gospel and ten letters of Paul (the Pastorals were not included). He was excommunicated but founded his own network of churches which flourished for several centuries. Marcion's canon stimulated the mainline church to develop its own canon.

During the last half of the second century, the four Gospels were collected out of what was by then a growing body of gospel literature. By 200 CE, these had been added to the Pauline letters to produce the core of an emerging canon. The lists of New Testament books from this period regularly include the four Gospels along with Acts, thirteen letters of Paul, plus additional writings. It is that third category which was still fluid at this stage. No list from this period includes all of our General Epistles; and writings not found in our present New Testament were sometimes included.[7]

It took nearly two more centuries for the third division of the New Testament to stabilize. Not until 367 CE did a canon list appear which exactly agrees with the canon we have inherited. In that year, Bishop Athanasius of Alexandria circulated among his churches a list of twenty-seven books corresponding exactly to our own (although not in our order) and declared that they alone should be read as New Testament. His declaration did not settle the issue for the whole church, but by 400 CE his list, for all practical purposes, had prevailed. There is a touch of irony in the fact that, by the time the New Testament canon had taken shape, the persecution of Christians had ended and the Roman government was officially sponsoring the production of biblical manuscripts. These developments will be examined more closely in the next chapter.

* * *

New Testament Suggestions for Further Reading

Borg, Marcus J. *Meeting Jesus Again for the First Time.* San Francisco: HarperSan Francisco, 1994.

Bornkamm, Günther. *Jesus of Nazareth.* Translated by Irene and Fraser McLuskey with James M. Robinson. Minneapolis: Fortress Press, 1995.

Bruce, F. F. *New Testament History.* New York: Doubleday, 1969.

Ehrman, Bart D. *The New Testament: A Historical Introduction to the Early Christian Writings.* Second edition. New York/Oxford: Oxford University Press, 2000.

Ferguson, Everett. *Backgrounds of Early Christianity.* Second edition. Grand Rapids MI: Eerdmans, 1993.

Harris, Stephen L. *The New Testament: A Student's Introduction.* Sixth edition. Boston: McGraw-Hill, 2008.

Jeremias, Joachim. *The Parables of Jesus.* Revised edition. New York: Scribner's,

---

[7]Of the books eventually canonized, the ones most frequently missing at this stage are 2 Peter, 3 John, Jude, and to a lesser extent Hebrews and James. Examples of books ultimately excluded from the canon but sometimes included at this stage are the *Apocalypse of Peter*, the *Epistle of Barnabas*, and the *Shepherd of Hermas*.

1963.

Mills, Watson E., et al., editors. *Mercer Dictionary of the Bible*. Macon GA: Mercer University Press, 1990.

Powell, Mark Allan. *Fortress Introduction to the Gospels*. Minneapolis: Fortress Press, 1998.

Roetzel, Calvin J. *The Letters of Paul: Conversations in Context*. Fourth edition. Louisville: Westminster/John Knox Press, 1998.

Sanders, E. P. *The Historical Figure of Jesus*. New York: Penguin Books, 1993.

Soards, Marion. *The Apostle Paul: An Introduction to His Writings and Teaching*. New York/Mahwah: Paulist Press, 1987.

Stein, Robert H. *Jesus the Messiah: A Survey of the Life of Christ*. Downers Grove IL: InterVarsity Press, 1996.

Wenham, David. *The Parables of Jesus*. The Jesus Library. Downers Grove IL: InterVarsity Press, 1989.

Wright, N. T. *The Challenge of Jesus: Rediscovering Who Jesus Was and Is*. Downers Grove IL: InterVarsity Press, 1999.

Part three

Church History

• 9 •

Early Christianity (100–500)

By the close of the first century, the apostles and other eyewitnesses to the life and ministry of Jesus were gone. The Christian religion was about to undergo a significant transition in the second century of its existence.[1]

Separation from Judaism

As we saw, Christianity began as a sect within Judaism. Relatively soon there was a mission to the Gentiles and the issue was raised whether or not to admit them without requiring circumcision, the key ritual marking Jews as Jews. The decision of the Apostolic Council not to impose that requirement meant that in the long run Christianity was destined to become a separate religion. Yet that separation did not take place immediately. For quite some time Christianity remained in close relationship with the Jewish synagogue. Jewish Christians continued to practice their traditions and to participate in synagogue life. Even Gentile Christians considered themselves to have been incorporated into Israel and adopted the Jewish scriptures as their own.

In the period following the fall of Jerusalem and the destruction of the Temple (70 CE), however, tensions began to increase. Christians saw that catastrophe as retribution for the Jews' rejection of Christ. Jews tended to blame the Christians. The survival of Judaism after the disaster was secured largely by a newly established academy of Jewish scholars at Jamnia, near the Palestinian coast, which took the lead in restructuring the Jewish faith. The reorganization was chiefly along Pharisaic lines, and the Judaism which emerged was much more uniform and less tolerant of diversity than earlier. Christians felt less and less welcome in the synagogues. Near the end of the

---

[1]We are indebted to several works for this unit on the history of Christianity. Much of the basic structure of these chapters was taken from Justo González, *Church History: An Essential Guide*, (Nashville: Abingdon Press, 1996). Material was gleaned from this source as well as from González's *The Story of Christianity*, vols. 1 and 2 (San Francisco: Harper Collins, 1984 and 1985) and R. Dean Peterson, *A Concise History of Christianity*, 2nd ed. (Boston: Wadsworth, 2000).

century, the rabbis added to the synagogue liturgy a "benediction against the heretics" which effectively made it impossible for Christians to participate and sealed the break between Judaism and Christianity. In spite of this break, the Jewish roots of Christianity are still evident in a number of Christian practices which were carried over from Judaism.

The Old Testament. To this day, Christians and Jews share the Old Testament scriptures and both regard these writings as sacred and authoritative. The term "Old Testament" by definition is Christian in origin. Christians believe that the Old Testament contains important theological concepts and provides the important context for understanding the life and ministry of Jesus the Messiah.

Worship. Earliest Christian worship was modeled after the style of worship in the Jewish synagogue. Reading of scripture, singing, praying, and exhortation were all standard synagogue practices. These practices were brought into Christian worship, although with a different focus. Christian worship centered on the person and work of Christ.

Baptism. Many people might think that baptism originated with John the Baptist. But, in early Judaism, whenever a gentile wanted to convert to Judaism a ceremony was involved which included circumcision and a ceremonial washing. This washing was considered the entrance into the Jewish fellowship. In the same way, the early Christians used baptism as a rite of initiation into the Christian fellowship.

Imperial Persecution

Almost from its inception, Christianity encountered opposition. The Acts of the Apostles indicates that the first group to persecute Christians was Jewish religious leaders who refused to accept that Jesus of Nazareth was the Messiah. In the earliest days of Christianity Rome considered the religion to be another sect of Judaism. Judaism was a legally acceptable religion in the Roman Empire; therefore, Christians were free to practice their faith. While they encountered opposition from Jews, the Romans paid them little attention. That changed in the latter half of the first century.

Nero. The first Roman emperor to persecute Christians was Nero, who ruled from 54 to 68. Early Christian tradition indicates that both Peter and Paul were martyred in Rome during Nero's reign. Although Nero's persecution was confined to the city of Rome itself, it was nevertheless a severe persecution as described by the Roman historian Tacitus. Writing in the early part of the second century, Tacitus describes the horrible treatment that Christians received from Nero as he blamed them for a fire that swept through the city in the summer of 64.

> But all the endeavors of men, all the emperor's largesse and the propitiations of the gods, did not suffice to allay the scandal or banish the belief that the fire had been ordered. And so, to get rid of this rumor, Nero set up as the culprits and punished with the utmost refinement of cruelty a class hated for their abominations, who are commonly called Christians. Christus, from whom their name is derived, was executed at the hands of the procurator Pontius Pilate in the reign of Tiberius. Checked for the moment, this pernicious superstition again broke out, not only in Judaea, the source of the evil, but even in Rome, that receptacle for everything that is sordid and degrading from every quarter of the globe, which there finds a following. Accordingly, arrest was first made of those who confessed [to being Christians]; then, on their evidence, an immense multitude was convicted, not so much on the charge of arson as because of hatred of the human race. Besides being put to death they were made to serve as objects of amusement; they were clad in the hides of beasts and torn to death by dogs; others were crucified, others set on fire to serve to illuminate the night when daylight failed. Nero had thrown open his grounds for the display, and was putting on a show in the circus, where he mingled with the people in the dress of a charioteer or drove about in his chariot. All this gave rise to a feeling of pity, even towards men whose guilt merited the most exemplary punishment; for it was felt that they were being destroyed not for the public good but to gratify the cruelty of an individual.[2]

Two important items should be noted here. First, Tacitus suggests that Nero was to blame for the fire but used the Christians in Rome as the scapegoats in order to escape the blame himself. Second, he indicates that Christians were a "class hated for their abominations." This can only be interpreted as misunderstandings Romans had about Christian religious practices and indicates that Christians were hated by many of the people in the city of Rome.

Domitian. After the death of Nero in 68, Christians enjoyed a relatively quiet period in which there was little or no persecution. But that changed during the reign of Domitian, who ruled Rome from 81 to 96. Toward the end of his reign, Domitian started to demand that he be worshiped as a god.

---

[2]Henry Bettenson, ed., *Documents of the Christian Church*, 2nd ed. (London/Oxford/New York: Oxford University Press, 1963) 1-2.

Because Christians believed in only one God and that their worship should be exclusive of other gods, many refused to comply. It should be added that Jews were in the same dilemma under Domitian. Eventually, a widespread persecution of Christians and Jews erupted throughout the empire. Modern scholarship suggests that rather than being initiated by Domitian himself, the persecution tended to be initiated by local rulers attempting to curry favor with the emperor. According to tradition, the book of Revelation was written during this time by the apostle John who had been exiled to the island of Patmos.

Trajan. Trajan was the emperor of Rome from 98 to 117. Largely in response to a question from Pliny the Younger, governor of Bithynia, Trajan formulated a policy for dealing with the large numbers of Christians in the Empire. Pliny wrote:

> It is my rule, Sire, to refer to you in matters where I am uncertain. For who can better direct my hesitation or instruct my ignorance? I was never present at any trial of Christians; therefore I do not know what are the customary penalties or investigations, and what limits are observed. I have hesitated a great deal on the question whether there should be any distinction of ages; whether the weak should have the same treatment as the more robust; whether those who recant should be pardoned, or whether a man who has ever been a Christian should gain nothing by ceasing to be such; whether the name itself, even if innocent of crime, should be punished, or only the crimes attaching to that name.[3]

Trajan's policy said that the efforts of the Empire should not be expended on searching out Christians. Christians were to be punished only if they were brought before the authorities and charged with practicing Christianity. They were to be examined, asked to recant of their Christian practices, and worship the Roman gods. If they refused to do so, they were then to be punished. The important thing to recognize about his policy, which was followed for the next two centuries, was that Trajan did not want the Roman authorities to expend time and money to hunt down Christians.

Diocletian. It is a frequent misunderstanding to assume that the early Christians were persecuted continually during the first three centuries. Persecution of Christians at the hands of the Romans was frequently brutal, but sporadic. While Trajan's policy remained intact for 200 years, there were

---

[3]Bettenson, ed., *Documents of the Christian Church*, 2nd ed., 3.

periods of severe persecution under Severus (193–211), Decius (249–251), and Valerian (253–260). According to many interpreters, the most severe persecution of all came during the reign of Diocletian, who ruled Rome from 284–305. During this period, Christians were expelled from the Roman legions out of fear that they were disloyal to Rome because of their refusal to participate in emperor worship. Diocletian also ordered that Christian buildings be seized and that copies of Christian scriptures be destroyed. Eventually, Christians were subject to torture and death.

Martyrs and Apologists. Christianity continued to grow despite periods of persecution. Because Christianity differed from the pagan religions practiced in Greco-Roman society, Christians were misunderstood. They tended to be withdrawn from society, refusing to involve themselves in the normal social intercourse in their respective communities. Therefore they appeared to non-Christians to be reclusive and suspicious. Furthermore, many in Roman society misunderstood the practices of Christianity.

There are several examples which serve to illustrate how non-Christians misunderstood various practices within Christianity. One charge made against Christians was that they were "atheists." To the modern mindset it seems odd that such a charge would be leveled against Christians. But since Christians refused to believe in the gods of the Greek and Roman pantheons and were unwilling to participate in the state cult of emperor worship, they were believed to be "atheists." A second charge made about Christians concerned their observance of the Lord's Supper. Christians talked of the bread and wine being the body and blood of Christ. Many nonbelievers hearing this began to think that Christians practiced cannibalism in their worship services. Christians were also perceived to be disloyal to Rome and even subsequently a threat to the very well-being of the Empire itself. This charge came from their worship of Jesus of Nazareth, considered an insurrectionist by the Romans. Christians holding an insurrectionist in such high regard would naturally be viewed with suspicion. Along with these charges came other sensationalized charges such as incest, infanticide and various practices of immorality.

Since much of the Roman animosity against Christians grew out of a misunderstanding of their religious practices (admittedly very different from Roman paganism), some early Christian theologians began to produce writings defending the religion against these false charges. These writers are called "Apologists." The writings of the Apologists provide an important source of information for helping to understand early Christianity and the social and political forces that were working against it. Typically, the Apologists would describe the various misunderstandings about Christians and then respond to those charges attempting to explain the traditions and beliefs of Christians. This was done to defend the Christian religion and to show that when properly understood, it posed no threat to the Roman Empire's well-being. It is interesting to read the writings which have survived from some of these Apologists. They provide a fascinating glimpse into the first few centuries of Christianity when Christians were struggling to survive during various periods of persecution and continuous ostracism. The Apologists provide a very different portrait of the Christian religion than that of later centuries when Christianity became entrenched within the power structure of Europe and other parts of the world.

Justin the Martyr, frequently called simply "Justin Martyr" was the principal Apologist of the second century. He was martyred for his faith in 165. An interesting characteristic of Justin's thought is that he argued that there were points of contact between pagan philosophy and Christianity. He believed that the pagan philosophers of his day had received truth but that Christianity was the ultimate and fullest expression of that truth. Justin is famous for several significant writings. His essays titled *First Apology* and *Second Apology* are concerned with rebutting various charges against Christians. Justin's *Dialogue with Trypho,* provides a good glimpse into Christian and Jewish relations in the middle of the Second Century. Recounted as a discussion with a Jewish rabbi named Trypho and his six companions, Justin provides an account of his own conversation and then a defense of the Christian interpretation of the Old Testament and the divinity of Jesus.

Another important "martyr," though not usually considered an Apologist, was Ignatius of Antioch. Ignatius was born around 35 making him one of the "Apostolic Fathers," a group of early Christian writers traditionally regarded as having some contact with the Apostles. Church tradition says that Ignatius studied with John, who is traditionally identified as "the beloved disciple," one of closest of Jesus' disciples. Ignatius was arrested in Antioch in the early part of the second century and was transported to Rome for execution. During the journey, he wrote seven letters, which have survived the centuries and provide an important glimpse into his thoughts about his faith and his impending martyrdom. These letters are an important early witness to developing ideas concerning the function of the office of bishop in the church. Ignatius's letters also provided encouragement and strength to other Christians who were called upon to suffer for their beliefs throughout the successive centuries of Christian history.

Polycarp (ca. 69–135), a young friend of Ignatius, provides another famous example of early Christian martyrdom. According to tradition, as an old bishop toward the end of his life, he was identified by the authorities as a Christian. At first his disciples encouraged him to hide arguing that his flock needed his leadership and guidance. However, after a few days he had to change hiding places and he soon became convinced that arrest was the will of God for him. Once arrested, he was asked to recant of his faith, curse Christ, and he would be set free. His reply was one of the most famous statements in early Christianity: "For eighty-six years I have served him, and he has done me no evil. How could I curse my king, who saved me?"[4]

One of the most famous stories of martyrdom from the third century was the story of Perpetua and Felicitas. Perpetua was a young, wealthy woman who, along with her servant girl Felicitas and several other companions was arrested for being Christian. One of the most endearing aspects of this story is the fact that Perpetua was a new mother and was nursing a young baby. In the *Martyrdom of Saints Perpetua and Felicitas*, there is a moving account of a visit from Perpetua's father to the jail where he begged her to recant of her faith. Yet, she was resolute and along with the others died in the arena.

Competing Expressions of Christianity

In addition to the problem of persecution encountered by the Church from Rome, there was also a problem within the fellowship. Questions related to the person of Jesus himself, how a person becomes a Christian, and other matters of doctrine began to cause deep divisions among Christians. Eventually, an official theology evolved among the Church leaders. Expressions of the faith that differed were called "heresy," referring to false doctrine. "Orthodoxy" is the term for what most Christians have traditionally understood to be correct doctrine. During the period from 100 to 313 there were several important heresies which created problems for the early Christians.[5]

Judaizers. The Judaizers were Jews who believed that Jesus was the

---

[4]Quoted by González, *The Story of Christianity* 1:44.

[5]For a good discussion of some of these competing versions of Christianity, see Bart D. Ehrman, *Lost Christianities: The Battles for Scripture and the Faiths We Never Knew* (New York: Oxford University Press, 2003).

Messiah. However, they believed that in order for Gentiles to be true followers of Jesus, they first had to convert to Judaism, which included the ritual of circumcision. They represented a significant challenge to Paul's understanding of how Gentiles are to be incorporated into the Church and are in the background of several of the New Testament books including Galatians. Although the Jerusalem Council, described in Acts 15 formally sided with Paul's understanding of how Gentiles should be incorporated into the Church, the Judaizers remained an alternate expression of Christianity for several centuries and their ideas were later manifested in groups such as the Ebionites and the Elkesaites.

Gnosticism. One of the principal threats to orthodox Christianity in its early centuries came in the form of a movement called Gnosticism. Because there were so many variations of this movement, it is really hard to define it in a simple way. Some New Testament scholars argue that the roots of Gnosticism were present in the first century and that some of the New Testament writings were aimed at countering this movement, which may have already been a threat to orthodox belief. However, it is generally believed that Gnosticism did not exist in a mature form until well into the second century.

While Gnosticism took many different forms, the form that presented a challenge to orthodox Christianity blended together a variety of ideas gleaned from many different sources. There were traces of Greek philosophy, eastern religion, and Greco-Roman mystery religions, mixed together with some of the teachings of Christianity. It takes its name from the Greek word *gnosis*, which means "knowledge." Gnosticism taught that a special kind of secret knowledge was necessary before one could acquire salvation or spiritual enlightenment. Gnostics made a clear distinction between the flesh and the spirit. The physical universe was created by a lesser god and was totally evil. The Gnostics taught that each human being has a divine spark which is entombed in an evil body of flesh. The flesh is evil, incapable of doing anything good. The spirit is represented by this divine spark. Salvation consisted of freeing this divine spark from its fleshly prison.

Since the flesh was considered evil, the Gnostics had two different approaches toward ethics. Some Gnostics taught that since the flesh was evil, the person needed to do whatever necessary to keep the flesh in check. These Gnostics devoted themselves to intense asceticism, attempting to deny the body its natural cravings. Other Gnostics had the opposite idea.

They taught that since the body was evil, there was no way that the flesh could ever be tamed. Therefore, they lived a life of libertinism, indulging in whatever their flesh craved.

Gnosticism's understanding of the person of Christ made it a serious challenge to orthodox Christology. Gnostics taught that the Son of God could not possibly be a real human being since the flesh is inherently evil. They believed that Jesus just appeared to be human, a concept referred to as *Docetism*, from a Greek word meaning "seem" or "appear." In reality, what appeared to be a human body was simply an illusion. This belief challenged the very essence of the atonement, indicating that Christ did not really suffer and die on the cross, a serious challenge to early Christian understandings about salvation.

Marcionism. Another threat to orthodox Christian belief in the second century was Marcionism. Marcion (d. ca. 154), the son of a bishop, went to Rome around 140 and was active in the church there. He eventually came under the influence of a Gnostic teacher and developed ideas similar to Gnosticism. Consequently, he was expelled from the Roman church, prompting him to begin his own church. His movement gained in popularity and his ideas were spread all over the Empire in the middle of the second century. He was so popular that Marcionism was still an active movement and threat to orthodox belief almost a century after his death.

Although influenced by Gnosticism and some of the Gnostic teachings, Marcion was not really a Gnostic himself. He believed that there were two competing Gods in the world. The creator of this world, the God of Judaism was an evil, inferior, incompetent God. The God of Christianity was a benevolent, superior God. Therefore, Marcion rejected Judaism, the religion of the Old Testament, and taught his followers to disregard anything Jewish. Regarding the New Testament, Marcion taught that only Paul correctly interpreted Jesus' life and teachings. Furthermore, from Galatians 1:8-9, Marcion surmised that there was only one true Gospel, which he believed was the Gospel of Luke.

Marcion was one of the first to propose a "canon" of scripture for his followers to read as the true interpretation of the Christian faith. His canon consisted of ten of the Pauline Epistles (he did not include the Pastoral Epistles) and a synopsis of the Gospel of Luke. Many scholars believe that the "Muratorian Canon," usually dated in the last half of the second century, was an orthodox response to Marcion's canon and teachings.[6]

Safeguarding Orthodoxy. Because heresy became such a threat to the existence of orthodox Christianity, the Church developed ways to safeguard orthodoxy. At least three responses to heresy gradually emerged over time. The first means for protecting orthodoxy was to develop a "canon" of scripture. As we have seen in the previous chapter, it took several hundred years for the writings of the New Testament to be accepted universally by all Christians. As heretics produced writings that challenged orthodox Christian beliefs, Christians began to collect writings that had apostolic connections to protect the orthodox faith. The fact that the canonized books of the New Testament had traditions that connected them directly to the apostles and were eventually accepted universally by the Churches, provided Christianity with a method for judging the soundness of doctrine.

A second method for safeguarding orthodoxy was to develop "creeds." A creed is a short statement of belief which was used for teaching doctrine in the churches. When a new convert to the faith became a member of the Church, he/she went through a period of instruction called "catechism." Creeds were used for the pedagogical purpose of teaching the catechumens. One of the first to appear and be used by Christians was a confession of faith called the "Roman Symbol." The use of the term "symbol" has its derivation in a Latin word which related to the concept of a "password" used for security reasons in a military camp. Therefore, the "creed" became a test of membership in the Church. Acceptance of the creed was necessary for full membership.[7]

The old Roman Symbol, which probably originated in the fourth century, but was based on earlier traditions, eventually evolved into what has come to be called the Apostles' Creed. The name that this confession of faith gradually developed was no coincidence. Early Christians believed that the theology of the Apostles' Creed was indeed the theology of the Apostles. One version of the Apostles' Creed reads:

I believe in God Almighty,

---

[6]Much of the information for this discussion of Marcion was gleaned from Hendrik F. Stander, "Marcion," in *The Encyclopedia of Early Christianity*, ed. Everett C. Ferguson (New York: Garland Publishers, 1990).

[7]Stander, "Marcion," 135, in Ferguson, ed., *The Encyclopedia of Early Christianity*.

And in Christ Jesus, his son, our Lord
Who was born of the Holy Spirit
and the Virgin Mary,
Who was crucified under Pontius Pilate
and was buried
And the third day he rose from the dead
Who ascended into heaven
And sits on the right hand of the Father
Whence he comes to judge the living and the dead
And in the Holy Spirit
The holy church
The remission of sins
The resurrection of the flesh
The life everlasting.[8]

A third safeguard to orthodoxy developed by early Christians was an episcopacy. The word "episcopacy" refers to an authoritarian hierarchy in the Church. Very early in the history of Christianity local churches began to be grouped together and put under the authority of a bishop. The earliest bishops were either apostles or persons who had a direct tie to one of the apostles. Bishops also tended to be well schooled in theology either by studying with an apostle, or in an area where an apostle had lived.

Gradually, five bishoprics rose to prominence: Rome, Constantinople, Jerusalem, Antioch, and Alexandria. The reasons these bishoprics developed such power is obvious. The emperor and the power base of the Roman Empire were located in Rome. In the fourth century, the capital was moved to Constantinople, thereby making it the major center of power for the Empire. Jerusalem was the city where Christianity began. Antioch was the city from which Paul departed for his missionary journeys and an important city for early Christians. Finally, Alexandria was an important city because of its reputation for scholarship and learning. Gradually, the bishops of Rome and Constantinople gained prominence over the other bishops.

Bishops gained power because of their connection with an apostle. As the apostles died, they appointed bishops to succeed them. Those bishops in turn passed down that apostolic authority to those succeeding them, and so on. This belief is called "apostolic succession." A bishop could therefore

---

[8]An early version of the Apostles' Creed taken from Peterson, *A Concise History of Christianity*, 80.

claim authority because that authority had been handed down to him from the apostles.

The second-century bishop of Lyons named Irenaeus wrote a treatise, titled *Against Heresies*, in which he claimed that as a youth he had seen Polycarp, Bishop of Smyrna, who had been taught by the apostles and had numerous contacts with those who had been with Jesus. Irenaeus was concerned about heresy and in order to combat it, he argued that the bishops transferred their apostolic authority down to their successors. He said that there was an unbroken line of succession among the bishops that extended back to the Apostles. He said that Peter and Paul established the Church at Rome and that they transferred their authority to Linus who was followed by others in an unbroken line of succession to the twelfth in the line, who was bishop of Rome when Irenaeus wrote his treatise.[9]

The bishop was therefore more than an administrator. The bishop served as the spiritual authority over the churches and the bishop's word was the final word on theology. They had, and often exercised, the authority to dismiss priests who were teaching doctrines not in accord with the bishop's interpretation of orthodox, apostolic Christianity. But, what happens if the bishops disagree with each other in theological matters? That became an important question during the fourth century.

Imperial Christianity (313–476)

The fourth century brought significant changes to the Christian religion. Christianity entered the century as a persecuted religion. But by the end of the century it had become the favored religion of the Roman Empire. This major development was the result of events which began with the accession of Constantine (306–337) as emperor of the Empire.

Constantine and the Edict of Milan. The story of how Constantine came to embrace Christianity is an interesting one. Beginning his reign in 306 with the death of his father Constantius, Constantine embarked on a series of political and military maneuvers which ultimately led to his accession as sole ruler of the Roman Empire in 324. The most important event during that period was the Battle of Milvian Bridge fought in 312. Tradition has it that before the battle, Constantine had a dream or vision in which a voice

---

[9]Kenneth Scott Latourette, *A History of Christianity* (New York: Harper & Brothers, 1953) 131-32.

spoke to him saying that he was to go forth and conquer under the sign of the cross. Reportedly, Constantine ordered that crosses be painted on his soldiers' shields and other equipment. His victory in the battle gave him sole control of the Western portion of the Empire and he credited the Christian God for his success.

The following year, Constantine and Licinius, the ruler in the East, issued the Edict of Milan, which called for an end to the persecution of Christians and a return of all property seized in earlier persecutions. In 324, when Constantine gained complete control of the Empire, he gave to Christianity an official sanction that made it equal with the other religions of the Empire.

Christianity and Imperial Support

Constantine's attitude toward Christianity created an entirely new environment for the religion, now over three centuries old. In those three centuries Christianity encountered and overcame tremendous obstacles. But the most startling changes were about to take place.

Although Christianity was never made the official state religion of Rome during Constantine's reign, he did show favoritism to the religion and it was during his reign that the most significant changes began to occur.[10] Large amounts of wealth and power began to make their way into the Church. Church buildings began to be constructed which were much more ornate and lavish than had ever been built before. With many important politicians and other dignitaries joining the churches, the simple worship style began to give way to a more organized liturgy. The Empire began to do favors for the Church and the Church reciprocated. Things were definitely different!

According to church historian Justo González, Christians reacted to these new dynamics in several different ways. Most accommodated themselves to Christianity's new position in the Empire. They believed that Constantine was the answer to their decades of prayer asking God for deliverance from persecution. One of the chief spokespersons for this position was Eusebius of Caesarea. Eusebius was an important theologian and church leader in the fourth century. He is best remembered for authoring the first history of Christianity. But Eusebius's history of the Church is not ob-

---

[10]Christianity became the official state religion of the Roman Empire during the reign of Emperor Theodosious I who ruled from 379 to 395.

jective history like that which most twenty-first century students are used
to reading. Eusebius's history serves as an apology for Constantine's
administration. He lavished praise on the emperor and indicated his belief
that Constantine became emperor by divine decree from no one other than
God. In short, Eusebius believed that Constantine was a part of God's grand
purpose for the Church and a positive influence.

On the other hand, there were many Christians who were slow to accept
these changes to Christianity and even sought to resist them. They believed
that wealth, power, and prestige served only to hurt the witness of the
Church and damage the purity of the faith. Many of these Christians
believed that the pursuit of pure Christianity could no longer be possible in
society and they began to withdraw to remote regions (usually the desert
areas) of the Empire.

As the monastic movement developed, it took two different forms. The
earliest type of monasticism to develop is called *eremetical* monasticism.
Eremetical monasticism refers to individuals who left society and went to
the mountains or deserts by themselves to live solitary lives devoting themselves to the pursuit of holiness. These people were called "monks," from
a Latin word which means "alone." Monks usually practiced asceticism,
denying the desires of the flesh out of their belief that only the spiritual
appetite should be fed. While it is impossible to know who the first monk
was, the father of monasticism is usually considered to be Anthony of Egypt
(ca. 251–356). *Cenobitic* monasticism developed later as monks began to
live and work together in monasteries. Pachomius (ca. 290–346) built the
first monastery at Tabenisi. He is also remembered for developing a *Rule*
or guide for practicing monasticism.

Another response to Constantine that some Christians manifested was
to break away from the Church and form their own Christian communities,
claiming that they were the *true* Church. One of the questions that
Christians disputed during Constantine's era concerned the status of the
lapsed, or Christians that renounced the faith in various ways during persecution. Some believed that ministers who renounced Christ in order to
escape persecution should not be restored to the Church except through
rigorous means of penance. Others tended to be more lenient toward these
ministers. Donatus, a fourth century Christian leader from North Africa,
believed that the ministerial duties such as baptism and communion performed by the lapsed ministers were invalidated by their lapsed status. A

schismatic movement called the Donatists arose around these concerns.[11]

Theological Development

During the early centuries of Christianity significant discussions about theology occurred. This was due in part to the rise of certain heretical groups discussed earlier and by theological controversy among the bishops. As Christians encountered heresy they were forced to think about theological issues.

Arianism and the Council of Nicea. The fourth century in particular was a century of theological development. One of the most important theological events to occur during that century was the Council of Nicea (325), the first "ecumenical" council in Christian history. It is called an "ecumenical" council because it brought together bishops from all over the Empire.

The Council of Nicea was the result of a dispute which arose in the city of Alexandria between Arius, a priest and Alexander, his bishop. Arius taught that Christ had not existed coeternally with the Father but instead had been created by God as the "firstborn of all creation." Arius's famous phrase to describe his belief was "there was a time when he was not." The technical term used to describe this position is *heteroousios*, meaning that Christ was of a "different substance" than the Father. Arius was a popular priest, young and well educated. His ideas developed a large following and caught the attention of Alexander, who ordered Arius to stop his teaching. Alexander believed that Christ had existed coeternally with the Father and was of the "same substance," or *homoousios*. Alexander, and others that opposed Arius, believed that Arius's teaching dangerously deemphasized the divinity of Christ, hence making him less than fully God.

When Arius refused to stop teaching his ideas, the controversy spilled out into other parts of the Empire. It became such a threat to the unity of Christianity and hence the Empire, that it eventually came to the attention of the Emperor Constantine. Constantine decided that the best way to resolve the issue was to bring together all the bishops into a council and let the issue be discussed. The council's decision would then be definitive.

Meeting in Nicea in 325, several hundred bishops, mostly from the eastern part of the Empire, came together to discuss the issue. During the course of the discussions three positions developed. Representing Arius's

---

[11]González, *Church History: An Essential Guide*, 34-35.

position was Eusebius of Nicomedia. The most important leader of the opposing party was Athanasius, who became bishop of Alexandria three years later when Alexander died. A compromising position was held by Eusebius of Caesarea (discussed earlier) who argued that Christ was of "similar or like" substance with the Father (*homoiousios*). After hearing the arguments and discussions for days, Constantine finally grew impatient and took the initiative to rule in favor of Athanasius and the *homoousios* party. The council issued a creed referred to today as the Nicene Creed. It is repeated regularly in many Christian churches today, almost 1700 years after the council met.

The Council of Nicea did not destroy Arianism. It remained a strong presence well into the Middle Ages. For the rest of the fourth century disputes arose between the two parties. Further doctrinal disputes would divide Christians for centuries to come. There were six more ecumenical councils which met over the next five centuries.

Important Theologians. The early centuries of Christianity produced a number of brilliant theologians whose work shaped the future of Christian theology. Irenaeus, Tertullian, Clement of Alexandria, Origen, and Cyprian were important theologians in the second and third centuries. Irenaeus, mentioned earlier, was bishop of Lyon in Gaul (modern-day France) and was greatly concerned about combating heresy. He was not an original thinker but attempted to teach his parishioners the theological concepts passed on to him. He believed that by teaching the theological tradition passed on to him, he would strengthen his flock against heresy. Tertullian was an important theologian in Carthage, North Africa. Much of his writing was also concerned with defending orthodox Christian theology against heresy. Clement of Alexandria, like Justin Martyr mentioned earlier in this chapter, attempted to explore Greek philosophy and its possible connections with Christian theology. His successor, Origen carried that tradition even further. Many of Origen's writings are philosophical. Although many of his more extreme doctrines were later rejected by orthodox Christianity, he remained an important influence on later theologians, especially in the East. Cyprian was bishop of Carthage when persecution broke out under the Emperor Decius in 249. Rather than face persecution, he escaped and hid with the hope that he could continue in his leadership role as bishop. Although he was martyred in a later persecution period (258), he was criticized for having fled. As a result, much of his writing concerns the issue of the "lapsed," or those Christians who desert the faith during periods of persecution but later desire to return to the Church.

Several theologians in the fourth century also deserve mention. Athanasius of Alexandria became bishop upon the death of Alexander. He became the great champion of Nicene orthodoxy throughout North Africa. Athanasius's letter to the churches in his charge called the "Festal Letter" in 367 serves as the earliest listing of the twenty-seven New Testament books as we now have them. During the last half of the fourth century the champions of Nicene orthodox theology were three theologians referred to as the "Cappadocian Fathers": Basil of Caesarea, his brother Gregory of Nyssa, and Gregory of Nazianzus. Sometimes forgotten by historians, but nevertheless an important contributor to theology of the fourth century, was Macrina, the sister of Basil of Caesarea and Gregory of Nyssa. The work of the Cappadocians built upon the contributions of Athanasius, particularly concerning the doctrine of the Trinity. Their work greatly influenced the conclusions of the second ecumenical council, the Council of Constantinople which met in 381.

Ambrose was an influential figure in western Christianity. He was a Roman public official who became Bishop of Milan. He was known for his preaching ability and for his defense of Nicene orthodoxy against Arianism. Ambrose may best be remembered for his influence on Augustine, arguably the most influential theologian in the first millennium of Christian history.

Augustine's journey to Christian commitment was an interesting one. He was born in Tagaste in North Africa. His father was a devotee of the pagan religions of his day whereas his mother, Monica, was a Christian. In his famous writing *Confessions* he describes how he came to accept the claims of Christianity. Educated in his youth as a Christian, Augustine eventually abandoned those teachings as he moved to Carthage to continue his education. There he took a mistress who gave birth to an illegitimate son. His intention was to study rhetoric (public speaking) in order to become a lawyer. He also began to study philosophy.

Augustine soon became attracted to Manicheism, a heresy based on the teachings of Mani, who taught a radical dualism between the world of the spirit (light) and the material world (darkness). In many ways Manicheism was similar to Gnosticism. After nine years as a Manichean, Augustine became disillusioned with its teachings.

After a move to Rome for a short period of time and then to Milan, Augustine became attracted to Neoplatonism, a popular philosophy in the Roman Empire at the time. Neoplatonism taught that by discipline, study, and meditation one could achieve unity with God, the ultimate source of all things. Evil consists of moving away from God and is not identified with the material world. Neoplatonism helped Augustine with some of his questions, but he eventually rejected its teachings.

It was during this time that Augustine began to attend church in Milan to hear the preaching of Ambrose. He also began to study the New Testament. According to the *Confessions*, he was in a garden one day contemplating his spiritual questions when he heard a child's voice say, "Take up and read." He saw a copy of the New Testament on a nearby bench and he picked it up and read from Romans 13 where it said, "Not in reveling and drunkenness, not in debauchery and licentiousness, not in quarreling and jealousy. But put on the Lord Jesus Christ and make no provision for the flesh to gratify its desires." This led to Augustine's conversion experience and not long thereafter, he and his son were baptized.

Desiring to start a life of monasticism, Augustine sent his mistress back to her home, took his son and some friends and moved back to North Africa to the city of Hippo where they entered a monastery. It was not long before he was ordained as a priest and eventually elevated to the position of Bishop of Hippo.

Augustine was a prolific writer and an original thinker. His *City of God* was written during the days as the Roman Empire was beginning to crumble. It served as his defense of Christianity during the demise of the Empire. His theology set the stage for later theologians in western Christianity.

Two other significant contributors to early Christian theology were Jerome and Chrysostom. Jerome was a monk in Palestine who produced the *Latin Vulgate,* the translation of the Bible into Latin, which became the official Bible of Roman Catholicism. John Chrysostom was a native of Antioch. The name Chrysostom means "golden mouth" and brings to mind the fact that Chrysostom is best remembered for his preaching ability. He served as Bishop of Antioch but eventually became bishop of Constantinople. Many of his sermons were preserved and still survive today. They reveal his courage in refusing to accede to everything the emperor wanted. They also reveal a champion of the common people in the city of Constantinople and his concern for their well-being.

By the beginning of the fifth century Christianity had become a major force in the Roman Empire. But an ominous future lay ahead for Rome. The story of Christianity's survival as the Roman Empire collapsed and its subsequent rise to power in Europe is told in the second major phase in the history of Church, the Middle Ages.

THE EXPLOSIVE DECADES

PERCENTAGE OF CHRISTIANS IN THE ROMAN EMPIRE

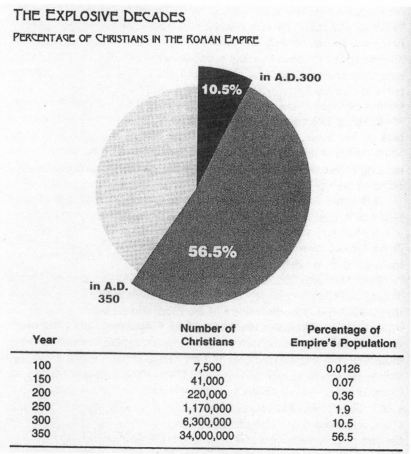

Year	Number of Christians	Percentage of Empire's Population
100	7,500	0.0126
150	41,000	0.07
200	220,000	0.36
250	1,170,000	1.9
300	6,300,000	10.5
350	34,000,000	56.5

These estimates are based on 40 percent growth per decade, and roughly correspond to figures found in early church documents. For more details, see Rodney Stark, *The Rise of Christianity: A Sociologist Reconsiders History* (Princeton NJ: Princeton University Press, 1996). The chart is adapted from *Christianity History* issue 57 (17/1): 26, and is used by permission.

• 10 •

Medieval Christianity (500–1500)

The demise of the Roman Empire is a convenient place for marking the transition of Christianity from its earliest centuries into the Middle Ages. This next era of Christian history would last for a millennium, 500–1500.

The Early Middle Ages (500–1000)

Barbarian Invasions. The fall of the western portion of the Roman Empire was a complicated event with a variety of causes. One of the most important factors contributing to its final demise was the invasion of various Germanic tribes, which came from regions beyond the Danube and Rhine Rivers in modern-day Germany. The Romans called these Germanic tribes "barbarian" after the Latin word *barbarus* which means "foreign, strange, or ignorant." These tribes invaded the western portion of the Empire in two different ways. Many of the invasions were the result of violent clashes between the Roman legions and these warlike tribes. In other instances, they simply migrated peacefully into the regions of the Empire.

As these people made their way into the eastern edge of the Empire, their powerful kings began to settle in certain regions and claim the territory for themselves. Several of these groups became well known for their influence on the later history of Western Europe. For example, the Vandals settled in the region called Spain today. Arian missionaries had earlier evangelized them, so they had a tendency to persecute orthodox Christians. They established a settlement in North Africa and from there invaded Rome, sacking the city in 455. Another group settling in the Toledo area of Spain was the Visigoths, also Arian in their theology.

The Franks settled in Gaul and gave that region its modern name of France. Originally pagan, they eventually converted to orthodox Christianity largely due to their king named Clovis. What led Clovis to convert to the Christian faith is not fully known. He was surrounded by a large number of Christians. But his conversion was much more than simply good politics. Clovis's wife Clothilda was a Christian and according to Clovis's biographer, she pleaded with him to forsake his pagan gods and accept the God of Christianity. He refused but allowed her to have their firstborn son baptized. The child tragically died shortly after its baptism and Clovis blamed the baptism for the child's death. Later, another child was born and surprisingly, Clovis consented to its baptism. Again, after the baptism the child became gravely ill and Clovis thought baptism would kill it as well. But this time the child recovered. The turning point for Clovis (like Constantine) came on the eve of a battle in which he was outnumbered and sure to lose. Reportedly, he prayed, "Jesus Christ, Clothilda says thou art the son of the living God, and thou canst give victory to those who hope in thee. Give me victory and I will be baptized. I have tried my gods and they have deserted me. I call on thee. Only save me."[1] Clovis won the battle and on Christmas Day in the year 496 he was baptized into the Christian faith. That same day, three thousand men in his army were also baptized.

The invasions of the Germanic "barbarian" tribes brought about the end of the Roman Empire in the west. The final blow came in 476 when the last emperor, Romulus Augustulus, was deposed. Although it may sound as if this era were bad for the Church, there were some positive factors in spite of the challenges. First, the Germanic tribes brought new subjects for the Church to proselytize, although many of these tribes had already been converted to Arian Christianity. Western Christianity eventually gained converts from many of the Arian tribes.

Second, the turmoil created in Roman society by the barbarian invasions forced the hierarchy of the Church to evolve even further. This gave greater structure to the Roman Catholic Church and laid the foundation for Christianity in the Middle Ages. Furthermore, as the hierarchy developed, many people in society began to look to the leaders of the Church for stability. The bishop of Rome, called *papa* in Latin by the people, began to acquire more prestige and power as the Empire began to collapse. The "pope" brought a sense of stability to the minds of the people in Roman society who were fearful in such a time of turmoil and social upheaval.

Third, the barbarian invasions divided eastern and western Christianity. The imperial capital had been in Constantinople (formerly Byzantium) since Constantine had moved it there in the fourth century. The barbarian invasions blocked the western portion of the Empire from the influence of the emperor in Constantinople. This gave Western Christianity (centered in Rome and eventually called "Roman Catholicism") the ability to develop

---

[1]Quoted in Roland H. Bainton, *Christendom: A Short History of Christianity and Its Impact on Western Civilization, Vol. I*, (New York: Harper and Row, 1966), p. 145. Clovis's biographer was Gregory of Tours (538–593/4).

its own distinctive characteristics. Eastern Christianity (eventually called "Eastern Orthodoxy"), now blocked from western influence, developed characteristics of its own as well.

Eastern vs. Western Christianity. As Christianity progressed through the Middle Ages, distinct differences began to develop between Christianity in the East and West. As seen above, the Germanic invasions into the Empire created a rift in communications between East and West. Furthermore, the cultural differences served to create theological differences.

In the West, Latin became the dominant spoken language and a culture developed which emphasized precision in theology. When councils met to discuss theological issues, western theologians saw the council decrees as settling the issues rather than prompting more discussion and speculation as they were viewed in the East. In the East, the Greek language was predominant, and eastern theologians tended to be more philosophical and speculative in their writings. They placed a great amount of emphasis on art and the mystery of God. Furthermore, eastern theologians thought that the basic problem of humanity was that people had lost their divinity as a result of sin. The work of Christ was to restore that lost divinity to humans. Western theologians believed that the human problem was sin itself. The work of Christ was to pay the penalty for sin. Therefore, the most important aspect of Christ's work for the East was the resurrection, which they viewed as providing a restoration of lost divinity, whereas the West placed great value on the cross, which verified that sin's price had been paid.[2]

Finally, there were differences in church and state relations in the two regions. The emperor continued unimpeded to reside in the East in Constantinople until the Muslims conquered the city in 1453. The State dominated the Church there. In the West, the Church stepped in to fill the vacuum in Rome created in the fourth century when Constantine moved the imperial capital. Therefore, the Church dominated the State in the West.

The differences between the two regions became more acute at some times than others. The most important crisis came in 1054. That date marks the formal break between Eastern and Western Christianity. One of the issues leading to the division involved an addition to the Nicene Creed called the *Filoque Clause*. The *filioque* in Latin means "and from the Son."

---

[2]See R. Dean Peterson, *A Concise History of Christianity*, 2nd ed. (Boston: Wadsworth, 2000) 110, for this discussion of the differences between East and West.

The West inserted it into the Nicene Creed after the statement which says that the Spirit proceeds from the Father. Aside from the theological changes that this created, the East refused to accept the *Filioque Clause* because it had not been voted on in an "ecumenical council" composed of all bishops. Their refusal to accept the addition forced the pope in 1054 to excommunicate the Patriarch of Constantinople, who then proceeded to do the same to the pope. The sacking of Constantinople in 1204 by the western Crusaders in the Fourth Crusade forever sealed the division between East and West.

Conflicts with Islam. In Arabia, in the early seventh century, a new religion began to develop under the leadership of Muhammed, an Arab merchant. Inquisitive about religious issues, Muhammed had been in contact with Christianity, Judaism and Zoroastrianism, three religions that were prevalent in that part of the world in the seventh century. These three religions shared several things in common, bringing them into sharp contrast with the polytheistic native religions of Arabia: (1) belief in one God; (2) belief in a collection of scriptures considered to be divinely inspired; (3) belief in an afterlife in which the righteous will be rewarded and the unrighteous punished.

Muhammed began a quest for the "true" religion. This search led him into the wilderness for periods of time in which he claimed that "Allah" (Allah is the Arabic word for God) revealed truth to him in a series of ecstatic visitations. Muhammed began to identify himself as a "Muslim," meaning "one who submits to Allah," and began to teach others about his revelations. He resisted the claim that he was starting a new religion. Instead, he contended that he was preaching the completion of the truth revealed first to the Hebrew Prophets and then to the person of Jesus, who was a great prophet, but not divine.

At first Muhammed's message fell on deaf ears with the people of his native Mecca. Polytheism was prevalent among their religious traditions. So Muhammed moved in 622 to Medina, a nearby city that became receptive to his preaching. Very shortly thereafter, Muhammed and his followers led a military campaign back to Mecca where he captured control of the city. Soon the city converted to the Muslim faith. Muhammed forgave his former enemies but outlawed all idols in the city. By the time of his death in 632, most of Arabia was in Muslim hands.

Following Muhammed's death, the Muslim religion began to spread beyond Arabia under the leadership of the "caliphs" or successors of Muhammed. By the middle of the seventh century, all of Arabia, Syria,

Palestine and Egypt were in Muslim hands. During the second half of the seventh century Muslim armies continued along the northern part of Africa. Carthage fell in 695 and in 711 a small group of Muslim armies crossed the Straits of Gibraltar and into Spain. Charles Martel finally stopped the Muslim advance in 732 at the Battle of Tours in France.[3]

The Muslim conquest of what had previously been Christian strongholds was significant for Christianity. First, the spread of Islam hastened the division between Eastern and Western Christianity. The Muslims, though relatively tolerant of Christians in many quarters, effectively isolated Constantinople from the West and kept the emperor from having any contact or influence there. Second, the conquest by the Muslims of many areas that had once been important Christian territories (such as Jerusalem) set the stage for the Crusades, which began several centuries later. Third, the Muslim invasions forced Christianity to turn its attention north. It is no coincidence that within two hundred years, Christianity would be accepted formally in Russia, and following the Fall of Constantinople in the fifteenth century Moscow would proclaim itself the "Third Rome."

The Late Middle Ages (1000–1500)

Development of the Papacy. The story of the papacy during the late Middle Ages is a tale of both a rise to power as well as a fall into decadence. The tenth century represents one of the most corrupt eras in the history of the Papacy. During the first part of the century a rapid succession of popes (seventeen between 897 and 955) occurred with numerous assassinations and political intrigue. The Papacy had become a political prize for the ruling families in Italy. It was not uncommon for a pope to have his rivals executed.

One of the most bizarre examples of the decadence of the period came in 897. The "Cadaveric Council," as it came to be called, was presided over by Pope Stephen VI. Formosus, one of Stephen's rival predecessors and already dead, was exhumed. His remains were then dressed in papal robes and his body was paraded through the streets of Rome. He was then placed on trial, and posthumously condemned for a variety of crimes, followed by the

---

[3]See Justo Gonzalez, *The Story of Christianity*, vol. 1 (San Francisco: HarperSanFrancisco, 1984) 248-50.

mutilation of his body. His remains were then thrown into the Tiber River.[4]

The so-called "Pornocracy" of the church occurred from 904 to 964. During these years the papacy was controlled by three women, who provided sexual favors to a number of weak-willed popes in exchange for wealth, titles, and land. One of the women bore an illegitimate son who was fathered by Pope Sergius III. The child later became Pope John XI.[5]

During this dark era in Roman Catholicism, an effort at reform was underway in the monasteries. Duke William III of Aquitaine began a monastery at Cluny in France. He appointed as abbot a monk named Berno, who had a reputation for reform and strict discipline in monastic circles. Through the leadership of Berno and his successors, Cluny spawned numerous other monasteries and this revival of monasticism eventually led to greater stability in the Church.

As the late Middle Ages progressed, three popes should be recognized for their contributions. They represent the height of papal power in the Middle Ages. Pope Gregory VII (1073–1085), known as a reformer, is perhaps best remembered for his clash with Henry IV, emperor of the Holy Roman Empire. The controversy generated between these two men concerned the issue of "investiture." By the eleventh century, the tradition had developed whereby the emperor "invested" or selected individuals to serve in high church offices such as bishop or abbot. In return, the emperor expected homage from the person appointed, thereby solidifying his power against potential enemies. The system worked well for the emperor.

Gregory VII disagreed with the practice, however. He believed that the appointment of ecclesiastical offices was the prerogative of the Church. He reasoned that when the emperor chose a bishop the person filling that office had more of a political obligation than spiritual, thereby compromising the spiritual integrity of the office.

The matter came to a head in the winter of 1077. Gregory forbade Henry to appoint any more ecclesiastical offices. Henry, however, convened a council and called for Gregory to be deposed as Pope. Gregory, who had his own political allies that were opposed to the emperor, then excommunicated Henry and placed him under the "ban." This meant that all those who were Henry's subjects were released from their oaths of allegiance to

---

[4]Gonzalez, *The Story of Christianity* 1:275.

[5]William Ragsdale Cannon, *History of Christianity in the Middle Ages*, (Grand Rapids: Baker Book House, 1960), p. 133.

him. In fact, Gregory's ban *forbade* anyone from obeying him. Henry eventually became desperate with the loss of support. He made his way across the Alps to the papal palace in Canossa, Italy, seeking forgiveness from Gregory. The pope made Henry stand in the snow for three days in sackcloth and ashes begging forgiveness before finally allowing him inside and granting him absolution. Through a political twist of fate several years later, Henry succeeded in having Gregory removed from power where shortly thereafter he died in exile. The episode stands as a remarkable illustration of papal power in the Middle Ages.

Innocent III (1198–1216) might be regarded as the most powerful pope in history. Certainly, he represents the height of papal power in the Middle Ages. He was the most powerful man in Europe during his reign. He was the first to use the phrase "Vicar of Christ" to describe the papal office. Innocent III also called the Fourth Lateran Council into session in 1215. Though the belief had been around for centuries, this council officially confirmed "Transubstantiation" as the theological definition of the Mass. Transubstantiation is the belief that when the priest elevates the "host" (the bread) during the Mass and pronounces the words of institution, "This is my body," the bread and wine are transformed into the body and blood of Christ in their substance while the "accidents" (or appearance) remain bread and wine.

Boniface VIII (1294–1303) was a third Middle Ages pope who believed in the absolute power of the papacy. He is best remembered for a papal bull (official papal opinion) called *Unam Sanctam* (1302). It formally declared that outside of the Church there is no salvation or forgiveness of sins. Therefore, when a person is excommunicated from the Church they are severed from their spiritual salvation. Consequently, the salvation of every human depends upon his or her submission to the pope's authority. Boniface further declared that in the world there are two "swords," the sword of temporal authority and the sword of spiritual authority. The clergy wields the sword of spiritual authority while the sword of temporal authority is in the hands of the secular rulers to be used for the Church and under its direction. *Unam Sanctam* declares that the pope is the Supreme Head of the Church and all on earth are subject to him. Ironically, for all of Boniface's protestation of papal supremacy, he came into conflict with the powerful king of France, Philip IV whom he ultimately tried to excommunicate. Philip ordered Boniface's arrest and even though Italian troops secured his release three days later, he died within a month a broken man.

The Crusades. The Crusades were a series of military campaigns from 1095 to 1291 to recover the Holy Land from the Muslims. The motives of the Crusades were mixed—partly religious, but also economic and political. Pope Urban II proclaimed the First Crusade in 1095. He promised forgiveness of sin and eternal life to those who died in the endeavor. On the journey toward Jerusalem, the Crusaders raped and pillaged throughout the countryside. Innocent villagers were killed for no reason as the bloodthirsty army pressed forward. Four years later, Jerusalem fell to the Crusaders and remained in Latin hands for approximately 100 years.

The Fourth Crusade was notable. Instead of attacking the Muslims, the Crusaders detoured into Constantinople and sacked the city in 1204, attempting to establish Latin Christianity there. This disastrous episode further eroded relations between Greek-speaking Christians in the East and Latin–speaking Christians in the West and weakened the Empire in the East.

After the Seventh Crusade, the crusading spirit in Europe died. Generally, the Crusades were a tragic failure because the Holy Land remained in Muslim hands except for a brief period following the First Crusade. Still, there were some important results of the Crusades. First, they served to further ill feelings between Christians and Muslims. Second, they created a further division (which has never been overcome) between Eastern and Western Christianity. Third, the power of the papacy grew. The popes called the Crusades into being, appointed the leaders and promised spiritual favors to those who volunteered. Fourth, the Crusades created a renewed interest in Christian piety. The veneration of relics became popular in Europe with crusaders claiming to bring back such things from the Holy Land as bones and other remains of martyrs and biblical characters and pieces of Jesus' cross. Fifth, new monastic military orders blending monasticism and warfare developed with names such as the order of Saint John of Jerusalem and the Knights Templar. Some of these new orders continued to be active in Europe long after the Crusades ended. Sixth, the attention to the Muslims and the rhetoric used to describe them as "infidels" created a renewed interest in heresy in Europe which was ultimately addressed with the organization of the Inquisition. Seventh, contact with the Muslim world opened the eyes of many in Europe to new ideas, especially in the areas of theology and philosophy. The writings of the Jewish philosopher Maimonides and the Muslim philosopher Averroes had an important impact on the theological and philosophical development in Europe in the thirteenth century. Eighth, the Crusades introduced new economic and social reforms in Europe. Commerce and trade routes were opened and a "middle class" began to rise in Europe.[6]

Scholasticism. The late middle ages saw an important innovation in the field of theology called Scholasticism. Scholasticism became the theological method of the academics in the universities in Europe during the centuries 1100–1500. It sought to combine the use of ancient philosophy with medieval theology in order to make rational sense of certain theological concepts.

Anselm of Canterbury is usually considered to be the originator of this movement. Anselm was famous for his motto, "I believe in order that I may understand," and also developed the famous ontological argument for the existence of God. He reasoned that if the idea of God is in the human mind, and there is nothing greater than that concept that can be conceived, therefore God must exist in reality. Anselm also developed the satisfaction theory of the atonement which sought to understand how the death of Christ on the cross provides salvation for humans. He reasoned that God was angry at humanity because of sin and Jesus, a perfect God/man died on the cross to appease God's wrath.

The most famous scholastic scholar was the great Thomas Aquinas, perhaps the greatest intellectual mind of his era. Aquinas believed that both faith and reason were necessary for understanding God. He also believed that rational thinking and the study of nature were important for obtaining knowledge of God. He is considered by many to be Roman Catholicism's greatest theologian and his famous work is called the *Summa Theologica*, represents the pinnacle of medieval scholasticism.

The Renaissance. On the heels of Scholasticism in the late Middle Ages came another movement which had an impact on theology but was much broader than just a theological innovation. The word *renaissance* means "rebirth." It was a cultural movement which attempted to revive the best of classical antiquity, particularly ancient Greece and Rome. The ancient Greco-Roman culture had been neglected in Western Europe for centuries. In fact, it was the Renaissance scholars who coined the term *Middle Ages* to refer to the centuries between their time and the ancient world.

The Renaissance affected almost every aspect of life in Western Europe including art, literature, architecture and certainly theology. Because of

---

[6]The results of the Crusades were taken from Gonzalez, *The Story of Christianity* 1:298-300.

their interest in the ancient world, Renaissance intellectuals learned Greek which subsequently led to an ability to read the New Testament in the Greek language rather than Latin. The person most credited with this innovation was Erasmus of Rotterdam, who produced the first complete edition of the Greek New Testament based on the best manuscripts available to him in his day.

The impact of this movement for the history of Christianity cannot be overlooked because it ultimately led to a questioning of the Church's authority in matters of faith. For example, a Renaissance scholar named Lorenzo Valla used historical analysis to prove that a document called the "Donation of Constantine," which purported to have been written during the era of Constantine, could not have been written then, but instead came from the eighth century. The "Donation of Constantine" supposedly contained the wishes of Constantine which granted land and authority over all the other bishops to the pope. Proving this document a forgery thereby undercut an important papal claim that had been used by popes for centuries and led to further questioning of the pope's ultimate authority over other Christians.

Early Reformation Movements. Although the Protestant Reformation did not begin until the sixteenth century, several early reform movements deserve attention. Two of these movements are most notable.

John Wycliff was an English Catholic priest and professor at Oxford. Wycliff lived in the fourteenth century during a time when there was a tremendous amount of corruption in the papacy and the Church's hierarchy. He became critical of the pope and began to disagree with the Church on a number of issues. First, he disagreed with the Church about the Bible. He believed that the Bible was the possession of all Christians and that any Christian should be able to read and interpret the Bible for him/herself. The Church taught that the Bible belonged to the clergy of the Church because they were the only ones with the proper training to allow its interpretation. They believed that it would be dangerous for the laity to read and interpret the Bible for themselves because that would possibly encourage heresy and would create anarchy within the Church.

Wycliff's ideas about the Bible led him to the conclusion that the Bible should be translated into English. Although he probably did not do any of the translating himself, he inspired the translation of the Latin Vulgate into English by his followers called "Lollards," who completed the project just after his death in 1384.

Wycliff also disagreed with the doctrine of transubstantiation. He believed that Christ was present only spiritually during the Lord's Supper and not physically as the doctrine taught. Furthermore, he believed that immoral or incompetent clergy, including the pope, should be replaced if they failed to carry out their offices properly; then, if the Church would not replace them, the secular rulers should.

Needless to say, Wycliff raised the eyebrows of many of those in positions of power within the Roman Catholic Church. Although he died of natural causes in 1384, the Lollards continued to preach his ideas throughout the English countryside. Eventually, their preaching became so controversial that they were forced to go underground. Wycliff's ideas became so threatening to the power structure of the Church that the Council of Constance, which met from 1414 to 1418, posthumously declared him to be a heretic. They ordered his body to be exhumed, and his bones burned to ashes and the ashes scattered. Wycliff's ideas and the work of the Lollards made them true forerunners of the Reformation a century later.

John Hus (1374–1415) was contemporary with Wycliff and was greatly influenced by his thought. Hus was from Bohemia in Eastern Europe. A professor at the University of Prague, and every bit as outspoken as Wycliff, Hus believed that Scripture is the final authority for the Christian life and that both the Church and the clergy of the Church should be reformed based on Scripture. He also rejected the doctrine of transubstantiation and became a vocal opponent of it. He preached sermons in which he vehemently opposed the corrupt morals of the clergy and frequently made the pope the chief target of his sermons.

Hus became a folk hero in Bohemia and soon had a large following of the people and the monarch in his region. This eventually came to the attention of the Roman Catholic Church. In 1414 he was invited to appear before the Council of Constance to defend his views. He was given safe-conduct to the Council. But when he arrived the safe-conduct was rescinded and he was arrested. He was tried and condemned as a heretic. In 1415 he was burned at the stake. When Hus's followers in Bohemia heard of his death they rebelled. The Catholics finally quelled the rebellion but not without first making some concessions. The "Bohemian Brethren" in Bohemia, along with the Lollards in England, became important voices advocating reform of the Church more than a century before the Protestant Reformation of the sixteenth century.

In the millennium called the Middle Ages, the Church gained great wealth and power and became entrenched as a political force in Western

Europe. In the East, the orthodox expression of Christianity achieved the same status until 1453 when the Muslims gained control of Constantinople. Christianity in the East never recovered its power. In the West, the sixteenth century brought about a wave of reform creating a new expression of Christianity called "Protestantism," the focus of our next chapter.

• 11 •

The Reformation

As we saw in the previous chapter, the movement of reform in Western Christianity began many years before the sixteenth century. It could be said that early reformers like Wycliff and Hus planted the seeds of reform that sprouted and blossomed in the sixteenth century with Martin Luther in Germany. The Reformation was not a monolithic movement. There were several independent movements in Western Europe, working simultaneously toward reform in the sixteenth century. They shared a common foe in the Roman Catholic Church, but these different movements also experienced turmoil and conflict among themselves at times.

The varied movements which taken together constitute the Protestant Reformation can be divided into two categories. Magisterial reformers like Martin Luther, Ulrich Zwingli, John Calvin, and Henry VIII in England, used the power of secular governments and rulers ("magistrates," thus "Magisterial Reformation") to accomplish their reform goals. Radical reformers, such as the Anabaptists, represent the second category. They were opposed to any kind of government efforts to carry out the spiritual reform goals for which they worked.

Magisterial Reformers

Martin Luther. The story of Martin Luther is one of the most interesting in the history of Christianity. He was born in 1483 in Eisleben, Germany, to parents of very humble means. Luther's father was a miner and eventually became manager of several mines which provided a certain measure of financial security for the family. A precocious child, Luther excelled in his schooling despite a schoolmaster who would be considered cruel by today's standards. It was not unusual for the children in Luther's class to receive severe beatings for unprepared lessons or for misbehavior. After completing his early schooling, Luther entered Erfurt University in 1501. He completed the B.A. degree in 1502 and the M.A. in 1505.

Throughout his childhood Luther's harsh treatment by his father coupled with a stern schoolmaster gave him a fear of authority figures. Gradually, this fear began to impact the way Luther viewed God. He began to see God as a vengeful, wrathful God rather than loving and benevolent.

As Luther increasingly became aware of his sinfulness, he became even more frightened of God. His fear of God grew more acute during his years at the University.

Upon completion of his university education, Luther intended to pursue a career in law. That changed very suddenly. One night, while walking in the midst of a thunderstorm, Luther was struck by lightning. Already made aware of the transience of life by the death of a friend, this experience terrified Luther and made him fearful of his own mortality in ways he had not been before. Picking himself up from the ground he cried out, "Save me Saint Anne (the patron saint of miners), I will become a monk." Luther began to see this experience as a divine sign and because of his fear of God, he responded immediately. He entered an Augustinian monastery in Erfurt in 1505.

As a monk, Luther began preparation for the priesthood, which included studying theology. But the more he studied, the more his view of a vengeful God terrified him. He began to obsess about his own sinfulness and inability to find a sense of forgiveness. He would go into the confessional and confess sometimes for hours at a time and then come out saying that he felt worse than he did before entering. He even began to torture his body by self-flagellation, beating himself until he passed out. Still, he could not find any peace in his soul.

In 1508 Luther left Erfurt for Wittenberg where he became a lecturer in theology and began to study for his doctorate. This became a turning point in his life. One evening, while preparing a lecture on the Pauline epistle of Romans, Luther read the phrase in 1:17, "the just shall live by faith." This discovery became the key for which he had been looking. For the first time he understood that justification before God did not depend on his own righteousness. In fact, Luther began to believe that a human being could never be righteous in his/her own strength. Rather, by placing faith in Christ alone, Luther believed that God pronounced the sinner righteous. Suddenly, Luther had an entirely new understanding of God. No longer seeing God as cruel and vengeful, Luther now saw God as loving, benevolent, and willing to provide forgiveness of sin and the means by which that forgiveness could be attained, namely, the sacrifice of Christ on the cross.

After completing his doctorate, Luther remained at Wittenberg. As he focused his attention on theology, Luther increasingly came to believe that the Roman Catholic system of the sacraments was inadequate for dealing with human sin because it was based more on human works than faith. With his new theology of salvation by faith alone, Luther began to attack the Church and the sacramental system. He became so vocal in his attack that he eventually captured the attention of the Church's hierarchy.

Luther's new ideas about justification by faith eventually brought him into direct conflict with the Roman Catholic Church. The first episode involved a man named Tetzel, who came to Wittenberg to raise funds for the Church by the practice of selling indulgences. During the Middle Ages, the Church developed the practice of selling indulgences in order to raise extra income. The theory behind the practice was based on lives of the Saints. The Church believed that the Saints had built up more merit than they actually needed to cover their own sins. Therefore, the extra merit was stored in the "Treasury of Merit" in heaven. The Church believed that the pope had the authority to tap into the Treasury of Merit and assign various amounts of forgiveness to those who bought indulgences.

Luther's personal struggle with sin and his view of the inadequacy of the Roman Catholic system for providing him the peace he sought led him into a public confrontation with Tetzel. On 31 October 1517 (All Saints' Eve), Luther posted on the church door at Wittenberg a formal challenge for debate. This document contained 95 *Theses* on the topic of indulgences that Luther wanted to debate with a representative from the Roman Catholic Church. Within a matter of weeks copies of the 95 *Theses* were published all over Europe. The Protestant Reformation had begun!

At first, the Church sought to silence Luther through his monastic order. But that proved ineffective. Many of Luther's faculty colleagues began to adopt his new theological ideas. In a more concerted attempt to silence Luther, the Church sent one of its champion debaters, John Eck, a revered Catholic theologian, to engage him in a public debate. To the surprise of the Catholic authorities, Luther won the debate. When he became critical of the pope, Leo X, and when the German people began to follow Luther, the resulting upheaval led to his excommunication in June, 1520. By the next year, the entire matter came to the attention of emperor Charles V of the Holy Roman Empire.

In the sixteenth century, the seven most powerful nobles in Germany had the authority to elect the emperor. In 1521, Luther was called to appear at the emperor's annual meeting with his electors in the city of Worms. At this yearly meeting, in a moment of high drama with all the emperor's electors present, Luther was called upon to recant his writings and attacks on the pope. In response Luther exclaimed:

Unless I am convicted by Scripture and plain reason—I do not accept the authority of popes and councils, for they have contradicted each other—my conscience is captive to the Word of God. I cannot and I will not recant anything, for to go against conscience is neither right nor safe. God help me, Amen.

Supposedly, Luther also added the famous words, "Here I stand, I cannot do otherwise."[1] The Edict of Worms, issued on 25 May 1521, formally condemned Luther's teachings. He was now at odds with both the pope and the emperor.

Luther probably would have been arrested and executed had it not been for his popularity with the German people and with the elector from his home region of Saxony, Frederick III. Frederick was a supporter and friend to Luther. He was instrumental in the founding of the University of Wittenberg and in the invitation for Luther to teach there. When Luther was excommunicated in 1520 Frederick refused to support the order. After the Diet of Worms Frederick had Luther "kidnaped" and hidden for protection at the Wartburg Castle, near Eisenach. These years in hiding proved to be some of Luther's most productive. A most significant publication from this period was a complete translation of the New Testament into German.

Luther's reform efforts in Germany continued for another twenty-five years until his death in 1546. By that time, a thriving Protestant movement was in place and Germany would never again be completely in the hands of Roman Catholicism. Historians note that in the last years of Luther's life his personality became very different from that of his early years. He became somewhat irascible, crude, and stubborn with his ideas. This may have been due partly to his declining health and partly also to the political pressure under which he found himself at times.

There remained another side to Luther's work and life. As his reform work was beginning in Germany, he began encouraging priests to marry. The monasteries emptied and Luther began matching priests with nuns from the convents. Luther himself married Katherine von Bora and together they had six children. They bought an old monastery building for a home and, along with their own children, raised four orphaned children. In addition, they rented rooms to some of Luther's students. Altogether, the household

---

[1]Roland H. Bainton, *Here I Stand: A Life of Martin Luther*, (Nashville: Abingdon Press, 1950), p. 185.

numbered twenty-five at its peak. His family was one of the great joys of his life.

How should Luther be evaluated? First, he can be credited with igniting the spark that flamed the Protestant Reformation of the sixteenth century. Other movements paralleled his, but Luther's reform in Germany paved the way in Europe for other reform movements to take hold. Second, Luther developed a fresh understanding of the doctrine of salvation with his ideas of justification by faith alone. It could be argued that he returned to Pauline theology, which the Roman Catholicism of the Middle Ages had modified to such an extent that it was no longer recognizable as Pauline. Third, Luther effectively became the founder of the Lutheran denomination, one of the major denominations within Protestantism today.

Ulrich Zwingli. While Germany was occupied with the Lutheran reform movement, Switzerland was engaged in its own reform. The Swiss Reformation began in Zurich with Ulrich Zwingli (1484–1531). A contemporary of Luther, Zwingli developed his disagreements with the Roman Catholic Church in a different way. Zwingli did not have the emotional and spiritual struggle that was present in Luther's journey to reform. He was born in Wildhaus, Switzerland where his father was mayor of the town. After studying with an uncle who was a priest, Zwingli furthered his education at the Universities of Basel, Bern, and Vienna. He was greatly influenced by the Renaissance humanist scholars who sought to study the best of ancient Greek and Roman culture.

Zwingli completed his M.A. in Classics (Humanism) in 1506 and became priest at Glarus where he began to study the New Testament closely. At Glarus, Zwingli volunteered as chaplain to mercenary troops provided by the Swiss to other countries. His first experience in war was with an army that was victorious in battle and that subsequently looted and pillaged the defeated enemy. A few years later he saw war from the perspective of a defeated, demoralized army. These experiences prompted Zwingli to begin speaking out against Switzerland's practice of providing mercenary soldiers to other nations.

In 1516 Zwingli became a priest in Einsiedeln where his Protestant views continued to develop. The city was famous for a shrine to the Virgin Mary, which attracted large numbers of religious pilgrims. Zwingli observed the way that many of the pilgrims were treated, especially by indulgence sellers who were active in the city. He began to oppose the idea that pilgrimages and indulgences were efficacious for salvation and began preaching to the pilgrims who came to visit the shrine.

Two years later, in 1518, Zwingli received appointment as priest to the largest church in Zurich. By that time, he had thoroughly embraced Protestant theology. His pathway to Protestantism was not the anguished spiritual struggle of Luther. Instead, Zwingli came to his Protestant faith through careful study of the Greek New Testament in the style of the Humanists of his day. He eventually gained the support of the city council in Zurich which supported his Protestant ideas and he began to reform the city by purging it of any trace of Roman Catholic practices or traditions.

Though a contemporary with Luther, a word should be said here about the difference between Luther and Zwingli, especially regarding their views of the Lord's Supper. In 1529, the supporters of both movements brought the two reformers together in Marburg, Germany. The goal was for the two men to reach an accord thereby presenting a united front against the Roman Catholic Church. They were able to agree on almost every point except their respective views of the Lord's Supper. Both men rejected transubstantiation. But Luther believed that the body of Christ was present in the bread and wine while Zwingli believed that the Lord's Supper was symbolic of Christ's body. This difference, and the inability to resolve it, forced the two movements to go their separate ways.

The city council of Zurich continued to embrace Zwingli's reforms. In 1531 the five Catholic cantons in Switzerland launched an attack on Zurich. Zwingli joined the efforts to defend his city and was tragically killed in battle in a town called Koppel. Within a month the Peace of Koppel was signed. The result was that each canton in Switzerland would have the freedom to choose between Catholicism and Protestantism.[2]

John Calvin. Following the death of Zwingli, John Calvin became the most important name associated with the Reformation in Switzerland. Calvin was born in 1509 in Noyon, France. His father had an important job as secretary to the Bishop of Noyon, a position that paid well, thereby providing the necessary funds for Calvin's schooling. He studied for a career in law at the Universities of Paris, Orléans, and Bourges. During his schooling, like Zwingli before him, he became thoroughly influenced by the

---

[2]For a good discussion of Zwingli's Swiss Reform movement see Justo L. Gonzalez, *The Story of Christianity*, vol. 2 (San Francisco: Harper Collins, 1985) 46-52, and R. Dean Peterson, *A Concise History of Christianity*, (New York: Wadsworth, 2000) 207-10.

spirit of humanism and its attention to ancient culture.

Very different from Luther, Calvin wrote little about any kind of inner struggle with sin or a spiritual crisis. It is not known when Calvin made his formal break with the Roman Catholic Church. It is clear that he was Protestant by 1534 because in that year he fled from France due to persecution of Protestants. He finally settled in Basel, Switzerland.

In 1536, Calvin wrote the first edition of his *Institutes of the Christian Religion*. One of the most important theological works in Christian history, it brought him immediate attention and fame. Originally published as a manual that could be easily concealed in one's pocket, it went through a number of revisions. The final edition, which occupied four volumes, was published in 1559. Reading the different editions of the *Institutes* provides an interesting picture of how Calvin's theology grew and developed from 1536 until 1559.

A significant turning point in Calvin's life came in 1536 when he visited Geneva. There he met William Farel who had initiated a Protestant reform in the city. Farel, needing help, requested that Calvin stay in Geneva and join the reform movement. Calvin agreed to stay, and remained there for two years, but it was a turbulent period. Almost immediately, Calvin began writing laws which he expected the city council to endorse. He sought to establish a "theocracy" in Geneva which would be governed by the same laws as the ancient Hebrews in the Old Testament. His vision included such things as "blue laws" (which forbid any business dealings on Sundays), forced church attendance, a confession of faith to which all citizens of Geneva were expected to assent, training of children in Protestant ideas, and a system of lay inspectors who would observe the conduct of the citizens and report any moral problems to Calvin. The laws proved so unpopular that the people initiated a riot against the city government. Although the annual election of 1537 favored Calvin and his supporters, a year later the opposition won and took over the council. Calvin and Farel fled to nearby Strasbourg.

Calvin spent three years in Strasbourg which proved to be his happiest and most peaceful. Though he turned his attention to writing, he always yearned to return to Geneva to complete the experiment with theocracy he started there. That opportunity came in 1541. The political situation with the city government changed once again and Calvin was invited to return. This time he was assured that there would be support for his reform efforts. Following his return, in 1541, he remained there until his death in 1564.

During those years, his dream of creating a "theocracy" was realized, although by modern democratic standards it was an oppressive, restrictive place to live. Nevertheless, Calvin should be regarded as one of the greatest reformers of the Reformation era, especially because of his keen theological insights and writing.

Calvin's theology found in the *Institutes* was systematized by his followers years after his death. Students of Calvinism have used the acrostic "TULIP" as a mnemonic device to remember the salient points of his theological system. The first letter stands for "Total depravity," the belief that all humans are totally depraved by original sin, meaning that there is nothing good that humans can do for salvation under their own power. Second, "Unconditional election" represents one of the most controversial points in Calvinism. This is the concept that before the world and human beings were ever created God predestined or "elected" certain people to salvation and others to eternal damnation. Third, "Limited atonement," is the idea that the death of Christ makes atonement only for the elect. That follows logically. If only the elect can be saved, then Christ's death could only be applicable to them. Fourth, "Irresistible grace" is the notion that if a person is one of God's elect, God's grace will be irresistible when that person is confronted with it. Fifth, "Perseverance of the saints" indicates that the elect will persevere in their salvation until the end of their lives making loss of salvation impossible.

John Calvin ranks as one of the greatest figures in the history of Christianity. Many have disagreed with his theology but all acknowledge the importance of his influence. The English Puritans were influenced by his theology. They brought that influence across the Atlantic Ocean to the Massachusetts Bay Colony. John Knox was a student of Calvin and took Calvin's theology back to Scotland where his reforms of the Church of Scotland led to the rise of Presbyterianism. One segment of the early Baptists of the seventeenth century was thoroughgoing Calvinist in its theology. Calvin has certainly left his mark on Christianity since the sixteenth century.

The English Reformation. Although it was magisterial in nature, the English Reformation was very different from both the German and Swiss reform movements. One could argue that the German and Swiss reforms were religiously motivated with political effects. The English reform, on the other hand, was a politically motivated movement that had religious conse-quences. The English reform began with the king, Henry VIII. The story of how he reformed the Church in England is most interesting indeed.

Henry VIII was happy as a Roman Catholic. In fact, when Luther's reform began in Germany, Henry was initially critical of it. His support for the Roman Catholic Church earned him the title "Defender of the Faith" from Pope Leo X in 1521. Although Henry certainly never intended to break away from the Roman Catholic Church, events began to take place which eventually made separation a necessity in his mind as he became fixated on having a male heir.

Henry's older brother Arthur, the original heir to their father's throne, married Catherine of Aragon (daughter of Ferdinand and Isabella of Spain) as a political arrangement between England and Spain. But Arthur died four months after the marriage. At this point Henry assumed the throne and it was determined that he would marry Catherine to keep the alliance between Spain and England intact. Church law prohibited marriage to a brother's widow. Therefore, a special dispensation from the pope was needed for the marriage to proceed. The pope willingly granted the dispensation. However, of six children born to Catherine and Henry, five died leaving only a daughter, Mary, to survive infancy. Henry became convinced that the failure to have a male heir from Catherine was because of God's judgment on what he now became convinced was an illegitimate marriage. Therefore, Henry began to seek an annulment from the pope, claiming that the marriage was illegal in the first place. To make matters worse, by this time Henry was involved in a romance with Anne Boleyn and he began to desire marriage to her.

The pope would probably have granted the annulment except for a political problem. Catherine was the aunt of Charles V, the emperor of the Holy Roman Empire whose armies were present in Italy and were protecting the pope. He simply could not risk angering Charles V. Granting the annulment would have been an embarrassment to the Spanish in general, and to Catherine and Charles V in particular. Therefore, the pope refused to grant the annulment.

Henry then decided to take matters into his own hands. In 1533 he married Anne Boleyn in spite of the pope's objection. The following year he asked Parliament to pass the Act of Supremacy which severed the Church of England from Rome and made the monarch of England the sole head of the English Church. The Reformation had arrived in England! Henry VIII eventually married four other women and finally got a male heir, Edward VI, from his third wife Jane Seymour. Henry died in 1547 leaving Edward, his nine-year-old son as king.

Henry had not been a theologian, although he was surrounded by those who were already influenced by the Reformation that was in full force on the Continent. The Act of Supremacy gave the king unparalleled powers to change the religious landscape in England. One event which brought social and cultural change almost immediately was the suppression of the monasteries whereby Henry ordered the monasteries closed and took possession of their vast landholdings.

The major theologian of the English Reformation was Thomas Cranmer, archbishop of Canterbury during the reigns of Henry and Edward. Through Cranmer's influence and guidance the English Church began to develop its own distinctiveness. He insisted that the Bible be translated into English and a copy placed in every church in England (the "Great Bible," 1538–1540). Cranmer became a major advisor to Edward VI and, because Edward was so young and impressionable, a considerable amount of reforms took place. Worship services in English churches began to be in English rather than Latin. Cranmer also wrote a *Book of Common Prayer* which was decidedly Protestant. The reform movement was in full force in England until Edward VI died suddenly only five years into his reign. His successor brought a screeching halt to the Protestant reformation in England.

Edward's successor was his half-sister Mary, the daughter born to Catherine of Aragon and Henry. She had grown up with an intense hatred for her father because of the embarrassment he had caused her mother and her mother's family in Spain. Mary also grew into adulthood with a strong commitment to the Roman Catholic Church. When she acceded to the throne in 1553 she was determined to return the Church of England to the Roman Catholic Church. She married Philip, who later became king of Spain, forming an alliance that gave her the political strength to carry out her aggressive efforts in England. She officially returned the Church of England to the papal fold in 1554. To make matters worse for Protestants, she began a systematic persecution throughout England of those who resisted her efforts. Many Protestants were imprisoned. A large number of Protestants fled to the Continent to Geneva and became thoroughly immersed in the reform of John Calvin. These "Marian Exiles" would later return to England and give rise to the beginning of the Puritan movement.

More than three hundred Protestants were martyred during Mary's reign, the most famous of which was Thomas Cranmer. Mary had him arrested and forced him to recant his Protestant views. In a trial in the Church of St. Mary in Oxford, he was condemned to be burned at the stake. In 1556 he was taken to the platform and before the fire was started given a chance to speak. It was expected that he would affirm his recantation and ask forgiveness for his sins. Instead, he withdrew his recantation and called the pope the Antichrist. He became one of the most important Protestant martyrs in England. Mary's persecution of Protestants was so severe that she earned the nickname "Bloody Mary."

England would probably be Roman Catholic today if Mary had lived longer. She died in 1558, however, after only five years as queen. Her successor was her half-sister Elizabeth I, the daughter of Henry and Anne Boleyn. Elizabeth came to the throne realizing that there was much political and religious instability in England. She was politically wise and understood that in order to survive she needed to forge a compromise. Her *via media* came in the form of the *39 Articles*, passed by Parliament in 1563. Elizabeth sought to steer a middle course between extreme Protestantism and Roman Catholicism. The Church of England today owes much of its distinction to Elizabeth I. She issued a new *Book of Common Prayer* and her "middle way" brought stability to England for the rest of the sixteenth century. She died in 1603 after forty-five years on the throne. Because of her, the Church of England (the "Anglican Church" in England and "Episcopal Church" in the United States) became Protestant, but not in the more aggressive style of the Protestantism in Germany and Switzerland.[3]

Radical Reformers

The Radical Reformation, embodied primarily in a group known throughout Europe as "Anabaptists," was different from the Magisterial Reformation. The Anabaptists were not as interested in "reform" of the church as they were in "restoration" of " New Testament Christianity. Therefore, they did not rely upon the magistrates to aid them in carrying out their reform movement. As a matter of fact, one of the distinguishing characteristics of the Anabaptists was their insistence upon complete separation of the institution of the church from the institution of the state.

The Anabaptist movement began in Zurich, Switzerland. Several of Ulrich Zwingli's students to whom he had taught Greek, began studying the

---

[3]See Peterson, *A Concise History of Christianity*, 219-24.

New Testament closely, especially on the topic of baptism and discovered that infant baptism is never mentioned in the New Testament. What they found was that the New Testament model of baptism is "believer's baptism," the idea that a person should make a personal faith commitment to Christ and then be baptized as a symbol of that commitment. Infant baptism as a practice developed in the early centuries of Christian history and represented a diversion from the true New Testament pattern. Convinced that the proper understanding of baptism must be recovered, about a dozen men came to the home of Felix Manz on the evening of 21 January 1525. According to an eyewitness account, Conrad Grebel baptized George Blaurock, who in turn baptized Grebel and the others present. This marks the birth of the Anabaptist movement.[4] The name "Anabaptist" was assigned to this group by its enemies as a term of derision. It is formed from the Greek prefix *ana* meaning "re" or "again," and *baptizo* meaning to immerse (baptize) in water. Therefore, the Anabaptists were the "rebaptizers."

As the message of Anabaptism spread, the movement grew in number. As the numbers increased, both Protestant and Catholic leaders became concerned. From the perspective of both Roman Catholicism and other Protestant leaders, Anabaptism was a radical movement and a dangerous threat to a well-ordered society. Because there was complete union between church and state in Europe in the sixteenth century, when a child was baptized shortly after birth, the record of that baptism in the parish church served as the record of that child's citizenship in the State. Therefore, rejection of one's infant baptism was tantamount to rejecting citizenship. Their enemies believed that the order of society could be disrupted if such a movement were allowed to continue. Consequently, the Anabaptists became targets for persecution from Catholics, Lutherans, and the followers of the Swiss Reformers alike. Some historians estimate that tens of thousands lost their lives holding to their Anabaptist convictions. Interestingly, the more the movement was persecuted, the larger it grew in Europe.

The Anabaptist vision of the church was very different from that of the Magisterial Reformers in several areas. In addition to different views of baptism (Luther, Zwingli, and Calvin retained the practice of infant

---

[4]For a good discussion of the beginnings of Anabaptism see William R. Estep, *The Anabaptist Story. An Introduction to Sixteenth-Century Anabaptism*, 3rd ed. rev. and enl. (Grand Rapids MI: Eerdmans, 1996) 10-11.

baptism), the Anabaptists had an entirely new concept of the nature of the church. The Magisterial Reformers (and Roman Catholicism for that matter) considered every member of society to be a member of the church. Infant baptism tied it all together. But the Anabaptists believed that only those who have had a personal faith experience with Christ can be members of the church. Baptism served as the outward symbol of a person's Christian rebirth and their becoming a part of the church.

Discipleship was another area where the Anabaptists differed from the Magisterial Reformers. Anabaptists believed that human beings have a free will to follow Christ. They placed a great emphasis on the Sermon on the Mount and the importance of following the commands of Jesus literally. Luther and the other Magisterial Reformers placed most of their emphasis on the conversion experience and forgiveness of sin. The emphasis on discipleship and following the teachings of Jesus literally led the Anabaptists to such views as pacifism (Jesus' was arrested in the Garden of Gethsemane and refused to fight) and refusal to swear oaths in court (Jesus commanded against swearing oaths in the Sermon on the Mount). This in turn led to more persecution and suspicion for their rejection of military service and swearing oaths.

The Anabaptists also believed that the church should be entirely separate from the state. In fact, they were one of the first groups in history to argue for separation of church and state. So extreme were they in this position that they refused to allow their members to serve in secular government positions. Furthermore, the Anabaptists tended to live in communities separate from society in general. Some of this may have been due to the persecution they received. Nevertheless, a strong sense of community existed among the Anabaptists who valued their fellowship with one another. This sense of community provided comfort and strength during times of persecution.

A group of Anabaptist extremists in the German city of Münster in 1533 forever tarnished the reputation of the Anabaptists in Europe. Led by Jan Matthys, these fanatics believed that they could establish the Kingdom of God in the city. They captured control of the city and held it for two years. They also introduced the practice of polygamy and other sordid practices. Finally, their grasp on the city was broken and the leaders of the group were arrested and executed. But the memory of Münster would taint the name "Anabaptist" for centuries to come. It has only been in the last century that historians have begun to see the movement for its value as a legitimate part of the sixteenth-century Reformation. Today, the descendants of the Anabaptists are found in groups such as the Mennonites, Amish, and Hutterites. Although these groups are different from one another, they owe their heritage to the Anabaptists of the sixteenth century.

Balthasar Hubmaier, from the frontispiece to *Balthasar Hubmaier*, trans. and ed. by H. Wayne Pipkin and John H. Yoder (Scottdale PA: Herald Press, 1989) and used by permission.

The Roman Catholic Reform

One of the frequently forgotten aspects of the Reformation of the sixteenth century is the fact that the Roman Catholic Church, though staunchly opposed to Protestantism, did in fact undergo a spiritual reform. The Roman Catholic Reform of the sixteenth century can be seen in a variety of movements within the Church. There were spiritual renewal movements led by groups such as the Oratory of Divine Love, founded in 1517 in Rome. Spiritual renewal also came through mystics such as Saint Teresa of Avila (1515–1582) and Saint John of the Cross (1542–1591), both of whom wrote of their mystical experiences with God.

One of the most important events to bring about reform in the Roman Catholic Church of the sixteenth century was the founding of a new monastic order called the Society of Jesus or "Jesuits." The founder was Ignatius Loyola (1491–1556). Loyola was born in Spain into a wealthy family. He became involved in the military and was wounded in battle with the French. During his long recovery he began reading certain types of devotional literature. He reported that one night he had a vision of the Virgin Mary and the Christ Child. This experience led to a profound conversion in which he vowed to serve Christ for the rest of his life. Loyola eventually gathered a group of followers and formed a new religious order which would be intensely loyal to the pope and at his disposal anywhere in the world. The pope granted his blessing to the new order in 1540 and the Society of Jesus was born. Loyola became the author of a famous devotional book called simply *Spiritual Exercises* which served as a guide to spirituality for the Jesuits.

The Jesuits soon became famous throughout the world for two things. First, they were devoted to education. Many Jesuits serve as teachers and Jesuit schools are some of the best in the world. Second, Jesuits are famous for their missionary activity. They heroically carried the Gospel to other parts of the world where many from Europe dared not go. The Society of Jesus remains an active, important monastic order in the Roman Catholic Church almost five centuries after its founding.

A second major event which brought reform to the Roman Catholic Church was the Council of Trent which met sporadically from 1545 to 1563. The council met for the purpose of addressing questions raised by Protestants. Had moderates in the Church been stronger, the Council might have made it possible to win back many of the Protestants. But the Council of Trent was dominated by conservatives and any hope of reunion between Catholics and Protestants was lost forever.

Doctrinally, the Council of Trent rejected almost all of the important Protestant developments and ideas. While it did affirm the doctrine of justification by faith, so important to Luther's thought, it said that faith must always be accompanied by good works. It also established the "twin towers" of authority making the Bible and tradition equal in their authority over Christians. It declared that the Latin Vulgate was the official Bible of the Church. The council upheld papal authority and declared the seven sacraments as administered by the Church to be the means by which the grace of God comes to humans. The Council also reaffirmed the doctrine of transubstantiation and that Latin was to be the language of the Mass.

The Aftermath of the Reformation

The Council of Trent made any hope of reunion between Catholics and Protestants impossible. For thirty years (1618–1648) Europe was torn apart by wars between Catholic and Protestant factions. Finally, the Peace of Westphalia (1648) ended this bitter period of warfare.

Protestantism continued to grow in many places throughout Europe. Following the sixteenth century there were now three major divisions in Christianity: Roman Catholicism, Protestantism, and Eastern Orthodoxy. Protestantism established itself around three major ideas. First, all Protestants agreed that Scripture alone (*sola scriptura*) was the only source of spiritual authority. This made it distinct from both Catholicism and Orthodoxy which taught that tradition was equal to Scripture in authority. Second, Protestants taught that salvation comes by faith alone (*sola fide*) and not through any kind of human works. Third, Protestants introduced a new doctrine into Christianity, the doctrine of the "priesthood of the believer." This doctrine involved three things: the believer has a direct relationship with God and does not need an intermediary such as a priest; the believer has the ability through the guidance of the Holy Spirit to interpret Scripture for her/himself; and believers are ministers to one another, thereby blurring the lines of distinction somewhat between clergy and laity.

After fifteen hundred years, Christianity had grown from the simple faith of the disciples of Jesus to being a major world religion. For the next 500 years Christians would continue to create diverse ways to practice Christian religion. The story of Christianity in the modern era is the topic to which we now turn.

Modern Christianity

The birth of "Protestantism" during the Reformation era established an entirely new branch of Christianity with new expressions of Christianity and new ways to live out the Christian life. During the modern era, Protestantism continued to evolve into diverse denominations and groupings of Christians.

The Seventeenth Century

The seventeenth century began with war between Catholics and Protestants in Germany. The two sides battled one another sporadically for three decades. The Peace of Westphalia in 1648 formally marked the end of the war with a treaty guaranteeing religious freedom for Catholics, Lutherans, and Calvinists. One might say that the Peace of Westphalia brought an end to the Reformation era and the beginning of the modern era. Unfortunately, freedom was not granted to the Anabaptists. They continued to be harassed and persecuted by both Protestants and Catholics for years to come.

The Enlightenment. One of the most significant movements to impact Christianity in the seventeenth century was the Enlightenment. Enlightenment thinkers began to stress the importance of human reason and autonomy, which eventually led to challenges to the Church's authority and new ways of interpreting Christianity. The Enlightenment thinkers generally had two presuppositions. First, they believed the world was created like a machine which functions according to "natural laws," such as the law of gravity. Isaac Newton, whose experiments demonstrated the law of gravity, believed that the order of the universe proved the existence of God. Second, Enlightenment thinkers believed in the importance of human reason. They held that through reason, along with observation of the universe and experimentation, ultimate truth could be discovered. Truth is not so much "revealed" by God but instead discovered through the power of human reason.

Lord Herbert of Cherbury was an early Enlightenment thinker who attempted to blend together religion and enlightenment rationalism. He is usually considered the father of Deism, which could be considered the religion of Enlightenment thinkers. In his famous book, *On the Truth* (1624), Herbert held that there were five natural laws of religion that can be discovered through reason. (1) There is a God; (2) God should be worshiped; (3) the primary expression of worship should be a virtuous life; (4) humans have a duty to repent from sin; (5) there is an afterlife where deeds will be judged.[1]

Influenced by Herbert of Cherbury, Deists developed a way of viewing Christianity that placed complete emphasis on human reason. The only expression of Christianity that had any value was a Christianity that could be proven to be rational. They affirmed that God created the universe and that it was a perfect creation, but the universe was created to operate on natural laws. They believed that God never intervened in the universe through "miracles" which requires a suspension of the laws of nature. For God to interfere in the universe would be tantamount to admitting that the world was not perfect, and it was unreasonable to assume that a perfect God would create an imperfect universe. Deists also denied the Trinity and regarded Jesus as a human being only instead of the traditional understanding of Jesus as both God and man. They placed a great emphasis on the moral teachings of Jesus. Finally, Deists rejected the divine inspiration of the Bible.

Puritanism. Another important movement that developed in the seventeenth century was Puritanism. In some ways, Puritanism was the seventeenth-century continuation of the English Reformation from the sixteenth century. As we saw in the previous chapter, following the death of Henry VIII's son Edward VI, Henry's daughter Mary came to the throne and sought to return the Church of England to the Roman Catholic fold. She persecuted Protestants causing many to flee from England to Europe where they could worship unhindered. Many of these "Marian Exiles" ended up in Geneva and were greatly influenced by John Calvin's teachings and his ideas of a theocratic society.

When Elizabeth I came to the throne of England, many of the English Protestants returned from Europe expecting Elizabeth to hasten a return of the Church of England to a Protestant trajectory. Unfortunately for them, she crafted a *via media* between Catholicism and Protestantism. These returning Protestants, now thoroughly imbued with Calvin's reforming ideas, became frustrated that Elizabeth was not "purifying" the Church

---

[1]Herbert, Edward," *The Oxford Dictionary of the Christian Church*, ed. F. L. Cross, 3rd ed. ed. E. A. Livingstone (Oxford UK: Oxford University Press, 1997) 756b-57a.

enough. This desire to purge the Church of anything that resembled Roman Catholic practices gave them the name "Puritan."

Many Puritans stayed within the Church of England hoping that gradually the Church would be further reformed. But, in the early decades of the seventeenth century following the death of Elizabeth I, the Puritans found themselves to be the targets of persecution. Many journeyed to America where they established a colony in Massachusetts Bay. This became one of the most productive colonies in the New World. From the influence of John Calvin they sought to implement a theocracy in Massachusetts Bay calling the colony a "city set on a hill." But, by the beginning of the eighteenth century, the colony had lost much of its spiritual vitality and Puritanism was relatively dead in Massachusetts Bay.

Some Puritans became so frustrated by the lack of significant reform that they began to separate and establish their own autonomous churches. These "Separatists" were much more radical in their reform goals and less patient in their ability to work within the Church of England. One group of Separatists led by John Smyth left England for Holland where they could worship in freedom. When they arrived in Holland they were befriended by a group of Mennonites. Eventually, Smyth became convinced of the importance of "believers' baptism." He proceeded to baptize himself and then the members of his congregation in 1609, thereby becoming the first "Baptist" church. Three years later in 1612 the congregation split and a group led by Thomas Helwys returned to England establishing in London the first Baptist church on English soil.

Arminianism. The seventeenth century also saw the birth of "Arminianism" as a response of opposition to the theology of John Calvin which had developed a strong following. During the last half of the sixteenth century, following his death, Calvin's theology became highly systematized by his later adherents. This rigid Calvinism eventually drew a response from Jacob Arminius of Holland, who disagreed with the way that Calvin's theology was being portrayed. Favoring a significant role of human free will, he began to lecture against Calvin's concept of predestination. The lectures led to a national controversy in Holland. Arminius died in 1609 and following his death his followers issued a document called the *Remonstrance* (1610). It stated the "Arminian" position in five articles, each disagreeing with the major points of Calvinism.

The controversy became so heated that the Calvinists met together in the city of Dort. The Synod of Dort, as the meeting came to be called, met from 1618 to 1619. The Calvinists condemned the theology of Arminius and issued five statements in response to the Arminian points. This gave rise to "five-point Calvinism," mentioned in the previous chapter with the acrostic TULIP.

For centuries, the Calvinism/Arminianism debate has raged among Protestant Christians. Several Protestant denominations have their roots in these two theological viewpoints. For example, Presbyterianism is rooted in the theology of Calvinism and is based on the "Westminster Confession," which was written by English Calvinists in 1646. On the other hand, John Wesley, a thoroughgoing Arminian and critic of Calvinism, founded the Methodist denomination giving it a strong Arminian focus theologically.

The Eighteenth Century

There were three important movements in the eighteenth century, all related to one another, and all "evangelical" in nature. By "evangelical" it is understood that all three of these movements emphasized a personal faith experience in Christ. These three movements were responses to the rationalism that developed in Protestant circles during the sixteenth and seventeenth centuries and tended to emphasize the importance of emotion in the Christian experience.

Pietism. The first of the eighteenth century evangelical movements is Pietism. It began in Germany toward the end of the seventeenth century with the preaching and writing of Philip Jacob Spener (1635–1705). Spener was a Lutheran pastor who underwent a personal conversion experience and eventually came to the conclusion that all the Lutheran churches in Germany were in need of an evangelical awakening. He organized the *Collegia Pietatis* which met in his home twice each week for prayer and Bible study. He also wrote a book called entitled *Pia Desideria,* which explained his Pietist ideas and became immensely popular. Because of its popularity *Pia Desideria* became a major primary source for Pietism in Germany.

Another important advocate of Pietism was August Hermann Francke (1663–1727). Influenced by Spener, he became an advocate of Pietism. In 1695 he became a professor at the University of Halle which, because of his presence on the faculty, became a center for Pietism in Germany. He also served as pastor of a congregation in Halle where he devoted himself to the practice and promotion of Pietism. The University of Halle also developed a commitment to missions during the eighteenth century. From Halle came sixty missionaries sent to foreign countries to spread the Christian faith.[2]

One student educated at Halle was Count Nicolaus von Zinzendorf (1700–1760). Zinzendorf was from a wealthy, pietistic family. In 1722 he began to use one part of his land as a shelter to a group of refugees from Bohemia who were escaping persecution. He organized these refugees into a community, which attempted to live according to the ideas of Pietism as Zinzendorf had learned at Halle. The community eventually called itself "Moravian Brethren," and developing an intense missionary zeal, they began sending missionaries to other countries.

Methodism. The principles of Pietism eventually came to the British Isles through the influence of the Moravians on John Wesley (1703–1791). Wesley was born into a very large family; he was the fifteenth child. He enrolled at Oxford and became involved with several student colleagues in a group they called the "Holy Club." Their desire was to devote themselves to prayer, Bible study and Christian service. Soon, their friends gave them the nickname "Methodists" because of their discipline and methodical attention to various devotional practices such as prayer and Bible study.

Wesley graduated from Oxford and in 1735, along with his brother Charles, set sail for the colony of Georgia to do mission work. On the journey across the ocean from England to Georgia, the ship was caught in a ferocious storm. Wesley feared for his life but noticed that a group of Moravians on board was peaceful and content in the midst of such impending peril. Seeing the calmness of the Moravians and recognizing his own terror during this storm intrigued Wesley who began a process of spiritual introspection. His central concern was whether or not there was more to the Christian experience than simply practicing the disciplines of the faith such as prayer, Bible study, and caring for the poor.

Wesley's work in Georgia did not progress very well. Following a failed romance which impacted his work in the church he served, Wesley decided to return to England. Upon his return, his mission failure, coupled with his inward spiritual struggle, led him to seek out the Moravians in England. On 24 May 1738 while attending a Moravian worship service on Aldersgate Street in London, Wesley experienced his faith in a way different than he had ever experienced before. In his journal he wrote, "I felt my heart strangely warmed."[3]

---

[2]Peterson, *A Concise History of Christianity*, 261.

[3]Wesley, *Journal*, 24 May 1738; cited by Gonzalez, *The Story of Christianity*

Susanna Wesley, mother of John Wesley who may have had more impact on his life than anyone else. She was the mother of nineteen children, eight of whom died in infancy. She was a strong disciplinarian and believed that all her children should be educated. From the Drew University Library collection. Used by permission.

With a new outlook toward his faith, Wesley began to preach the importance of a personal conversion experience within the Church of England. Gradually, the churches began to close their doors to him so he took to preaching in the fields. He rode thousands of miles on horseback to preach all over England. He organized a system of lay-ministers to do follow-up for his evangelism. Although Wesley desired that the movement remain within the Church of England, it eventually became separated and took the name Methodism. Methodism also made its way to the American Colonies where it achieved great success largely due to the efforts of Francis Asbury (1745–1816) who had been sent to America by Wesley for the purpose of organizing the movement there. Asbury eventually became one of the first Methodist bishops in America.

The First Great Awakening. The American Colonies served as the setting for the third eighteenth century evangelical movement. The First Great Awakening, as it is frequently called, was a series of revivals of religion which occurred in the American Colonies during the middle decades of the eighteenth century. By the beginning of the eighteenth

2:212.

century, religion was at low ebb in the Colonies. Puritanism, so prevalent in New England during the early seventeenth century, was essentially dead as a movement. A Dutch Reformed pastor in New York, Theodore Frelinghausen, who was influenced by German Pietism, began to preach about the lack of piety in his congregation. He began to emphasize the importance of personal, heartfelt faith. This emphasis on Pietism and personal conversion led to an outbreak of revival in his church which spread to the other Middle Colonies. Frelinghausen is usually regarded as the initiator of the First Great Awakening in the American Colonies and provides the connection between this movement and Pietism in Germany.

One of the most important figures of the First Great Awakening was Jonathan Edwards. Edwards was educated at Yale College and served as pastor of a Congregational Church in Northampton, Massachusetts. He began to preach of the importance of personal piety much like Frelinghausen had earlier in New York. This led to a tremendous awakening in his congregation from 1734–1735. Edwards's writings about the revivals, especially his *A Faithful Narrative of a Surprising Work of God* (1737), serve as a theological explanation and justification of the revivals. He remains a most significant theologian from early America and is considered by many to be the major theological interpreter of the First Great Awakening. Edwards is probably remembered best for his famous sermon "Sinners in the Hands of an Angry God," preached for the first time in 1741.

Edwards's preaching was intellectually challenging with use of carefully worded manuscripts that he read to the congregation from the pulpit. By contrast, George Whitefield brought a completely different style from England to the American Colonies. Educated at Oxford and a member of the Holy Club with John Wesley, Whitefield made a total of seven preaching tours of the American Colonies, the most important of which occurred in 1740. Whitefield was a powerful preacher and his preaching attracted large numbers of people. Unlike Edwards, Whitefield often preached simple, extemporaneous sermons. Emotional excesses at some of the revivals eventually caused many of the churches to reject Whitefield's preaching. He was thereby forced to preach in open fields, where it was estimated that Whitefield preached to crowds as large as 30,000 with no voice amplification. Nicknamed the "Grand Itinerant," Whitefield was the first evangelist to capture the American public's attention and was the most important preacher of the First Great Awakening.

The First Great Awakening left a variety of permanent results on the

George Whitefield preaching in an open field. It was reported that his voice was strong enough to preach to 30,000 in an open field without amplification. From *Christian History* issue 38 (12/2): 10. Used by permission.

American religious landscape. First, the Awakening brought in large numbers of new converts to the denominations in America. The major Protestant denominations in the colonies at that time, Congregationalists, Baptists, and Presbyterians, experienced unprecedented growth as a result of the revivals. Second, the Awakening produced divisions in those same denominations. The controversial nature of the revivals with frequent emotional outbursts turned many away from supporting them. Third, the First Great Awakening underlined the importance of "voluntary" religion in America. America has never had a state church. Membership in a church is not automatic; it is voluntary. The Awakening helped to create such an environment. Fourth, as a result of the First Great Awakening, revivalism became an important characteristic of American religion. Fifth, the revivals produced new converts to the Christian faith and also many who decided to prepare for careers in ministry. This caused the birth and growth of educational institutions in the eighteenth century. Along with the spiritual awakening came many new candidates who expressed a desire to train for the ministry. Institutions such as Princeton, Brown, Rutgers, and Dartmouth were all formed in the eighteenth century due in large part to the influence of the revivals and the need to train new ministers. Sixth, the revivals left a legacy of humanitarian concern in American religion and promoted mission work among slaves as well as among the Native Americans. Finally, the First Great Awakening contributed to the growing "democratization" of American religion, creating an atmosphere whereby those who were dissatisfied with their current denominations simply left to join dissenting groups.

The Nineteenth Century

In his classic seven-volume series *A History of the Expansion of Christianity*, church historian Kenneth Scott Latourette referred to the nineteenth century as "The Great Century" and devoted three of his seven volumes to that period.[4] Indeed, there was a remarkable amount of activity and energy within the Christian religion during that century, particularly in the American context. While it would be impossible here to describe all of the important Christian movements during that century, several deserve mention.

The Second Great Awakening. One of the most important religious events in America during the early decades of the nineteenth century was the Second Great Awakening. Like the Awakening of the eighteenth century, the Second Great Awakening was a series of revivals that placed emphasis on personal piety and heartfelt devotion to God. The most important evangelist of the Second Great Awakening was Charles G. Finney. Originally planning for a career in law, Finney was converted to Christianity and felt a calling to preach. His crusades, particularly on the frontier in early nineteenth century America, were attended by large, emotional crowds. Unlike Jonathan Edwards, who believed a revival was "a surprising work of God," Finney believed that a revival was "the result of the *right* use of the appropriate means."[5] In other words, Finney believed that it was possible to *make* a revival happen by doing certain things. His "new measures," included such things as praying for the unconverted by

---

[4]Kenneth Scott Latourette, *A History of the Expansion of Christianity*, vols. 4–6 (reprint: New York: Harper & Row, 1970).

[5]Charles G. Finney, *Lectures on Revivals of Religion*, as cited by Edwin S. Gaustad, in *A Documentary History of Religion in America*, vol. 1 (Grand Rapids MI: Eerdmans, 1982) 337.

name in his services; the "anxious bench," where all of the unconverted were segregated from the other worshipers; and massive advertising before he ever came to town. Finney's "new measures" became the prototype for how evangelists would conduct revival meetings in the nineteenth and twentieth centuries.

The Second Great Awakening provided some lasting results for American Christianity such as numerical growth for certain denominations, particularly Baptists, Methodists, and Presbyterians. But, the most important lasting impact of this movement was its legacy of attention to the social evils of American society. Emphasis on temperance in alcohol use, poverty, and the abolition of slavery can be traced to the enduring effects of the Second Great Awakening.

The emphasis on personal piety in the Second Great Awakening and the success of the revivals also led many American Christians to begin looking beyond the borders of America to those in other parts of the world. The result was the birth of the modern missions movement. Two of the pioneers in the early missions movement were Adoniram and Ann Hasseltine Judson. Originally appointed by the Congregationalist denomination as missionaries to India, they became Baptists and subsequently moved their missions emphasis to Burma. By the end of the nineteenth century, American Christians were serving as missionaries not only in Burma, but also in Africa, Asia, Central and South America.

Liberalism and Fundamentalism. As the nineteenth century progressed, theologians began to look for ways that Christianity could meet the challenges of modernity. This was due in part to the popularity of Charles Darwin's *Origin of the Species* (1859) and *The Descent of Man* (1871). The response came in the form of "Liberalism," a movement which sought to reassess Christianity through the lens of modernity. One of the first to reinterpret the Christian religion in light of modern ways of looking at the world was the German theologian Friedrich Schleiermacher (1768–1834). Schleiermacher believed that the essence of Christianity was not to be found in doctrine or morals. Instead, he believed that Christianity, at its very foundation, is rooted in the feeling of absolute dependence upon God and that all Christian beliefs could ultimately be traced to that root source.

Liberalism had an impact on other concerns of Christianity as well. For example, the modern study of the Bible known as "higher criticism" was a result of Liberalism's influence as scholars began to use the same tools to study the biblical materials as were used to study other kinds of literature.

One result of this new methodolology was the Documentary Hypothesis, made famous by Julius Wellhausen (1844–1918). Wellhausen studied the Pentateuch carefully and questioned the traditional Mosaic authorship theory believing that the Pentateuch evolved over several centuries and was the work of numerous authors and editors from different historical periods in Hebrew history.

As might be expected, this new approach to scripture and theology was met with opposition in many theological circles. Fundamentalism was the movement which arose to counter Liberalism. Named after the publication of a series of articles called *The Fundamentals*, Fundamentalists argued that there were five important Christian beliefs which could not be compromised: (1) the virgin birth of Jesus; (2) the verbal/plenary inspiration of the Bible; (3) the bodily resurrection of Jesus; (4) the visible second coming of Christ; and (5) the satisfaction theory of the Atonement.[6] Fundamentalism has remained a powerful movement in Christianity to the present. Its effects can be seen in several of the major denominations in America such as Baptists, Presbyterians, and Methodists. Its influence is also seen in a growing number of nondenominational churches.

The Twentieth Century

The Social Gospel Movement. Several important movements during the twentieth century should also be highlighted. At the beginning of the century, some Christians (especially in America) became highly sensitive to the poor in society. The Industrial Revolution had created a large class of poor people, particularly immigrants in large cities, who had to endure terrible living conditions in tenement housing or unsafe, unhealthy working conditions in their employment. Walter Rauschenbusch (1861–1918) was a German Baptist pastor who served as pastor of a congregation in one of the slums of New York City called "Hell's Kitchen." There he saw poverty in some of its worst forms. It made such an impression upon him that he began writing and lecturing about ways the Christian Gospel implies that believers must work to alleviate the suffering of the poor. For Rauschen-busch, simply converting everyone to the Christian faith by evangelism

---

[6]Gleaned from R. A. Torrey and A. C. Dixon, *The Fundamentals: A Testimony to the Truth*, (Grand Rapids: Baker Book House (reprint), 1988). The "satisfaction theory of the atonement" is the belief that the death of Christ *satisfies* the wrath of God which is aimed at humans for their sinfulness.

would not take care of all of the social ills in society. He called for a more radical remedy, a transformation of the social structures of society. Rauschenbusch referred to himself as a "Christian socialist." He wanted to see a systematic redistribution of wealth in society such that the differentiation between the haves and have-nots would no longer exist. Further, he thought that government should create and enforce laws which would oblige large corporations to pay better wages and provide safer working conditions. He lobbied for laws which would make cities create better housing situations for the underprivileged. Rauschenbusch became a pioneer in what came to be known as the Social Gospel Movement. This movement remained popular for the first two or three decades of the twentieth century and was helpful in bringing about many reforms of the political and economic sectors of society.

Neoorthodoxy. Liberalism provided an optimistic outlook toward the world and humanity and was a popular movement in the closing decades of the nineteenth century and the early decades of the twentieth century. However, the horrors of World War I shattered this optimism and led theologians to reconsider Christianity once again and how it impacts the world. One of the most notable theologians of the twentieth century was Karl Barth (1886–1968). Barth precipitated a theological innovation called "Neoorthodoxy," as a reaction against Liberalism. It attempted to combine the critical study of the Bible and modern ways of viewing the Christian faith, with a strong doctrine of the reality of human sinfulness and need for salvation. Barth left an enormous impact with his thought. He was an organizer of the Confessing Church which produced the Barmen Declaration (1934) that formally opposed the Liberalism of the German Lutheran Church. Later, the Confessing Church provided a voice of dissent as other German churches capitulated to Nazism. Neoorthodoxy became the most innovative theological force in Protestantism during the middle of the twentieth century. Several other Neoorthodox voices also became important shapers of Christian thought and the reality of sin. They include Dietrich Bonhoeffer, who was executed by the Nazis as a result of his opposition to Hitler, and the Niebuhr brothers, H. Richard and Reinhold, who were important Neoorthodox voices in America.

Vatican Council II. The most important event in Roman Catholicism during the twentieth century was the convening of Vatican Council II (1962–1965), called into session by Pope John XXIII, the most progressive pope of the century. Convinced of the need for the Roman Catholic Church to open itself up to the modern world, John XXIII presided at the formal opening of the council but died before its completion. Nevertheless, Vatican II brought several important reforms to the Roman Catholic Church including the celebration of Mass in the vernacular of the people instead of Latin, and openness to dialogue with Protestants as well as religious traditions outside of Christianity.

Evangelicalism. The middle of the twentieth century saw the birth of the Evangelical movement in America which by the end of the century would be one of the strongest expressions of Christianity in America. Evangelicals were essentially as conservative as Fundamentalists theologically. They believed in the authority of the Bible and held to the notion of a personal relationship with God through Jesus Christ. However, they differed from Fundamentalists by their openness to the modern world. Fundamentalists rejected Darwin's theory of evolution, but many Evangelicals embraced it. Evangelicals were also more open to the Civil Rights Movement than many Fundamentalists as another example.

Carl F. H. Henry was one of the earliest Evangelical theologians. He founded a magazine called *Christianity Today* which highly acclaimed as being the major voice for the movement. The Reverend Billy Graham was also a famous name associated with Evangelicalism. He began work as an evangelist in 1949 with a crusade in Los Angeles which brought him immediate recognition in the press. Advisor to presidents and other international heads of state, Billy Graham was a "household name" through much of the latter half of the twentieth century.

Pentecostalism. At the end of the twentieth century one of the strongest expressions of Christianity was found in the Pentecostal movement. Participants in Pentecostalism claim to experience the presence of the Holy Spirit in the same way as the early Christians described in Acts 2. They claim that in addition to the salvation experience of God's grace, there is a "baptism of the Spirit" which is evidenced by sign gifts such as speaking in tongues (referred to as *glossolalia*). Other signs which accompany the presence of the Holy Spirit include healing and prophecy.

While the movement shares similarities with the earlier Holiness Movement such as its emphasis on the baptism of the Spirit, Pentecostalism's roots can be traced to the Azusa Street Revival in Los Angeles in 1906. Since then, the movement has grown steadily, with an explosion of growth in the last quarter of the century. For most of the century it tended to be a movement among the poor and lower classes (particularly in America); but during the last several decades it has experienced growth from both middle and upper classes.

Several features of the movement make it attractive to new converts. First, from its inception, Pentecostalism has had a tradition of racially integrated worship services and churches. While many Protestant denominations fought integration, Pentecostalism welcomed it. Second, Pentecostalism is open to women in positions of leadership within the church, including preaching and pastoral ministry, whereas some Protestant denominations are still reticent or even hostile toward women leaders. Third, Pentecostal worship services are very emotional and exciting, a feature that attracts many people.

At the end of the twentieth century Christianity was one of the largest religions in the world with almost two billion adherents. We have seen how over two millennia the religion has grown, been shaped by culture, and diversified to respond to its environment. As the twenty-first century begins there are three main branches of Christianity: Roman Catholicism, Eastern Orthodoxy, and Protestantism with varieties of expressions within those categories. Yet, there are some basic beliefs that all Christians share in common. We now turn to examine those beliefs.

* * *

Church History Suggestions for Further Reading

Ahlstrom, Sydney E. *A Religious History of the American People*. New Haven CT: Yale University Press, 1972.

Bainton, Roland H. *Christendom*. Volumes 1 and 2. New York: Harper & Row, 1964, 1966.

Bainton, Roland H. *The Reformation of the Sixteenth Century*. Enlarged edition. Boston: Beacon Press, 1985.

Cannon, William Ragsdale. *History of Christianity in the Middle Ages: From the Fall of Rome to the Fall of Constantinople*. Grand Rapids MI: Baker Book House, 1960.

Dowley, Timothy, ed. *Introduction to the History of Christianity*. Minneapolis: Fortress Press, 1995.

Gonzalez, Justo L. *The Changing Shape of Church History*. St. Louis: Chalice Press, 2002.

_____. *A History of Christian Thought*. Volumes 1, 2, and 3. Revised edition. Nashville: Abingdon Press, 1987.

_____. *The Story of Christianity*. Volumes 1 and 2. San Francisco:

HarperSanFrancisco, 1984 and 1985.

Jenkins, Philip. *The Lost History of Christianity*. New York: Harper Collins, 2008.

Latourette, Kenneth Scott. *A History of the Expansion of Christianity*. Seven volumes. New York, London: Harper & Brothers, 1937–1945; reprint: Grand Rapids MI: Zondervan, 1980.

_____. *A History of Christianity*. New York: Harper & Brothers, 1953.

_____. *A History of Christianity*. Two volumes. Revised edition. New York: Harper & Row, 1975; reprint: Peabody MA: Hendrickson, 1975.

Noll, Mark A. *A History of Christianity in the United States and Canada*. Grand Rapids MI: Eerdmans, 1993.

_____. *Turning Points: Decisive Moments in the History of Christianity*. Grand Rapids MI: Baker Book House, 1997.

Peterson, R. Dean. *A Concise History of Christianity*. Second edition. New York: Wadsworth, 1999.

Walker, Williston A. *A History of the Christian Church*. Fourth edition. Revised by David W. Lotz and Richard A. Norris. New York: Scribner's, 1985.

Ware, Timothy. *The Orthodox Church*. New edition. London: Penguin Books, 1997.

Part four

Christian Theology

• 13 •

Christian Practice and Belief

So far our introduction to Christianity has led us through the Old Testament/Hebrew Bible, the New Testament, and the history of the church. And yet you may still be wondering: But what do Christians *do*? What do Christians *believe*? We are finally in a position to answers these questions, beginning with Christian worship and practice and then moving toward belief.

Christian Worship

Sunday morning is where it all begins for most Christians. Christians typically meet together in churches to worship on Sunday, the first day of the week, because it is the day Jesus was raised from the dead. In addition to multiple times on Sundays, Roman Catholic churches offer Saturday evening Mass, usually around 5:00 or 5:30, as well as abbreviated services throughout the week (Monday through Friday).

Protestants normally begin the Sunday schedule of events around 9:30 A. M., when people meet together in small groups divided by ages or interests to study the Bible for about an hour. After small group Bible study or "Sunday School" everyone, young and old, gathers for corporate worship usually around 11:00 A. M.

If you were to randomly sample a variety of worship styles, say Roman Catholic, Eastern Orthodox, Pentecostal, Church of Christ, and Presbyterian, you would witness a vast sea of differences. You might ask, "How can all these different styles be identified with the Christian heritage? Is there anything that they all share in common?" Surprisingly, there is. Despite the enormous differences that separate one denomination's worship service from another, there are at least eight essential elements found in all Christian worship services, regardless of denomination or location.

Anytime and anywhere Christians get together for worship, music will be present. Music plays a central role in all Christian worship. From pipe organs to electric guitars, from traditional hymns to contemporary songs of praise, music is one of the most common expressions of worship for Christians. Although Church of Christ congregations forego the use of musical instruments, there is still music to be found; churches of that tradition conduct their corporate singing *a cappella* style. Church is one of the few places where people sing together as a group. Changing the style of music is often cause for the most strenuous contentions and divisions within churches, which, although it is regrettable, goes to show how important music is to people's experience of worship. The style and strength of the music will often be a deciding factor in whether or not someone will join a church.

Prayer is another essential feature of worship. Christians pray to God multiple times during a single service. Prayer is not just "filler;" it is not a momentary break in the action. Prayer lifts the soul to God. Worship connects our hearts with God and in prayer we speak directly to God, so prayer is, properly considered, the heart of worship.

Christian worship is also centered around the Bible. A third characteristic of all Sunday morning services is the reading of Scripture. Passages of Scripture are regularly read aloud; sometimes multiple selections are read from the Old Testament, New Testament, and the Gospels. Christians are people of the Book. Not only is the Bible read, a minister, priest, or pastor will take time in the service to expound upon a passage of Scripture, to interpret, apply, and proclaim it for today's listeners. Thus, a fourth mark of Christian worship is the message or sermon or homily. For many Protestant denominations, preaching the sermon, or delivering the Word, constitutes the high point of the service. This becomes visually evident by the location of the pulpit—often front and center on the platform.

The collection of tithes and offerings is a fifth common characteristic of Christian worship. At some point and in some manner, the people will be given an opportunity to give back in the form of offering a portion of their income to God and the church. Of course, there is the practical necessity of supporting the church so that the electric bills and other expense can be paid. But Christians give primarily out of a sense of obedience to God and gratitude for God's gifts and blessings. It is an act of worship. The idea of tithe, or giving a "tenth" of one's income, comes from Scripture (Leviticus 27:30 and Malachi 3:10, for instance) and has become a general rule of thumb for Christian giving.

In addition to these five essential elements, we should add a sixth umbrella component: liturgy. Liturgy refers to those corporate ceremonies, recitations, and rituals that help stabilize the worship service on a week to week basis. An example of liturgy might be reciting the Lord's Prayer, the Apostles' Creed, the Nicene Creed, or the Doxology (which is sung usually after the offering is collected). Other liturgies might involve the minister saying "The Lord be with you," to which the congregation responds, "And also with you." Sometimes after Scripture is read, the reader will conclude by saying, "This is the Word of the Lord" to which the congregation responds, "Thanks be to God." In some churches, the members are every Sunday asked to "Pass the Peace" which means they turn and greet people around them in the name of the Lord. Liturgy can include how and which candles are lit, the recognition and celebration of certain holy days (which we will address later), and even the colors that ministers and choir members wear at certain times of the year. These and other practices may or may not be spelled out in an order of worship. Some are unwritten patterns or traditional recitations. Liturgy refers to a whole complex of purposed and tradition-guided activities. Some church services are more "liturgical" than others, but all services participate in some form of liturgy, whether they call it that or not.

Many Christian services offer Communion or Lord's Supper weekly. In Roman Catholic and Orthodox services, the Communion or Mass, not the minister's message, is the high point of the service. We will list it as the seventh common element of Christian worship. We need to understand, however, that not every church does it every Sunday; some churches perform Communion once per month or once every quarter. Nevertheless, for all Christian churches and denominations, it is a very important and hallowed act.

The Communion event is highly charged with meaning. It involves the communal eating of wafers or bread and the drinking of wine or grape juice and the minister reading some variation of these words from Scripture:

> [T]he Lord Jesus on the night when he was betrayed took a loaf of bread, and when he had given thanks, he broke it and said, 'This is my body that is for you. Do this in remembrance of me.' In the same way he took the cup also, after supper, saying, 'This cup is the new covenant in my blood. Do this, as often as you drink it, in remembrance of me.' For as often as you eat this bread and drink the cup, you proclaim the Lord's death until he comes.   (1 Cor 11:23-26)[1]

The eating of bread that represents flesh and drinking the cup that

---

[1]Matt 26:26-29, Mark 14:22-25; Luke 22:17-20 and John 6:51-58 also record the event.

represents blood is surely the most mystery laden ritual that the church performs. The depth of its symbolism cannot be fully explored here. But we can summarize the main significance by looking at the three names by which it is called: Lord's Supper, Communion, and Eucharist. Each of these names provides a glimpse into the richness of the event's meaning:[2]

Breaking the Bread and Passing the Cup

The Lord's Supper. This title brings to mind the last meal that Jesus shared with his disciples in which he called the bread and wine his own body and blood to be poured out for humanity (Luke 22:20). So, the event is a memorial, but it is also a *supper* in the sense that it is nourishment, physically and spiritually. We consume the elements so as to remind ourselves that we do not live by bread alone (Matt 4:4), but are sustained and nourished by the Lord himself, his Spirit and his Word.

Holy Communion. To call it Communion is to emphasize the communal nature of this act; we eat and drink together, not alone. Almost nothing is more powerful for building friendship than the simple act of eating together. We are made friends with God and our fellow believers in this meal. We are bound in a community of faith with God and in a living community with one another. 1 Corinthians 10:16 asks, "The cup of blessing that we bless, is it not a sharing in the blood of Christ? The bread that we break, is it not a sharing in the body of Christ?" We are united in relationship with Christ through his sufferings remembered in the cup and loaf. The next verse adds, "Because there is one bread, we who are many are one body, for we all partake of the one bread." Through our relationship with Christ, we are united to one another when we share the bread and the cup.

Eucharist. Literally, "thanksgiving." Partaking in the meal is an act of gratitude to God for giving us new life through Christ's gift of his life for our sakes. As we eat the bread of Christ's body and drink the cup of Christ's blood, we directly confront the sobering sacrifice of the cross. One cannot help but eat in a spirit of humility and thankfulness.

Baptism is the other major mystery-laden tradition that should be mentioned in conjunction with the Lord's Supper. Jesus himself was baptized

---

[2]Michael Jinkins, *Invitation to Theology* (Downers Grove IL: InterVarsity Press, 2001) 240-41.

and commanded that his disciples be baptized "in the name of the Father and of the Son and of the Holy Spirit" (Matt 28:19) as a way of demonstrating that they have been buried with Christ in death and raised to walk in the newness of life (Rom 6:3-4, Col 2:12). Baptism, a word which is derived from the Greek term "to wash," is the initiation rite into the family of faith. As such, it is our eighth common element of Christian worship.

A sizeable disagreement has emerged over how exactly this initiation should be performed and what it should mean. Many Christians (including Roman Catholics, the Orthodox, and Protestants) practice "infant baptism" as a way of inducting babies into the family of faith, committing the child to God and to God's people, and for "the remission of sin." In this tradition, which goes back to the very early church, baptism is seen as a *necessary part of* the salvation process. Those who practice "believer's baptism," by contrast, view the act not as a necessity of salvation, but as a *sign of* salvation. It is a sign of the faith commitment one has already made. Thus, it should not be performed upon infants, who have no choice in the matter. It should be reserved for those who have consciously made a decision for Christ and willingly submit to baptism as believers. Generally, believer's baptism is performed by immersion, or dunking, whereas infant baptism is generally performed by effusion, or sprinkling, so as not to submerge the baby completely under water. The irony of the debate between infant baptism and believer's baptism is that those who practice infant baptism require that the individual, upon entering adulthood, publicly confirm the faith into which he or she was baptized and those who practice believer's baptism perform baby dedications in which the baby is prayed over and the parents are charged to rear the child in "the admonition of the Lord." Although there are real differences between the two traditions, both provide means for the church to be involved at the birth of a child and at the transition into adulthood.

Communion and baptism are called "ordinances" or "sacraments." An ordinance is another word for a commandment. Christ commanded that his followers should baptize one another and remember his death in the memorial meal (Matt 28:19, 1 Cor 11:23). He instituted the ordinances of baptism and Communion. Alternatively, it can be said that these two symbolic acts are sacraments. "Sacrament" comes from a Latin word that had multiple connotations: "ritual," "symbol," and even "mystery."[3] The

---

[3]Bernard Cooke and Gary Macy, *Christian Symbol and Ritual* (New York:

language of sacrament today expresses the fact that these acts are more than human inventions; they are means of God's mysterious and gracious involvement in our lives. Baptism and Communion, among other activities and events within the church, are ways that the presence of God is mediated to the faithful.

Major Days/Dates in the Christian Calendar

Christians begin their weeks by coming together for worship. So, there is a weekly rhythm of Christian practice. There is also a broader calendar that Christians have traditionally observed. To a greater or lesser extent, Christians recognize the following festivals and days of commemoration throughout the year.

Advent. Literally "the coming or arrival" of Christ, Advent prepares for the birth of Jesus. It begins on the fourth Sunday before Christmas. This special time leading up to Christmas is marked by the lighting of the Advent candles, decorations in the sanctuary, special music, readings, and traditions.

Christmas Day. If we can push past Mr. and Mrs. Claus, the elves, ribbons, lights, stockings, trees, and so on, we find that Christmas is a celebration of Jesus being born in a manger in Bethlehem. Christians sing familiar carols and meet for worship, often on the evening of December 24th as well as on the 25th.

Epiphany. On January 6th Christians commemorate the arrival of the wise men from the east who came looking for a newborn king and were led to him by a bright star. They brought Jesus gifts of gold, frankincense and myrrh. Epiphany means "the appearance."

Ash Wednesday. This day begins the season of Lent. In many churches, people come forward to be marked with ashes, an ancient symbol of sorrow and repentance. The day before Ash Wednesday is Mardi gras, or "Fat Tuesday." Final splurges and festivities are enjoyed before the start of Lent.

Lent. Forty days of fasting and devotion leading up to Easter. Those who practice Lent give up luxuries, typically in the form of foods—meat, eggs, milk, chocolate, and such—so that their thoughts and desires might be directed away from fleshly cravings and towards prayer, good works,

---

Oxford University Press, 2005) 38.

contemplation, and Scripture reading.

Palm Sunday. Christians recall Jesus' entry into Jerusalem during the last week of his life, when people welcomed him to the city by waving palms and laying them in his path. Palm Sunday is usually in late March and marks the beginning of Holy Week.

Holy Week. Also called *Passion Week*, the last week of Jesus' earthly life is marked by a number of events. Special days of this week include Maundy Thursday, when Jesus shared the last supper with his disciples and instituted the remembrance of that meal in celebration of the Lord's Supper or Communion. The word "Maundy" comes from the old English word for "commandment." It is a reference to Jesus' "new commandment" given at the last meal for the disciples to love one another. Good Friday solemnly remembers the day Jesus suffered crucifixion. Holy Saturday hallows the day the Son of God lay dead in the tomb. The start of Holy Week is one week before Easter.

Easter Sunday. Usually falling in late March or April, Easter Sunday celebrates the disciples' discovery that Jesus had been raised from the dead and was alive. Death was not the end of God's Son. Many churches keep vigils throughout Saturday night or hold sunrise services on Easter morning. The day is greeted with special worship celebrations, family meals, and in some older traditions, the exchange of flowers and eggs.

Ascension Day. This day commemorates Jesus being lifted up to heaven forty days after Easter Day.

Pentecost. When Jesus left his disciples for the last time after his resurrection, he promised them that his spirit would return to them and empower them. Pentecost celebrates the coming of the Holy Spirit upon the disciples. It falls on the seventh Sunday after Easter.

Trinity Sunday. On the first Sunday after Pentecost Christians in worship reflect on the triune God who is Father, Son, and Spirit. Typically, churches recite the Nicene Creed.

Ordinary Time. The term "ordinary" is derived from the word "ordinal" or numbered, numbering the Sundays between Epiphany and Ash Wednesday and then between Trinity Sunday and the first Sunday of Advent, by far the longest stretch of the church calendar. Ordinary Time is punctuated by minor feasts and saints days.

All Saints Day. The day before All Saints Day, "All Saints Eve," "All Hallows Eve" or "Halloween," has long overshadowed the day of commemoration it precedes. Nevertheless, November 1 remains a day of obligation in the Roman Catholic Church and a "major feast" in many

Protestant calendars. Christians remember saints both known and unknown on this day.

Christian Beliefs

We have briefly outlined some of the major features of Christian worship. Whenever we pause to think about what we are doing in worship and the beliefs that motivate our actions, we are doing theology. The root meaning of the word *theology* is "the study of God." Usually, knowing the root sense of a word is of great value, but in this case the utility is limited. How would one go about a "study" of God? Would you take notes while looking through a telescope? Of course, Christians study *the Bible* to know about God. But then are we studying a book, and not really God? And, are we studying "God" in general? Or does "the study of God" involve a specific God, to the exclusion of other gods? And is the study only of God? What about family, self, church, the earth? Are those things not relevant to theology?

The study of God really begins when we reflect on faith, practice, and worship. More particularly, theology involves clarifying and investigating our *convictions* about God, the world, and life. Convictions are at the core of our theology. If theology is about clarifying convictions, then we need first to know what convictions are. James McClendon, a recently deceased Baptist theologian formerly affiliated with Fuller Theological Seminary, and James Smith, a self-professed "secular atheist" philosopher, collaborated in the early seventies to study "convictions." McClendon and Smith asserted that convictions are central features of personal identity and that they can be defined as beliefs so persistent and so deep-rooted that to change them would change one's identity.[4] They are beliefs so central that to alter them would alter who you are. These kinds of beliefs are not like opinions, as in "I believe it might rain today." When the Christian says "I believe in God" she is not expressing an opinion about whether or not God exists, she is promising her mind, heart, soul and body to God.

A conviction calls out who we really are. In this sense a conviction indicates something performative, not academic. It is an *act* of faith, a

---

[4]James McClendon and James Smith, *Convictions: Diffusing Religious Relativism*, rev. ed. (Valley Forge PA: Trinity Press International, 1994) 5.

promise of fidelity, a *pledge* of allegiance.[5] At a wedding, the bride and groom are asked to take vows to have, to hold, and to cherish. These are not mere words; they are a binding act, a covenant. So also, one's conviction about God is not a mere intellectual conclusion, but a vow, an act of commitment, a binding of the self to another. Convictions name who we are, where we align our fortunes, and what we define our lives by—convictions name core identities.

Just as a person can be convicted of a crime, proven beyond a shadow of doubt to be guilty, so there are certain beliefs every person is convicted of and cannot simply give up or deny. Now a criminal can have his conviction reversed, but in doing so he also experiences a transformation of identity. No longer a criminal, confined to a cell and a serial number, the person is set free, declared innocent, and made "a new man." So also when someone "converts" to Christianity by repenting and accepting God's forgiveness in Christ, he or she also undergoes a change of conviction which produces a radical change in identity—the person is made a disciple, a baptized Christian. Convictions can change, but when they do, people change. This is the experience of conversion, to be changed from the inside out.

One other feature of convictions should not be overlooked: convictions are communal. Opinions may be your own, but convictions are shared. Convictions are not private possessions, although they can be deeply held by individuals. They come instead in communities and in conversation with broad and long traditions. When we say we believe in Jesus, we are affirming a Christian conviction, not a personal opinion; when we make faith in Jesus our own we are identifying with the greater Christian tradition and community. Conversion is not a private act. It might be personal, but not private—there is a difference. Whereas privately held opinions or beliefs tend to isolate us from one another ("You have your opinion and I have mine"), Christian convictions draw us together. We are brothers and sisters in the faith, believing in "one Lord, one faith, one baptism, one God and Father of us all, who is above all and through all and in all" (Eph 4:5-6). Professions of faith in Christ are made public in a church service; one must stand before the whole church and acknowledge Christ as Lord. And then one must be publicly baptized as a sign and enactment of that profession.

Christians share a common faith, but naming and talking about the

---

[5]Nicholas Lash, *Believing Three Ways in One God* (Notre Dame IN: University of Notre Dame Press, 1993) 18.

convictions of that faith is not an easy or risk-free task. Theology is concerned with identifying and reflecting upon our convictions, our core beliefs. Some of our core beliefs may be explicitly religious, others may not. All are included in theological reflection. As God is the creator of all and is concerned about all areas of our lives, so theology is concerned not just with those things we typically call "religious," but with all of life. Theology, then, is not about abstract ideas and arguments, but about core convictions—about *life* and how life answers to God.

Theology helps us to state clearly what we believe about God, life, purpose, and reality. In early Christianity, this task was often performed by creeds or "rules of faith." "Creed" is a term that has developed a bad reputation among some people. Critics see creeds as an exercise in authoritarianism—creeds present things to be saluted without question or discussion. But the word "creed" comes from *credo*, Latin for "I believe." A creed, in the plainest sense, is nothing more than a statement of one's beliefs, or better, it is a statement of a community's convictions. It gets at the core identity and tradition of a people in a simple and straightforward way. Of course, one could object to creeds by saying, "If you want to know what Christians believe, just read the Bible." But the Bible is a really big book! And, the Bible itself contains multiple summaries of beliefs and important statements of conviction. Examples might include Deuteronomy 6:4 "Hear, O Israel: the Lord our God, the Lord is one;" Peter's confession at Caesarea Philippi recorded in Matthew 16:16-8 and Mark 8:29, "You are the Christ, the Son of the living God;" the bold pronouncement of 1 Corinthians 8:5-6, "There is one God, the Father, from whom are all things, and for whom we exist, and one Lord, Jesus Christ, through whom are all things and through whom we exist." Other instances of summary statements or creedal affirmations include Philippians 2:6-11, too lengthy to quote in full here and 1 Timothy 2:5-6, "There is one God; there is also one mediator between God and humankind, Christ Jesus, himself human, who gave himself a ransom for all."[6]

Keeping these key scriptural statements in mind and reading the Scriptures as a whole, Christians have often summarized the basic story line and salvation message of the Bible in definitive statements of belief. One of the

---

[6]For further discussion on these key statements in the Bible, see Jaroslav Pelikan, *Credo: Historical and Theological Guide to Creeds and Confessions of Faith in the Christian Tradition* (New Haven CT: Yale University Press, 2003) 123-57.

most familiar is known as the Apostles' Creed.

The Apostles' Creed

I believe in God, the Father almighty,
    creator of heaven and earth.
I believe in Jesus Christ, God's only Son, our Lord,
    who was conceived by the Holy Spirit,
    born of the Virgin Mary,
    suffered under Pontius Pilate,
    was crucified, died, and was buried;
    he descended to the dead.
    On the third day he rose again;
    he ascended into heaven,
    he is seated at the right hand of the Father,
    and he will come to judge the living and the dead.
I believe in the Holy Spirit,
    the holy catholic Church,
    the communion of saints,
    the forgiveness of sins,
    the resurrection of the body,
    and the life everlasting. Amen.[7]

Before his death in 2006 at the age of 82, the esteemed Eastern Orthodox professor of Yale University, Jaroslav Pelikan, compiled and annotated a comprehensive collection of more than 200 Christian creeds and confessions. One of the more interesting of these is the Masai Creed composed sometime around 1960 in the context of an indigenous, seminomadic African tribe of Masai. The Masai Creed describes Jesus as one who was "born poor in a little village, who left his home and was always on safari doing good" and, though he was buried in the grave, "the hyenas did not touch him."[8]

Although there are a number of significant Christian creeds, without

---

[7]There are several translations of the Apostles' Creed, with minor differences between them. This one is the (Ecumenical) English Language Liturgical Consultation version. See online at <http://www.englishtexts.org/praying.pdf> p. 21.
[8]Pelikan, *Credo*, 328-29.

hesitation we can say that the most important is the Nicene Creed, the statement of beliefs issued by the Council of Nicaea in 325 (and slightly revised at the Council of Constantinople in 381).[9] Its importance derives from the fact that the Nicene Creed is one of the few statements of faith that is affirmed by every major branch of Christianity in the world. It was recognized as representing the essential message of the Bible and the faith before any major split had occurred in the Christian tradition—before Protestantism and Roman Catholicism parted ways and even before the Western Roman Church and the Eastern Orthodox Church divorced. Today Christians of all stripes still recite this ancient statement of faith, a sign of continued Christian unity.[10]

For three reasons, we will use the Creed of Nicaea as an outline to help guide our study of Christian theology. First, as we have already indicated, the Nicene Creed is perhaps the most universally recognized statement of what Christians historically confess. So, if we are going to give a broad overview of what Christianity affirms, then it is wise to appeal to the most universal of aids.

Second, in following the Creed we are doing nothing more than following the storyline of Scripture. "What the Scriptures say at length, the Creed says briefly."[11] Some Christians suspect that using the Creed might be a sly attempt to usurp the authority of the Bible. This was certainly not the intention of the writers of the Creed nor is it our intention. The Bible is the ultimate authority for faith and practice; the Nicene Creed simply tries to summarize, to condense, and to outline the basic story of the Scripture, but not to replace it. One of the greatest theologians of the church, Thomas Aquinas, assures us that the Creed is "no addition to Holy Scripture, but something derived from it."[12] In learning a foreign language, one might study a book of grammatical rules, recognizing all the while that learning

---

[9]An equally important creed is the Apostles' Creed. I have chosen to focus on the Nicene Creed, however, because it incorporates all the points of the Apostles' Creed but gives a more expanded consideration of them.

[10]We must make one qualification at this point: the filioque clause that was added much later to the Nicene Creed remains a challenge to this unity. The use of "and the Son" continues to be a point of divergence between western and eastern forms of Christianity. See the chapters on Christian History.

[11]Lash, *Believing Three Ways*, 8.

[12]Thomas Aquinas, *Summa Theologica* II.2, Q. 1, a. 9.

the rule book can never replace speaking the language. The Creed provides the rules of grammar by which we read Scripture and speak the faith.

Third, since space is limited, following the Creed serves as a pragmatic and fair way to cover the basics of Christian beliefs. If space permitted, we would outline book by book the theology of the Bible, how that theology was articulated in church history and how that theology functions for Christians today. This is far too grand a task for this text. But we must acknowledge that anything less than such a massive undertaking will be selective. Just as every preacher must select certain biblical texts for his or her sermon and leave out others, even when he or she is attempting to present the entirety of the good news, so every theology must ultimately be selective in some sense. Instead of selecting what to emphasize based on personal preference or subjective whim, we are going to allow the consensus of the early church, which culminated with the Council of Nicaea, to guide our reading.

Scripture, though dizzying in its scope and complexity, tells a simple story. The plot is one of creation, fall, and redemption. God creates the world; the world rebels against its creator; God attempts to heal the breach in the relationship through covenant with one people group, Israel; ultimately the Creator sends his own Son—God in the flesh—to bring the relationship between God and humanity together in one man (Acts 7:2-53; John 1:14; Col 2:13; 1 Pet 3:18). The newly restored relationship is lived out in the new people of God, the church, who are sent into the world to announce the good news of redemption (Matt 28:19-20; Acts 1:8). According to classic Christianity, this is the basic narrative of the Bible. As we read the Creed, we will see this same narrative shape. The Creed is not an abstract list of principles, but the condensed story of God's drama as revealed in God's Word.

The Nicene Creed

> We believe in one God,
> the Father, the Almighty,
> maker of heaven and earth,
> of all that is, seen and unseen.

> We believe in one Lord, Jesus Christ,
> the only Son of God,
> eternally begotten of the Father,
> God from God, Light from Light,
> true God from true God,
> begotten, not made,

of one Being with the Father.
Through him all things were made.
For us and for our salvation
    he came down from heaven:
    by the power of the Holy Spirit
    he became incarnate from the Virgin Mary,
    and was made man.
    For our sake he was crucified under Pontius Pilate;
    he suffered death and was buried.
    On the third day he rose again
    in accordance with the Scriptures;
    he ascended into heaven
    and is seated at the right hand of the Father.
    He will come again in glory to judge
        the living and the dead,
    and his kingdom will have no end.

We believe in the Holy Spirit, the Lord, the giver of life,
    who proceeds from the Father and the Son.
With the Father and the Son he is worshiped and glorified.
He has spoken through the Prophets.
We believe in one holy catholic and apostolic Church.
We acknowledge one baptism for the forgiveness of sins.
We look for the resurrection of the dead,
    and the life of the world to come. Amen.[13]

---

[13] *Book of Common Prayer*, 1979 U.S. edition, translation by International Consultation on English Texts, 326-27, 529-30; see also the English Language Liturgical Consultation, online at <http://www.englishtexts.org/praying.pdf> p. 16.

From Belief to Sin

We believe in one God, the Father, the Almighty, maker of heaven and earth, of all that is, seen and unseen.

We believe. It would be easy to overlook the first two words of the Nicene Creed and go straight to the phrase "one God." Surely, it might be argued, what is important about this first sentence is its object, *God*. But if we miss the opening phrase, "we believe," then we miss an important point: the Creed of Nicaea is a statement of faith; it is what we believe about God. It has meaning only "If you confess with your lips that Jesus is Lord and believe in your heart that God raised him from the dead" (Rom 10:9). The Creed is not an impartial news report about the Christian faith. The Creed attempts to put in words those things believers hold most dearly with heart, soul, and mind.

As we mentioned in the last chapter, the word "creed" comes from the Latin *credo*, "I believe." The rest of the Creed attempts to explain *what* we believe. Indeed, the rest of the Creed could be bracketed as a dependent clause of "we believe." You could put anything in those brackets and it might still be a creed: "I believe in…[*fill in the blank with love, money, rock 'n' roll, whatever*]." The Nicene Creed is a statement of *Christian* convictions; it represents where Christians stand and have stood for a long time.

Are Christian truths relative, then? No. The *people* who confess these truths are relative. The truths themselves stay the same. The Christian faith claims to be the true story of the world, but we recognize that not everyone will acknowledge our Gospel as truth—Muslims, Buddhists, and Hindus would not admit it, for instance. The Nicene Creed represents a certain group, a certain "we" who believe. Political creeds do the same. "*We* hold these truths to be self-evident…" The authors of the Declaration of Independence understood that not everyone holds "life, liberty, and the pursuit of happiness" to be basic or true. They knew that those ideals could be attacked, dismissed, or overturned. But, to the founders of America, they were self-evident. For Christians, convictions about God, Christ, love and death are just as self-evident. The fact that they are religious does not make them more irrational or capricious than political ideals. Both are convictions—core beliefs that shape the way communities think, feel, and understand everything else.

One God. Christianity is often classified as a monotheism, a belief in one God. But is that correct? The Nicene Creed opens with a confession of belief in one God, but then proceeds to discuss this God as "Father," "Son," and "Spirit", allowing a paragraph for each. So, which one is God: Father, Son, or Spirit?

> *The short answer*: All of them!
> *Response*: That is not monotheism, but tritheism, a belief in three gods.
> *Answer*: It's not tritheism. Christians claim that God is Trinity,
>   three in one.
> *Response*: Well, that solves everything!

The longer answer: A wise man once quipped: "If you deny the Trinity, you'll lose your salvation. If you try to understand it, you'll lose your mind!" The term "Trinity" is found nowhere in Scripture. But, this does not mean it is the invention of bored theologians. Talk of God as Father, Son, and Spirit sprouts up in many New Testament passages, most notably in Matthew 28:19, where Jesus commands his followers, "Go therefore and make disciples of all nations, baptizing them in the name of the Father and of the Son and of the Holy Spirit." Paul blesses the church at Corinth saying, "The grace of the Lord Jesus Christ and the love of God and the fellowship of the Holy Spirit be with you all" (2 Cor 13:13). So, when theologians speak of the Trinity, they are trying to faithfully express what they find in Scripture. As texts are compiled and collated, a broadly Trinitarian picture emerges: "[T]here is one God, the Father, from whom are all things and for whom we exist" (1 Cor 8:6); "[B]ut in these last days he has spoken to us by a Son, whom he appointed heir of all things, through whom he also created the worlds" (Heb 1:2); so that "When the Spirit of truth comes, he will guide you into all the truth" (John 16:13). Clearly, God has revealed God's self three ways, in three persons. And yet, "There is one God" (1 Tim 2:5; Deut 6:4). God is three and God is one. How might we comprehend this mystery?

Popular analogies for the Trinity abound. The comparison is sometimes made between the triune God and H_2O. Just as H_2O can come in three distinct forms (liquid, solid, gas), so God appears as Father, Son, Spirit. Or, just as the sun cannot be separated from its rays of light and its felt heat, so the Son is the ray of the Father and the Spirit is the heat of God. Or, to use a mathematical analogy: $1+1+1 = 3$, but $1 \times 1 \times 1 = 1$. These may all be good ways to stretch our minds—an exercise that must be done whenever we talk about the Trinity—but they all miss something central: the Trinity is about relationship. To talk about God as Father, Son, and Spirit is to talk about how God relates personally to creation. The analogies in this paragraph are impersonal.

The triune God of the Bible is relational—intimate with creation to the point of dying for it. "For God *so loved* the world that he sent his only begotten Son" (John 3:16). Christians do not worship a static, monolithic thing called "God." Christians know God as Father in the sense that God is a loving parent. God is Son in the sense that God also entered history as one of us, as our brother. God comes as Spirit in the sense that God inspires life, empowers or "gives spirit" to believers, and saturates our spirits. The triune God is relational and personal. So, should we conceive of the Trinity as three *persons*? The language of "personhood" is tricky.

To identify God as three persons certainly emphasizes the "threeness" of God and the relational nature of God. Humans can only have genuine relationships with persons, not with objects. However, theologians have hesitated to call God three "persons" because it gives the false impression that the Trinity is a little society or team consisting of three separate individuals, who have separate wills, memories, and personalities. The error in stressing the threeness of the Trinity to the neglect of the oneness is called *pluralism*. By contrast, we affirm that God is *one*, not three separate deities.

On the other hand, it is possible to over-correct the problem of pluralism by so emphasizing the oneness of God that the very idea of Trinity evaporates. The problem here is known as *modalism*. One analogy of the Trinity that might, if pushed, tend toward modalism is the analogy of one's name: just as most individuals have three names (first, middle, and last), so God has three names, Father, Son, and Spirit. The temptation is to present the Trinity in name only—God plays the part of father and son and spirit, but those are just names, roles, or masks behind which lies a true essence which is something different. Christians must affirm instead that Father, Son, and Spirit represent not merely names, but the reality of who God is.

"The phrase 'Father, Son, and Holy Spirit' is simultaneously a very compressed telling of the total narrative by which Scripture identifies God and a personal name for the God so specified; in it, name and narrative description not only appear together...but are identical."[1] This compact

---

[1]Robert Jenson, *Systematic Theology*, vol. I (New York: Oxford University

statement, offered by Robert Jenson, a leading American theologian who works as a Senior Scholar at the Center for Theological Inquiry at Princeton, means to suggest that Father, Son, and Spirit are names that arise out of the biblical story of God's involvement with human history. God is not only identified *by* the events of Israel's exodus and Jesus' resurrection but *with* those events. The triune God of Christianity is not merely mentioned in the passing of those events but is identified by and with what takes place.[2] It is not that something about God is being revealed in the event of Christ, but that the revelation *is* Christ. The revelation is the event and the event is the revelation. The God Christians worship is the God who speaks to Abraham, Jacob, and Isaiah and acts through Esther, Mary, and Peter. Indeed, instead of Father, Son, and Spirit acting as incidental characters in an earthly drama, Abraham, Jacob and the rest are characters in God's drama. This is the story of who God is and what God does through human lives and for humanity. Christians do not recognize some hidden and unknown deity behind the revelation. The biblical story of creation, Israel, Christ, and the church identifies the God who is Father, Son, and Spirit.

Language is limited. The distortions of pluralism or modalism arise when language is overextended and when analogies are stretched beyond their usefulness. The distortions come when we use language to "explain" God. God cannot be explained. God is fundamentally mysterious. When we talk about God, we are addressing the Creator of the universe, the Eternal One who is beyond all our thoughts and space itself. Augustine, the fifth-century North African bishop of Hippo, said in his masterly work on the Trinity:

> People who seek God, and stretch their minds as far as human weakness is able toward an understanding of the trinity, must surely experience the strain of trying to fix their gaze on *light inaccessible* (["unapproachable light" NRSV] 1 Tim 6:16), and the difficulties presented by the holy scriptures in their multifarious diversity of form, which are designed, so it seems to me, to wear Adam down and let Christ's glorious grace shine through.[3]

Press, 1997) 46.

[2]Jenson, *Systematic Theology* 1:59.

[3]Augustine, *The Trinity* III, trans. Edmund Hill (Brooklyn: New City Press, 1991) 97.

When the phrase "God in three persons, blessed Trinity" appears in the hymn "Holy, Holy, Holy," it works because it is in the context of *worship*. It turns our hearts in praise toward the mystery of the Trinity. When the same phrase ("God in three persons") is used as a straightforward, easy way of *explaining* the Trinity, outside the context of worship and song, it fails. The doctrine of the Trinity cannot be *explained* because, by its very nature, it is a way of representing the deep mystery of God.

Trinity is mystery, and we must resist the temptation to fix or explain it because it is mystery. Karl Barth, the famous Swiss theologian of the mid-twentieth century, bemoaned "the constantly increasing barbarism, tedium, and insignificance of modern Protestantism, which has gone and lost—probably along with the Trinity and the virgin birth—an entire third dimension (shall we say the dimension of. . . mystery)."[4] Barth, who was expelled from Germany in 1934 for opposing the Nazis, knew the danger of reducing the Christian faith to a few basic ideas that could be manipulated and used for whatever one wanted, say, to support German nationalism and racial superiority. The Nazis claimed that, unlike the "godless communists," they were not opposed to religion and would even accommodate religious faith as long as it did not interfere with social and political life—as long as it could be precisely defined and regimented and controlled.

But, mystery defies control.

Belief in God is itself a mysterious act—one that cannot be fully comprehended by believers or nonbelievers, however hard they try to figure it out. This statement is not intended to offend, but to point out that God is not an object to be intellectually known, but a Creator, Savior, and Sustainer to be encountered and worshiped. Belief is a giving of one's self, a sacred submission of the soul, a vow of one's fidelity. Believing involves and invokes mystery—Christians direct their bodies, hearts, prayers, and songs toward a God they cannot presently see but nonetheless sense and know.

Theologians and pastors cannot and should not *explain* the mystery of God the Father, Son, and Holy Spirit. So, should they then remain silent and say nothing about it? Such an alternative is no better than trying to explain the Trinity mathematically. The mystery of the Trinity is a very important doctrine, in fact, maybe *the* most important, so something should be said

---

[4]Barth quoted in Eberhard Busch, *Karl Barth: His Life from Letters and Autobiographical Texts* (London: SCM Press, 1976) 284.

about it. Let us offer three constructive ways of talking about the mystery.

* The Christian God is one "what" and three "whos."[5] To the question, "What are you talking about?" the Christian answers, "God. God is *what* we are talking about." To the question, "And who is God?" the Christian answers, "God is Father, Son, and Spirit. That is *who* God is." More technically, God is one being and three ways of being. We believe in one God who is revealed three ways, as Father, Son, and Spirit.

* God the Father is God over us; God the Son is God come to us; God the Spirit is God with us; God the Trinity is God for us.[6] This little saying represents well the most important point about the Trinity that we mentioned above, namely that when we say "Trinity" we are expressing in shorthand the fact that God is for us, cares about us like a good father, desires relationship with us like a good brother, and guides us by divine prompting spirit. Each member of the Trinity represents an aspect of how God relates to *us*—the creation, God's handiwork.

* Finally, the mystery of the Trinity is not: "How can three equal one?" The enigma is not mathematical. If we stop there, then we completely miss the real mystery. Rather, the real question is: *How can the God who fathered the world enter as a son of the world and give his life in order to bring new life and spirit to the world?* The answer is the story of the Christian faith, the story of the Bible. The point is that the mystery of the Trinity is best stated as a question, not as an answer. But, again, the mystery is not in the mathematical equation. It is in the discovery that *God has not abandoned us.* God has not walked away from the creation, even when it tried to tear itself away. Instead, the God who gave form and life to the world chose to come into the world in the form of a mere human, with all the trappings of gender, race, sweat, and blood. In accepting the conditions of human life, God also accepted a cruel human death. In order to reestablish relationship with the people of the world, God chose to die for them. Why would God do this? That is the mystery that is the Trinity.

The Father. Now we come to the first member of the Trinity, God the Father. When we use the word "Father," what do we mean? Is God a male? Put more bluntly, does God have a beard, chest hair, testosterone? Obviously not. "God is spirit, and those who worship him must worship in

---

[5]Anthony Meredith, *The Cappadocians* (Crestwood NY: St. Vladimir's Seminary Press, 1995) 44.

[6]I am indebted to Bob Patterson for this insight.

spirit and in truth" (John 4:24). Furthermore, Genesis 1:27 says that "God created humankind in his image, in the image of God he created them; *male and female* he created them." If both men and women were created in God's image, then apparently that image transcends gender distinctions. God does not have a gender nor is God neutered. God does not have a body with arms, legs, and feet: God is spirit.

The problem is not God, but language. Our language offers three possible pronouns: he, she, it. We have already established that God is personal, so calling God an "it" will not do. We are left with choosing either "he" or "she." But God is neither male nor female (and so it may be good to use feminine pronouns for God every now and then just to remind us of the fact). Nevertheless, the Bible uses masculine pronouns for God, and Jesus speaks of God as Father, not Mother. The point being made, however, is not about gender but about personal concern and relationship. The Bible and Jesus use personal and therefore gendered nouns and pronouns to express the fact that God is above all things personal, not impersonal. Jesus throws off any notions of God as distant and unmovable; Jesus reveals a Father who cares, invests, and feels. "As the Father has loved me, so I have loved you" (John 15:9). Jesus prays to "Abba, Father" (Mark 14:36).

Of course, the image of "father" does not instantly evoke positive images for everyone. Some people have lousy fathers, abusive fathers, or negligent fathers. Jesus is clear to define what he means when he calls God "Father." God is Father in the sense of being a loving parent, like the father in the parable of the prodigal son (Luke 15) who runs to us, throws his arms around us, and hosts a party on our behalf. This Father nurtures, gives good gifts, and protects his children. "Is there anyone among you who, if your child asks for bread, will give a stone? Or if the child asks for a fish, will give a snake? If you then, who are evil, know how to give good gifts to your children, how much more will your Father in heaven give good things to those who ask him!" (Matt 7:9-11). To call God Father is not to emphasize God's masculinity, but to acknowledge God's affectionate, parental concern for us. Hosea 11:4 also expresses well the parental character of God's love. In that passage the Lord says, "I led them with cords of human kindness, with bands of love. I was to them like those who lift infants to their cheeks. I bent down to them and fed them." There is something maternal about this paternal love—something magnificently parental.

Almighty. Is the statement, "God is almighty, all powerful," a good and true statement in and of itself? Can it stand alone? Most of us would nod our heads in agreement. "Yes," we would say, "God is almighty and all powerful, meaning that God can do whatever God wants to whomever God wants whenever God wants." If God is all-powerful then God can heal, give life, create, and save. Of course an all-powerful God can also cause sickness, destroy, and damn. If God is all-powerful then you can never know what God will do because God is free to change God's mind, to do what God wants. Maybe God has chosen to be good and to do good now, but tomorrow God may have a change of mind and decide to deceive, destroy, and kill. If God is almighty, then that is certainly an option. Theologian Karl Barth reminds us that when Adolf Hitler invoked God's name in speeches, he always referred to God as "the Almighty."[7]

Lord Acton was right: "Power corrupts, and absolute power corrupts absolutely."[8] We should be wary of any human or institution that claims power or strives for power at the expense of human dignity and welfare. Likewise, we should be wary of any theology that defines God primarily in terms of power or unlimited almightiness. Such a God we might fear, but we could never trust. For this reason, "almighty" is bracketed in between "Father" and "maker" in the Creed. It does not stand alone. First we know God as loving parent, then we recognize God as almighty—but only as a way of qualifying and describing God's fatherhood. "Almightiness" in this context affirms that the Father's love is effective; it means that God is able to fulfill God's role as father. None of us are able to do that; none of us can claim to be the perfect parent, son, daughter, or friend. But God can because God is almighty.

What is the effect of God's almighty fatherhood? What does God's fatherhood produce: objects of affection. The Father's love creates and seeks relationship with creation. The Father almighty is *maker of heaven and earth*. God's power has a direction according to God's role as Father, to the end that heaven and earth are created for the Father's sake.

Of all that is, seen and unseen. The writers of the Creed have, up to this point, been sparse with their wording, choosing each word and phrase carefully so as not to waste, repeat, or overstate. But, one cannot help but

---

[7]Karl Barth, *Dogmatics in Outline,* trans. by G. T. Thomson (New York: Harper & Row, 1959) 48.

[8]This commonly cited quote comes from a letter of Lord Acton to Bishop Mandell Creighton, 1887.

think that here they have repeated themselves unnecessarily. "All that is, seen and unseen" appears to be excess verbiage. Surely "all that is, seen and unseen" would be included in whatever exists in "heaven and earth." And yet, the Creed writers felt it necessary to delineate what was included in heaven and earth.

By this phrase the Creed is asserting what the Bible makes plain: there is only one world, the world breathed forth by God. God did not create the good parts and Satan the bad parts. There is no dualism of good and evil, God and Satan, light and dark. God creates and oversees all that is, seen and unseen. Colossians 1:16-17 speaks of this all-creating and all-encompassing Word of God:

> [F]or in him all things in heaven and on earth were created, things visible and invisible, whether thrones or dominions or rulers or powers—all things have been created through him and for him. He himself is before all things, and in him all things hold together.

There is no territory of existence independent of God. God encompasses all that exists. So, what about evil? Strictly speaking, evil does not enjoy the goodness of creation, and in that sense, evil does not exist. As Augustine of Hippo reasons, "I saw and it was made clear to me that you [God] made all things good, and there are absolutely no substances which you did not make." Whatever God makes is good; God made all things that exist; so "whatever things exist are good." Evil is not a thing that God made and so "for you [God] evil does not exist at all;" it is rather the shadow side of creation, the cessation of existence, the deterioration of what is good.[9]

"Evil" is the name we give to the corruption of what is good. Sickness is not a "thing" in addition to health; sickness is the corruption of health. Disobedience is not something added to obedience; disobedience names the failure to obey. Death is the absence of life, the end of life, and not something in addition to life. Likewise, evil is not an extra, an addition to God's good creation; it is the absence of goodness, a lack or corruption of goodness.

This explanation does not make evil any less problematic. Why do bad things happen? Why do people suffer? From where does this corruption and void come? The mystery of evil is deep, and dark.

---

[9]Augustine, *Confessions* VII.xii, translated by Henry Chadwick (New York: Oxford University Press, 1991) 124-25.

What Is Sin?

The brief exploration of evil segues well to a discussion of sin. At this point we digress from the Creed of Nicaea. But, understanding the nature of sin will better situate us to comprehend the next section of the Creed on Christ.

The Greek term for "sin" in the New Testament is *harmartia*, whose root meaning is "to miss the mark." *Harmartia* was originally an archery term; it referred to shooting an arrow and missing the target. Theologians have extended this archery metaphor by recognizing that there are two ways to miss the mark: overshooting (pride) and undershooting (apathy).

Pride. Humans often overshoot the mark by overestimating their own nature, abilities, and place on this earth. Pride is an overestimation of self-worth. Pride leads to the belief that the world revolves around *me* and that what I am doing is more important than what anyone else is doing. The proud self says, in effect, "I am god." I rule my own universe; I am master of my own destiny. Pride showcases itself in many venues; from genetics to economics, from intellect to morality, pride has no limits. American culture in particular feeds on pride's promises, perhaps most noticeably in pride of body—the fitness fetish, the dieting craze, our insatiable appetite for fashion and clothing. Our culture places a high premium on sex appeal, the pride of the body as a sensual object. Another form that this bodily pride takes is pride of youth. People go to great lengths—even submitting to surgery and toxic drugs (Botox)—to achieve and maintain young looks. From MTV, "the station of eternal youth," to glamour magazines canvassing the ends of checkout lines, the obsession with looking young permeates American society. So pride comes in all shapes and sizes; in the end all forms of pride are forms of self-exertion over others and over God.

Apathy. The opposite of pride might be despair and despondency, what we will call "apathy." It is possible to undershoot the mark by underestimating the self. By "apathy" we do not necessarily mean laziness, though that can be a symptom. Rather, apathy implies that the individual shrugs her shoulders at life, that she is listless, opinionless, lifeless. There is no center of the universe; life floats from day to day without meaning, direction, or purpose. Instead of seeing the self as the center of the universe, one does everything she can to forget the self. The apathetic individual avoids the nagging questions of meaning and purpose. Through alcohol, pornography, physical abuse, and even suicide she tries to escape the pressures of daily life, run from reality, and hide from God. But, apathy is not only marked by dark habits. As Karl Barth points out, apathy may even "disguise itself as ceaseless activity."[10] We can busy ourselves so much with work, sports, social events, extracurricular activities, hobbies and movie going that we lose our souls. If we stay busy enough, we will never have to confront who we are in silence, solitude, and reflection.

What We Are Missing. As can be implied from the discussion so far, identifying sin does not mean that we catalogue every possible wrong or offense. It is not a matter of *doing* or *not* doing certain things. Sin is a theological category, not a legal or even a moral one. Sin, in the end, means not knowing who we are in relation to our Maker; it means either thinking that I am God or that there is no God and no meaning to life. It is just as much about not knowing who we are as not knowing who God is. Nicholas Lash, the eminent Cambridge theologian, comments:

> Sin is refusal of relation, self-enclosure in a futile search for safety. There is nothing glamorous or esoteric about sin. Spreading like fungus from dying cites across the surface of the globe, its appearance is only the familiar bleak ugliness of egotism, of the attempt to transform other people, things, facts, institutions, ideas, and dreams into 'our' absolute and indestructible possessions.[11]

Gustavo Gutiérrez, writing out of his depth of experience of revolutionary politics in Latin America, says that "Insofar as it constitutes a break with God, sin is a historical reality, it is a breach of the communion of persons with each other, it is a turning in of individuals on themselves."[12] Sin, then, has two prongs: rejecting who God is and rejecting who we are. It means forgetting that we are created in God's image, the *imago Dei*. This is the target for which we should be aiming, and which we most often overshoot and undershoot.

---

[10]Karl Barth quoted in Jean Bethke Elshtain, *Who Are We?* (Grand Rapids MI: Eerdmans, 2000) 84.

[11]Nicholas Lash, *Believing Three Ways in One God* (London: SCM Press, 1992) 101.

[12]Gustavo Gutiérrez, *Theology of Liberation* (Maryknoll NY: Orbis, 1988) 85.

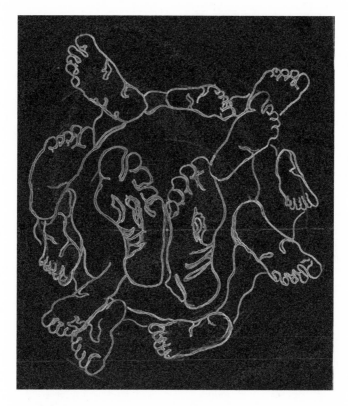

"Order My Feet," by Neil Grimm, used with permission by the artist.

To what does the "image of God" refer? To say that humans are made in God's image means that there is something in humans that reflects God; humans somehow mirror who God is. Some might suggest that the image is our moral sensibility, our capacity to know right from wrong. Others say it is our intellectual capabilities, our reason and capacity to invent. But it seems more reasonable that what we mirror about God is linked to the reason for which we were created. The Christian affirmation is that humans were created for relationship with God. As such, the *imago Dei* refers to the capacity for relationship with God.

We can only have true communication and genuine relationship with beings essentially like ourselves. For instance, you can love your dog and may even prefer him to other human beings. Even so, the relationship with a pet is rather one-directional. Your dog may reciprocate your affection, but you will never achieve a truly intimate relationship with a pet. Of course, you can have more of a relationship with your dog than with a pet rock. Nevertheless, a truly intimate relationship can be had only with another human being, another creature like yourself. Likewise, God could not have authentic relationships with us if we were no more than dogs or rocks to God. We are not God's guinea pigs. To have relationship with God means, most basically, that in some essential way we must be enough *like* God to relate and communicate. The eighth Psalm ponders this amazing truth:

> When I look at your heavens, the work of your fingers,
>   the moon and the stars that you have established;
> what are human beings that you are mindful of them,
>   mortals that you care for them?
> Yet you have made them a little lower than God,
>   and crowned them with glory and honor.

With this in mind, the ultimate sin is to refuse this stunning offer of relationship. Sin means not only refusing our Creator but our very nature, purpose, and destiny. St. Athanasius of Alexandria, at the ripe old age of twenty, wrote these profound words in 318 CE about the effects of sin:

> But men, having turned from the contemplation of God to evil of their own devising, had come inevitably under the law of death. Instead of remaining in the state in which God had created them, they were in process of becoming corrupted entirely, and death had them completely under its dominion. For the transgression of the commandment was making them turn back again according to their nature; and as they had at the beginning come into being out of nonexistence, so were they now on the way to returning, through corruption, to nonexistence again. The presence and love of the Word had called them into being; inevitably, therefore when they lost the knowledge of God, they lost existence with it.[13]

Athanasius makes clear that sin leads humans away from their calling, purpose, and existence into despair, purposelessness, and death. His words help complete our brief consideration of the nature of sin. And yet, our consideration has more than a few loose ends. There persist many questions about sin, its cause and its effect, that we have not answered. So, in an

---

[13]Athanasius, *On the Incarnation*, § 4, (Crestwood NY: St. Vladimir's Seminary Press, 2000) 29-30.

attempt to tie up some of these loose ends, we will consider, in no particular order, a number of key questions about sin.

Some Quick Conclusions regarding the Nature of Sin

* Are we sinful because we are finite, limited beings? No. The fact that we are human means that we will make mistakes, forget things, assume things, and so forth. We cannot know everything, we cannot be everywhere we need to be, we cannot do everything we need to do. We are fragile and limited in so many ways. This alone does not make us guilty of sin. Theologian Reinhold Niebuhr clarifies "that the world is not evil because it is temporal, [and] that the body is not the source of sin in man."[14] Genesis 1:31 reports that God created humanity with all its limitations and declared it to be "very good."

* Does the existence of Satan or demonic temptation explain sin? No. Regardless of Satan's origin or role in the universe, sin is something for which *we* are responsible, not someone else. We may be tempted by the devil, the world, or our own flesh, but only we can choose to give in to the temptation. Since sin is not about breaking a law but about a rupture in our relationship with God, no one else can be accountable for that relationship except us. "Against you, you alone, have I sinned, and done what is evil in your sight" (Ps 50:4).

* Is sinning *inevitable*? Yes. All people eventually turn astray. Romans 3:23 says, "For there is no distinction, since all have sinned and fall short of the glory of God." We also know from experience that no one always makes right decisions. People inevitably try to live without God. We are forever substituting what is good for us with what is convenient and attractive.

* Is it therefore *necessary*? No. Inevitability is not the same thing as necessity. Just as Satan cannot force anyone to sin, so God does not compel sin. Sin goes against God's will. By definition it is rebellion against what God wants, the essence of "things that the LORD hates" (Prov 5:16, or just read Amos). So, while all people do eventually fall into sin, we are responsible for our actions.

* Do we, by virtue of being born into a fallen world through fallen parents, *inherit* sin? This question is tied up in the question of "original sin."

---

[14]Reinhold Niebuhr, *The Nature and Destiny of Man*, vol. 1 (New York: Scribner's Sons, 1964) 167.

Traditionally, Christianity has affirmed the doctrine of original sin, or "the state of alienation from God into which all humans are born."[15] "Original" refers to more than the original sin of Adam and Eve; it refers to the way you and I are born. The doctrine of original sin is a way of recognizing that the world and the human race as a whole is somehow out of sync with God, that there is a systemic problem in our world and that no one escapes from the lure and effects of sin. The root problem is that the world is in need of redemption, recreation. The initial beauty and purity of creation has been shattered and all of us are born into a fragmented picture.

* Are we born individually *guilty* of sin? As with many of these difficult questions, there is room for diversity of opinion here. For me, the answer is "no." Humans are not born guilty of sin in a seminal way; sin is not communicated through sperm or the sex act that produces the child (although St. Augustine espoused something like this in a position called traducianism; he was trying to show just how hopeless and helpless we are before God). Another way of asking the question about who is guilty for sin is: Where do babies go when they die in infancy? If they are born guilty of sin, then they should be condemned to eternal separation from God. But surely it is not right, good, or just to condemn infants to eternal separation before they ever have a chance to willingly accept or reject relationship with God through Christ. This goes against the biblical truth that "God is love" and "there is no fear in love, but perfect love casts out fear; for fear has to do with punishment" but God's love has to do with mercy and forgiveness (1 John 4:16-18).

For sin to be sin, one must be personally responsible. The thirteenth-century master of Christian thought, Thomas Aquinas, said that "acts have the character of morality only insofar as they are voluntary."[16] In other words, you cannot be morally responsible for something you have no choice over like being born, breathing, and feeling hunger. These are nonmoral acts. Just being human is not sinful. Sin is "voluntary." Nevertheless, to return to the point about original sin, humans are born into a sinful world and therefore tainted from the beginning. Think of a corrupted computer program: all files opened in that corrupted program are instantly corrupted themselves. No file can remain untouched and pure in a corrupt system. The

---

[15]"Original Sin," *Pocket Dictionary of Theological Terms* (Downers Grove IL: InterVarsity Press) 87.

[16]Thomas Aquinas, *Summa Theologiae* II.1.18, *Selected Writings*, ed. by Ralph McInerny (New York: Oxford University Press, 1998) 574.

files are not themselves guilty of the corruption, but they do inherit the corruption. In Romans 5:12, Paul states, "sin came into the world through one man, and death came through sin, and so death spread to all because all have sinned." This great verse confirms that sin is both inherited and voluntary. It says that sin came into the world through the first humans and has since spread to all. But why has it spread? "*Because* all have sinned." Paul says sin has spread to all and corrupted all because all have chosen to sin and continue to choose to sin. We are all tainted by rebellion because we all choose to disobey.

> * Is there *social* inheritance of sin? Yes. I deny that we are born individually guilty of sin, but I want to make clear that we *are* born into a world that has badly missed the mark. We are born into a world that gets along fine without God. Humans have alienated themselves from communion with God and from true community with one another. So, we are born into families with prejudices and societies that perpetuate injustices. Before we are even aware, we may be learning or benefitting from those systems and prejudices. Even from early on, children are taught, directly and indirectly, to desire certain things (like money, fashion, success, popularity) and scorn other things (weakness, sympathy, simplicity, restraint). We adapt quickly to sinful institutions and desires. A clean computer file opened into a corrupt program will become corrupt itself; we cannot be born in this fallen world and not fall ourselves.

> * Is belief in sin something that Christians confess? Is there such a thing as a *Doctrine of Sin,* or a creedal affirmation of sin? No. There is no doctrine of sin. Christians do not *believe* in sin, which is to say we don't put our trust and hope in sin, we don't have faith in sin, we don't pledge our lives to sin. Christians *believe* in Christ, in salvation from death and forgiveness of sin. Sin is always unbelievable, or as Karl Barth would call it, the "impossible possibility." There is never a *good* reason to sin. Sin is *absurd*. Sin does not make sense: it does not make sense to rebel against our Maker and refuse to accept our own nature. Sin is what went wrong; it is against God's will. God does not make room for our rebellion, God does not bless sin as "okay"—God sends God's Son to snatch us from the jaws of sin and death. God's creation is good and orderly and sin is the intentional shattering of that goodness, the inexplicable disordering of that order. Sin means shooting oneself in the foot; it is our own self-destruction. Just as evil is a mysterious corruption and failure of the good, so sin is humanity's baffling refusal of God's good will. We should not doctrinalize sin or make it a Christian belief—to do so would be to explain it, classify it, and fit it into the system as if it were all part of the plan. Sin

does not fit; it never merits a *good* reason.

Even though it is always an anomaly and stands outside what is intelligible, the idea of "sin" *does* eventually appear in the Creed, in the phrase "the forgiveness of sins." But here it does not stand alone as something Christians independently affirm. We only really know the nature and pervasiveness of sin through the lens of forgiveness. Only when we see it through the forgiveness offered through Christ's sacrifice do we know what sin is and how to name it. For the purposes of our discussion, it makes sense to talk about the problem first (missing the mark of relationship with God, others, and ourselves) and then talking about the solution, Christ's forgiveness. Nevertheless, Christ and Christ's forgiveness come first, and only afterwards comes the idea of sin. Christians are people who are forgiven. When asked, "Forgiven of what?" believers then answer, "forgiven of sin." As we will see in the next chapter, sin is not the problem to which Jesus' death is the answer; rather the cross is the question mark placed on our very lives.[17] The cross not only overshadows sin, but all human strivings and efforts, including the good, the bad, and the anxious.

---

[17]This rephrases something Karl Barth says in *The Epistle to the Romans*, trans. Edwyn Hoskyns (New York: Oxford University Press, 1968) 35.

• 15 •

From Jesus to the Holy Spirit

If Christianity is about anything, it is about Jesus. In any given church, the centrality of Jesus asserts itself in paintings, carvings, and stained glass images. Outside of the church, books, hymns, T-shirts and tattoos all testify to the overwhelming importance of this man from Nazareth. Is there any religious symbol more universally recognized than the cross of Christ? The first question of the Heidelberg Catechism, an important confession of faith emerging out of the Reformation era in 1563, reads: "What is your only comfort in life and in death?" The answer, "That I belong body and soul, in life and in death, not to myself but to my faithful Savior Jesus Christ who at the cost of his own blood has fully paid for all my sins."[1] Who is Jesus and what did he do? These are key questions because, as the Heidelberg Catechism suggests, Jesus Christ is central to the Christian faith. Or rather, he is *the center* of the Christian faith. As another example of the centrality of Christ, the original formulation of the theological "Basis" for the Constitution of the World Council of Churches in 1948 was a simple affirmation: "The World Council of Churches is a fellowship of churches which accept our Lord Jesus Christ as God and Savior."[2]

Who Is Jesus?

The ubiquity and prominence of Christ today can be traced to Scripture's own testimony. According to Scripture,

at the name of Jesus
　　every knee should bend,
　　in heaven and on earth and under the earth,
and every tongue should confess
　　that Jesus Christ is Lord.　　　　　　　　　　　(Phil 2:10-11)

Reverence and worship are due him because, as both Heb 1:3 and Col 1:15

---

[1] Presbyterian Church U.S.A., *The Constitution*, part 1, *Book of Confessions* (Louisville: Office of the General Assembly, 1994) 29.

[2] See Henry Bettenson, *Documents of the Christian Churches*, 3rd ed (New York: Oxford, 1999) 426.

testify, when we see Jesus we are seeing God. The Gospel of Matthew reports that the disciples recognized the divinity of Jesus and "worshiped him, saying, 'Truly you are the Son of God' " (Matt 14:33). John's Gospel reports that Philip, one of the disciples, asked Jesus to "show us the Father, and we will be satisfied." Jesus answered, "Have I been with you all this time, Philip, and you still do not know me? Whoever has seen me has seen the Father. . . . I am in the Father and the Father is in me" (John 14:8-12).

The Christian message is not that Jesus was merely a great prophet of God or that Jesus was so moral and upright that he was likened to God, but that God himself became incarnate, or became flesh, in the person of Jesus (John 1:14; Phil 2:6; Col 1:15-20). First John 1:1-2 declares that the incarnation was real, that Jesus the Son of God was "heard," "seen with our eyes," "looked at and touched with our hands." This was no phantom, no fantasy, no illusion. To quote the eminent fourth century church father Athanasius again:

> He took to Himself a body, a human body even as our own. Nor did He will merely to become embodied or merely to appear; had that been so, He could have revealed His divine majesty in some other and better way. No, He took *our* body.[3]

Yet, what exactly does this mean? Here we are dealing with the mystery of the "incarnation"—God becoming human and pitching his tent among us. The logic of the incarnation was one of the first theological questions with which the early church had to wrestle. As we saw in our study of church history, the Council of Nicaea (325) declared Jesus to be fully divine. The Nicene Creed leaves no doubt. The Son is "God from God, Light from Light, true God from true God." The Son is God in the same way that the Father is God. Whatever it means to be God, Jesus the Christ *was* in the flesh. But, then the question arose: If Jesus was fully divine, was he really a human, or did he just appear to be human? It would seem that if a being were the fullness of divinity, then that being could not also be human without compromising some of that divinity. In what sense could the Son of God have been human? The Christian community of churches and bishops collectively responded with another council, the Council of Constantinople which met in 381.

The council was moderated by the esteemed theologian and patriarch

---

[3]Athanasius, *On the Incarnation* §8, p. 34.

of Constantinople, Gregory of Nazianzus (329–391), who offered this important rule with regards to the incarnation: "What has not been assumed has not been healed."[4] If one of the reasons God became human was to take humanity's place and suffer the punishment of death that humanity deserved for sin, then God needed to "assume" a full human personality, not merely a random body. God intended to heal the whole of the human person—body, mind, and soul—not merely the human body. So, God assumed or became a full-fledged human being, with body, mind, and soul. Gregory made this argument to the bishops, patriarchs, and church leaders assembled at Constantinople in 381 and the result was that the council affirmed Jesus as fully human. The incarnation was through-and-through, a total and complete affair. Whatever it means to be human—to smile, to need sleep, to get thirsty, to sweat—Jesus the Christ experienced all those things. Other councils followed Nicaea and Constantinople. At those later councils the full human and divine natures of the Son were further clarified and explained such that the Council of Chalcedon could finally declare that Christ exhibited "two natures without confusion, without change, without division, without separation."[5] The divine was not confused or blended with the human, nor were the natures divided so that half of Jesus was human and half was divine. Christ was one, unified personality, fully divine and fully human.

Now, to some readers, this discussion of the natures of Christ may sound tedious and hairsplitting. And for their efforts, the councils did not once and for all *explain* the incarnation. They did not offer a straightforward statement of *how* God became human. But that is precisely the point. The wonder of Christmas is that in a misplaced manger in the tiny town of Bethlehem, Mary, Joseph, and some shepherds witnessed something of incomparable mystery.

> But Mary kept all these things and pondered them in her heart.
> Then the shepherds returned, glorifying and praising God for all the things
> that they had heard and seen. . . .　　　　　(Luke 2:19-20 NKJV)

The early church realized that the best thing to do was to *protect the*

---

[4]Gregory of Nazianzus, "Letter 101," quoted in J. N. D. Kelly, *Early Christian Doctrines*, rev. ed. (San Francisco: HarperSanFrancisco, 1976) 297.

[5]Henry Bettenson and Chris Maunder, eds., *Documents of the Christian Church*, new ed. (New York: Oxford University Press, 1999) 56.

mystery of the incarnation, not dissect it. The proper response is to ponder the mystery and glorify God. We should not overstep the limit of Scripture's testimony about Jesus. We affirm, with the Bible, that Jesus is fully God and fully human, two natures meeting in one person.

In Jesus we see equally who God is and who humans are supposed to be. That God so intimately revealed both the character of God and humanity in this one life is the heart of the mystery. In the incarnation God blows apart boundaries and expectations. As one contemporary British theologian, John Milbank, poignantly writes:

> For Christianity did, indeed, explode all limits: between nations, between races, between sexes, between the household and the city, between ritual purity and impurity, between work and leisure, between days of the week…. But above all, with the doctrine of the Incarnation, Christianity violates the boundary between created and creator, immanence and transcendence, humanity and God. In this way, the arch taboo grounding all the others is broken.[6]

That God becomes human means the eternal becomes time-bound, the infinite becomes finite, the omnipotent and omnipresent becomes located in a particular man at a particular time in a particular place. As Milbank observes, the incarnation surely violates taboo; God surely crosses a line by condescending to our skin and blood and bones. This is the mystery of the incarnation.

What Did He Do?

The literary giant Ernest Hemingway was once challenged to write a story using only six words. He responded with this, "For sale: baby shoes, never used." Other authors have been asked to do the same. John Updike wrote, "'Forgive me!' 'What for?' 'Never mind.'" A six word summary of the life of Jesus might read: "He lived, he died, he rose." Alternatively we might say he reveals, reconciles, and rules.[7]

He lived. What did Jesus accomplish by living? What was his life's work? We might be able to encapsulate the meaning of Jesus' birth, life, ministry, teachings, and miracles by saying: Christ came to reveal God.

---

[6]John Milbank, *Being Reconciled* (New York: Routledge, 2003) 196-97.

[7]In classical theology, Christ's work as revealer, reconciler, and ruler is often presented under the headings of prophet, priest, and king.

Jesus represents the fullest revelation and the most complete unveiling of God. As 2 Corinthians 3:16 says, "when one turns to the Lord, the veil is removed." The God shown through Christ's actions, ministry, and words is a compassionate and caring God who risks all for his creation. This God, to whom Jesus prays and for whom Jesus speaks, comes as Father, *Abba*, Daddy. Jesus lets the little children come to him, cares for the lame and the blind, and eats with tax collectors and sinners to show the people that the Father cares for the young and the old, the innocent and the guilty alike. As Martin Luther observed, "God is the God of the humble, the miserable, the afflicted, the oppressed, the desperate, and of those who have been brought down to nothing at all."[8] A main component of Jesus' message is that the Father especially looks after the downtrodden and outcast and treats those he loves as his children. What is more, Jesus warns, "Truly I tell you, unless you change and become like children, you will never enter the kingdom of heaven" (Matt 18:3).

Jesus does not only reveal God, but God's kingdom. One of the most often repeated phrases in Jesus' teachings is "the kingdom of heaven" or "the kingdom of God." The very first sermon-like message of Jesus found in the Gospel of Mark is a brief announcement: "Jesus came to Galilee, proclaiming the good news of God, and saying, 'The time is fulfilled, and the kingdom of God has come near; repent, and believe in the good news'" (Mk 1:14-5). Jesus not only announces who God is, but what God's rule is like. Exactly what is the kingdom of God? Is it a territorial designation, with walls, a military, and a capital? Can the kingdom be physically located? Jesus himself replied to these questions in his encounter with Pilate, "My kingdom is not from this world. If my kingdom were from this world, my followers would be fighting to keep me from being handed over to the Jews. But as it is, my kingdom is not from here" (Jn 18:36). Elsewhere Jesus says, "The kingdom of God is not coming with things that can be observed; nor will they say, 'Look, here it is!' or 'There it is!' For, in fact, the kingdom of God is among you" (Lk 17:21).

Jesus resisted requests to define once and for all what the kingdom *was*, but he never tired of saying what the kingdom was *like*. "The kingdom of heaven may be compared to someone who sowed good seed in his field…The kingdom of heaven is like a mustard seed…The kingdom of

---

[8]Martin Luther, as quoted in William Placher, *Jesus the Savior* (Louisville: Westminster/John Knox, 2001) 77.

heaven is like yeast...The kingdom of heaven is like treasure hidden in a field...the kingdom of heaven is like a merchant in search of fine pearls...the kingdom of heaven is like a net...the kingdom of heaven is like the master of a household..." (Matt 13). The parables are meant to portray in vivid stories the new values and expectations of this heavenly kingdom come to earth. Not only the parables, but the sayings, actions, and miracles of Jesus point the way, not *to* the kingdom, but *of* the kingdom. The kingdom of God is not a destiny to be arrived at, but a way of living, speaking, traveling, and loving. "As the Father has loved me, so I have loved you; abide in my love" (Jn 15:9). As Jesus reveals who God is, he also reveals how we should respond to God; this is the new order of God. To say that the kingdom of heaven is not a geographically or ethnically plotted terrain is not to say it is just a metaphor, just a spiritual hope or a whiff of smoke. The life of Jesus was a life of action, of confrontation, of healing and calling. The kingdom of heaven presents a way of real engagement.

He died. Jesus functions not only as revealer but as reconciler. Through his life he reveals God's will, through his death he accomplishes God's will of reconciliation. Colossians 1:19-20 reads, "For in him all the fullness of God was pleased to dwell, and through him God was pleased to reconcile to himself all things, whether on earth or in heaven, by making peace through the blood of his cross." The Nicene Creed confesses "for our sake he was crucified." Jesus' death was no ordinary death. It did something, it meant something, it was "for our sake." In Christ's death we were reconciled with God (Rom 5, 2 Cor 5:17-21). We were made right with God; the breach in the relationship between humanity and God caused by sin was healed. The New Testament uses a vast array of metaphors and images to describe the significance of this reconciliation. We will look at three.

First, Jesus' crucifixion is presented in a number of New Testament passages as *the victory of God*. Christ's death saves us, rescues us from the powers of sin and death. Colossians 1:13 says, "He has rescued us from the power of darkness" and Colossians 2:13-15 adds, "he forgave us all our trespasses, erasing the record that stood against us with its legal demands. He set this aside, nailing it to the cross. He disarmed the rulers and authorities and made a public example of them, triumphing over them in it [that is, the cross]." The Son of God and Man was not stripped of his honor and defeated on the cross, rather on the cross Christ disarms the powers that be and makes a public spectacle *of them*. His death is not a disaster but a triumph, revealing the reason for which he was born. By submitting to death he conquers, deflates, and vanquishes it. The cross becomes an event not of Roman injustice but of Christ's glory, not of death's finality but of life's gift. It is a victory.

A second lens for viewing Christ's work of reconciliation on the cross is as a *mediation or substitution*. Jesus mediates between God and humanity for the purpose of reconciling the relationship. We were the ones who were in the wrong, who had rebelled and deserved to be cut off from God, but Jesus chose to die in our place, as our substitute. 1 Peter 2:24-25 expresses this understanding of Christ's death,

> He himself bore our sins in his body on the cross, so that, free from sins, we might live for righteousness; by his wounds you have been healed. For you were going astray like sheep, but now you have returned to the shepherd and guardian of your souls.

The substitution metaphor appears in two forms in the New Testament: legal and sacrificial. In the legal form of substitution, one imagines a courtroom setting in which the Law has declared us guilty and sentenced us to death when Jesus steps in to take our punishment and set us free (Rom 8:1-4, Gal 4:4-5). In its sacrificial form, Jesus lays down his life as a sacrifice for his friends. Jesus says, "I am the good shepherd. The good shepherd lays down his life for the sheep" (Jn 10:11). Also, Hebrews 9:26 says, "He has appeared once for all at the end of the age to remove sin by the sacrifice of himself." In either the legal or sacrificial form, the message of substitution is clear: Christ takes our place, pays our penalty, and makes a way to God.

Finally, the third way in which the New Testament portrays Christ's death is as a *demonstration of God's love for us*. While it is important to say "I love you" regularly, those words must be validated and reinforced by loving actions. There must be some demonstration of love beyond the verbal expression. God could have told the world, "I love you" in any number of ways. Yet the divine Creator loved the world so much that mere words could not express it. The Father had to send his only Son (Jn 3:16). Hebrews 1:1-2 frames God's decision this way, "Long ago God spoke to our ancestors in many and various ways by the prophets, but in these last days he has spoken to us by a Son." God chose to demonstrate redeeming love by sending the Son, God's own self, into the fray.

St. Paul asks his readers whom they would be willing to die for—

immediate family notwithstanding. For whom would you give your life? The list is fairly short for most of us:

> Indeed, rarely will anyone die for a righteous person—though perhaps for a good person someone might actually dare to die. But God proves his love for us in that while we still were sinners Christ died for us.
>
> (Rom 5:7-8)

While we were still enemies with God, running as fast as we could away from truth, Christ stretched out his arms, risking everything, even life, for our sake. It is the ultimate proof of our value to God. When confronted by this demonstration, the proper response is to return love in kind out of gratitude.

On a hill just outside the occupied city of Jerusalem around the year 30 CE Jesus of Nazareth was put to death alongside two other criminals by a standard form of Roman execution. What exactly does this one death *mean*? It means reconciliation between God and humanity in the ways we discussed—as the victory of God, as a mediation or substitution on our behalf, and as a demonstration of God's love. The variety of images found in the New Testament for describing this event, and the fact that the Scriptures never settle on just one as the preferred understanding of Christ's death indicates not an ambiguity on Scripture's part, but an important truth: there is a mystery about the meaning of the crucifixion just as there is a mystery about the incarnation. The mystery of Christ's death should not be finalized and cemented into one particular interpretation to the exclusion of all others. Rather, we must emphasize the plurality of New Testament interpretations and protect the mystery of the cross.

He rose. Christians preach Christ crucified. Yet we must say more: Christ did not remain crucified, the Christian witness is that he was resurrected. Resurrection is the crucial counterpart to the crucifixion. Christ is not still on the cross. 2 Timothy 2:8 homes in on the importance of the resurrection for the gospel: "Remember Jesus Christ, raised from the dead, a descendant of David—that is my gospel." Christ not only paid for sins on the cross but was raised from the dead so that we might have life. If Christ is not raised, then it is hard to argue convincingly that Christianity is a faith of new life, new hope. Christianity is a resurrection faith.

In the resurrection, Christ manifests himself as exalted ruler, Lord (Phil 2:5-11). As the Nicene Creed declares, "On the third day he rose again in accordance with the Scriptures; he ascended into heaven and is seated at the right hand of the Father. He will come again in glory to judge the living and the dead, and his kingdom will have no end." Death does not have the last word; Christ overcomes not only sin and the law for our sake, but death as well. As resurrected ruler of this world and the next, the Lord continuously sends his spirit to empower his people for new life and freedom.

"Rebirth of Hope," by Nell Grimm. This piece represents in part the resurrected Lord breaking bread with the disciples at Emmaus, an element inspired from a painting by He Qi, "Supper at Emmaus." But also notice the Phoenix, a medieval symbol of Christ's resurrection, grasping the cross in its talons. Used with permission from the artist and the owner, Timothy Brock.

The Holy Spirit

We now come to the third paragraph of the Creed and the third person of the Trinity: "We believe in the Holy Spirit, the Lord, the giver of life." Who is the Spirit and what does the Spirit do?

The doctrine of the Holy Spirit is intimidating to most believers because it is so abstract. God as spirit seems to make God unwieldy, invisible, and unpredictable—God the phantom. Christian theology must first of all dispel this idea by asserting that the Spirit is not just any spirit blowing about, but the *Holy* Spirit, God's Spirit. The Spirit has a definite identity, namely God's identity and activity. What, though, do we mean by the word "spirit"? An older variation of the word "spirit," Holy *Ghost*, still appears in various places like the Doxology, a traditional piece of verse sung by many Christians every Sunday after the tithes and offerings are collected.

> **The Doxology**
>
> Praise God from whom all blessings flow
> Praise Him all creatures here below
> Praise Him above ye heavenly host
> Praise Father, Son, and Holy Ghost

The word "ghost," derived from Old English, originally meant "spirit." Unfortunately, it has lost its status as a synonym for "spirit" in popular usage; the word "ghost" now conjures images of Casper the Friendly Ghost, not of divine presence.

The Old Testament Hebrew word for Spirit is *ruah*; the New Testament Greek word is *pneuma*. Interestingly, while both are translated "spirit," they also carry the sense of "wind" and "breath." In Genesis 1:2 both senses are present: "[D]arkness covered the face of the deep, while a wind [*ruah*, breath, spirit] from God swept over the face of the waters." In John 3:8 Jesus makes a similar play on words, "The wind [*pneuma*] blows where it chooses, and you hear the sound of it, but you do not know where it comes from or where it is goes. So it is with everyone who is born of the Spirit [*pneuma*]." Both Old and New Testament allow for flexibility of meaning— the Spirit is the breath of God, the wind of heaven. We have a hard time wrapping our minds around the idea of spirit. We can envision a Father and a Son, but how can we picture Spirit? Air, wind, and breath cannot be seen by the eyes, although their effects can be felt on the face, in the nostrils, and heard in the rustling of leaves. So it is with the Spirit. One might see the effects of God's Spirit at work, but no one can see God and live. When we raise the image of Spirit, we are closer to the mystery of God, who is not a body (a wrong impression we might get if we concentrate solely on God as Father or Son). God is eternal, ineffable, uncontainable, spirit.

New Testament scholar Gordon Fee has suggested a most concise characterization of the Holy Spirit with the title of his book, *God's Empowering*

Presence.[9] The Spirit is the presence of God, or *Emmanuel*, "God with us." God's presence is always an empowering, encouraging, uplifting presence. The Holy Spirit is the believing community's "Advocate" or "Helper," as Jesus tells his disciples during his last meal together with them (Jn 14:16, 26). Certainly the Pentecost event in Acts 2 testifies to Jesus' description of the Spirit. The outpouring of the Spirit upon Jesus' disciples on that day empowered them to share the good news of Christ and to come together as the church. The Spirit helped them and emboldened them to move forward and proclaim the good news that Christ had been raised. The Holy Spirit is God's empowering presence.

We have discussed who the Spirit is, but what does the Spirit do? The Nicene Creed suggests at least these pedagogical tasks of the Spirit:

> He has spoken through the Prophets.
> We believe in one holy catholic and apostolic Church.
> We acknowledge one baptism for the forgiveness of sins.
> We look for the resurrection of the dead,
>   and the life of the world to come.[10]

These lines are not just random leftovers that are placed at the end because they do not fit elsewhere in the Creed. These represent the work of God's Spirit. Here we will speak of the *works* of the Spirit, as opposed to the more traditional language of the *gifts* of the Spirit. The language of "gifts" is certainly biblical, but many Christians have distorted it by rigidly cataloguing each and every gift of the Spirit, as if there were a set inventory of gifts from which to choose, and then producing lengthy questionnaires to help eager believers determine which gifts they have been given. Augustine of Hippo, writing as bishop in the early fifth century, offers a wonderful corrective to this tendency to separate out and impersonalize the various gifts when he says "the gift of the Holy Spirit is nothing but the Holy Spirit. So he is the gift of God insofar as he is given to those he is given to."[11] The Holy Spirit does not dispense trinkets, magical powers, or

---

[9]Gordon D. Fee, *God's Empowering Presence: The Holy Spirit in the Letters of Paul* (Peabody MA: Hendrickson, 1994).

[10]"The 'Nicene' Creed" as found in Epiphanius, *Ancoratus*, 118, ca. AD 374. See *Documents of the Christian Church*, 2nd ed., ed Henry Bettenson (London, New York: Oxford University Press, 1963) 26 (or Bettenson's 1st ed., 1943, p. 37).

[11]Augustine, *Trinity* XV.36, Edmund Hill translation, p. 424.

angelic surprises; the Spirit gives himself to believers (Acts 2:37, 8:18, 11:15). The Spirit inhabits the life and actions of the obedient, empowers the church, and woos the hearts of unbelievers. It might clarify and broaden the scope to speak of the works of the Holy Spirit rather than the gifts.

Following the Creed, the first work that the gift of the Spirit produces is inspiration. God's empowering presence inspires. As the Nicene Creed states, the *pneuma* of God is the "giver of life" who has "spoken through the Prophets." Inspiration, as the opposite of expiration, literally means to breathe into, to give life to, to vivify. God's Spirit breathes life into the world and into the words of the prophets. The Holy Spirit inhabits the words of Scripture, such that they become living and active, sharper than a two-edged sword (Heb 4:12). These are more than words on a page; Christians rightly call the Bible the Word of God. The Spirit continues to speak the life-giving Word of God through the words of the Bible to those who will receive them. We need to also make clear that the inspiring and life-giving work of the Holy Spirit is not limited to the Bible, but enjoys a wider range. The divine Spirit inspires not only Scriptures, but people even today to speak and embody the word and work of God. Augustine writes, "Our enlightenment is to participate in the Word, that is, in that *life which is the light of men* (Jn 1:4)."[12] The inspiration of the Spirit opens hearts to Jesus Christ, illuminates the Scriptures, and to helps us "live according to the Spirit" (Rom 8:5; Gal 5:25).

The Holy Spirit also *gathers* the church. The Greek word for church is *ekklesia*. "Church" in our minds connotes a building, a steeple—open the door and there are the people. But *ekklesia* can be translated simply as a "gathering." The first "churches" were not bricks and mortar but gatherings of believers in homes. The Spirit gathers God's own people together for worship and mission. The Nicene Creed characterizes this particular gathering as *one, holy, catholic,* and *apostolic*. Christians confess that because there is only one God, there is only *one* church. Across the globe there are countless cathedrals, chapels, church buildings, worship centers, congregations, associations, and denominations. Nevertheless, all of these add up to one. The church as a whole and all the particular churches that constitute that whole are united in the worship of the one God. We must make "every effort to maintain the unity of the Spirit in the bond of peace" since "there

---

[12]Augustine, *Trinity* IV.1, Edmund Hill translation, p. 155.

is one body and one Spirit, just as you were called to one hope of your calling, one Lord, one faith, one baptism, one God and Father of all" (Eph 4:3-4).

The church taken as a whole is the church *catholic*. Catholic here does not refer exclusively to the Roman Catholics but to the church "universal," "whole," or "total." The church is not limited to one ethnicity or nationality, but transcends race, culture, gender, and age to include all, "for all of you are one in Christ Jesus" (Gal 3:28). In this sense the church is catholic.

The church is also called *holy*. The term can carry the idea of moral rectitude—and Christians are called to live righteous lives and to be pure of heart. But holiness also means to be set apart, called by God, divinely appointed. The Church has been set apart for a task: to proclaim the good news of God's love, redemption, and forgiveness to a hurting world. "So we are ambassadors for Christ, since God is making his appeal through us" (2 Cor 5:20). Finally, the adjective *apostolic* asserts that the church traces its roots back to the apostles of New Testament days. The Christian faith was not invented yesterday; it has a long and beautiful history that trails all the way back to Jesus' disciples. St. Irenaeus of Lyons, the disciple of Polycarp, the disciple of John, the disciple of Jesus, beautifully describes the apostolic transmission of the Word of life "which the prophets announced and Christ confirmed and the apostles handed over and the Church, in the whole world, hands down to her children."[13] For two thousand years now the good news of the church has been transmitted from one generation to the next, from one language to the next, from one culture to all cultures.

Some people may say that the first line of the Creed is the most difficult to confess. If you can confess God, and believe that God exists, then everything else should be a snap. Others say the most difficult line regards Jesus. Most people concede, even if vaguely, that God exists. But to say that this one person Jesus was God in the flesh is a whole other issue. To them, Jesus is the real sticking point of the Christian faith. In our opinion, the most difficult line of the Creed to confess is the one about the church. To say that the church is "one" although everywhere we see it divided, fractured into denominations, and disunited; to say that the church is "holy" although regularly we see Christian leaders who fail, deceive, and forget their mission; to say the church is "catholic" although too often we see dis-

---

[13]Irenaeus, *On the Apostolic Preaching* (Crestwood NY: St. Vladimir's Seminary Press, 1997) 100.

crimination, ethnocentrism, and cultural divisions; to say that the church is "apostolic" although we find Christians who do not know their heritage and go so far as to cut themselves off from their historical and biblical roots—to say these things takes real courage and real faith.

As we take note of the church's shortcomings, we must do away with our dreams and illusions about Christian community and deal with the reality of human behavior in community. Dietrich Bonhoeffer, a German pastor and professor who attempted to hold the believing church together under Nazi rule, admitted that we all enter the church with certain expectations and dreams. He wrote in his classic little book on *Life Together*, "God's grace speedily shatters such dreams."[14] "The sooner the shock of disillusionment comes to an individual and to a community the better for both" because "he who loves his dream of a community more than the Christian community itself becomes a destroyer of the latter."[15] Our illusions about others must be shattered so that our faith and trust in the Spirit's work can be built up. The Christian community is drawn together and united in the Spirit of Christ. "We belong to one another only through and in Jesus Christ."[16]

Forgiveness of sins represents a third act of the Spirit. The Spirit of God in Christ works to forgive, to reconcile, to bring peace and restoration (Acts 3:19, 1 John 1:9). Sin does not stand alone as something Christians affirm; indeed, only in the shadow of forgiveness can we see what sin is. Christians affirm the *forgiveness* of sins, where "sins" represents nothing more than the *object* of forgiveness. "This means that the marks of human unrighteousness and ungodliness are crossed by the deeper marks of the divine forgiveness; that the discord of human defiance is penetrated by the undertones of the divine melody 'Nevertheless.' "[17] Through the chaos of human perversion, destruction, and delusion, God *nevertheless* reaches us with water-calming arms of hope and love.

"Gospel" comes from eliding the old English phrase, "God's spell" or "good spell" (i.e., "good news"), into one word. The Greek word from

---

[14]Dietrich Bonhoeffer, *Life Together*, trans. John Doberstein (New York: Harper & Row, 1954) 26.

[15]Bonhoeffer, *Life Together*, 27.

[16]Bonhoeffer, *Life Together*, 21.

[17]Karl Barth, *Epistle to the Romans* (New York: Oxford University Press, 1968) 95.

which this phrase derives is *euangelion* (*eu*—good + *angelion*—message) and was used by the early church to title the four accounts of Jesus' life— the *euangelion* or gospels of Matthew, Mark, Luke, and John. Elsewhere in the New Testament, *euangelion* is used to describe the essential message of the Christian faith (Acts 20:24; Eph 6:15). The angel of the Lord who appeared to the shepherds the night Jesus was born announced, "I am bringing you good news of great joy for all the people: to you is born this day in the city of David a Savior, who is the Messiah, the Lord" (Luke 2:10-11). The news of Jesus is good news of great joy, the news of forgiveness and redemption. From the word *euangelion* we also get the word "evangelism," which too often carries the negative connotation of a high-pressure sales pitch. If we understand it rightly, though, evangelism is *not* about first convincing people that their lives are full of sin and void of meaning and then offering them a remedy for their guilt and waste. Evangelism is first of all an announcement of glad tidings—the happy news that God in Christ has forgiven the sins of the world, ours included—"he is the atoning sacrifice for our sins and not for ours only but also for the sins of the whole world" (1 John 2:2). The price has been paid so that the guilt and waste of pride and apathy have no power left in them. Reconciliation, not sin, is what Christians should preach and proclaim.

The good news of the Spirit's work of forgiveness provides an opportunity to highlight a countercultural impulse in the Christian faith. It could be argued that "and justice for all" names the highest American value. Americans expect above all for the government to ensure fairness and equality in every field of life. If someone cheats, steals, or kills, we want that person brought to justice so as to keep the balance in society. For Christians, however, justice can never be the highest priority because justice can only even the score, it can only give someone his or her due. It cannot bring healing, redemption, or reconciliation. While justice and fairness may be necessary for maintaining social order, they do not have the final word. Forgiveness stands as the highest Christian value. After the scales of the blindfolded Lady Justice have been balanced, still the gentle hands of the Spirit have work to do. One of the most important witnesses Christians can offer the world today is prison ministry: to people who "got what they deserved" Christians extend the offer of restoration. Even after justice has been served, convicts need to be restored to their God, their family and friends, their victims, and to themselves.

At his home synagogue in Nazareth, Jesus announced the purpose of his ministry by quoting from Isaiah 61:1-2a:

> The Spirit of the Lord is upon me,
>   because he has anointed me
>   to bring good news to the poor.
> He has sent me to proclaim release to the captives
>   and recovery of sight to the blind,
>   to let the oppressed go free,
> to proclaim the year of the Lord's favor.   (as quoted in Luke 4:18-19)

Elsewhere, Jesus commended visiting prisoners as the kind of action that would distinguish his true followers from false ones (Matt 25:35-36). Charles Colson's twin ministries of Justice Fellowship and Prison Fellowship work within prisons to set up Bible studies and Christian communities of support and outside of prison to end systematic abuses and unjust punishments. Such ministries witness powerfully to the possibilities of forgiveness and reconciliation.

Finally, the work of the Holy Spirit involves *the resurrection of the dead*. What can this mean? Does resurrection mean the same thing as the immortality of the soul? Does it mean physical bodies are to be dusted off and reassembled? Perhaps the best place to begin a biblical discussion of resurrection is 1 Corinthians 15, one of the most extensive biblical discussions we have on the topic. Paul sees it as an urgent task to clarify resurrection to the churches at Corinth, little home fellowships which he himself established over the course of about eighteen months in Corinth before sailing on to Ephesus. As he writes to his beloved but troubled Corinthians about resurrection, he seems to have in mind a couple of misunderstandings of the idea that he wants to correct.

First, there is the classical Greek view of life after death, which is basically a belief that the soul separates from the body at the moment of death and transitions into heavenly immortality. It has much in common with the standard Hollywood portrayal of life after death. At the moment of death, the soul springs forth from the exhausted body like a bird from a cage and flutters off to immortality. I call it the Hollywood view because in most movies about life after death, when someone dies, the audience sees the translucent soul lift out of the body and float up toward the sky or to some bleach-white space. The body is a prison for the soul, prone to disease, easily tired, limited in so many ways. The soul is your true self, the pure, essential, eternal "you" that is released at death. A strong body-soul dualism characterizes this view, a dualism that not only the Greeks but most

Americans take for granted. In this view, resurrection of the body is neither needed nor desired. The soul leaves the body far behind as it races off to eternity. Paul notices that there are some in the Corinthian house churches who "say there is no resurrection of the dead" (1 Cor 15:12).

The opposite of this Hollywood or Greek view might be something like a physicalist or literalist understanding of resurrection, in which the dead self is reassembled and resuscitated at the Last Judgment. The physicalist view avoids any body-soul dualism because there is no soul that departs the body, rather death strikes a final note for the whole self; when you die, you really die. The entire self—body, soul and all—must be reconstituted in the resurrection.

According to Paul, neither option is viable. Neither option represents Christian resurrection. "But someone will ask, 'How are the dead raised? With what kind of body do they come?'" (1 Cor 15:35). This seems like a logical question if resurrection is not the soul floating off to bodiless immortality or the body being magically reconstituted out of decay. What else could resurrection mean? Paul's answer, however, is sharp: "Fool! What you sow does not come to life unless it dies. And as for what you sow, you do not sow the body that is to be, but a bare seed" (1 Cor 15:36-37). He compares our present existence with the existence of a seed. Once it drops and is covered in the earth, it breaks open and spawns amazing new forms of life. Who would guess that those enormously strong and tall trees out your window, with their leaves, branches, bark and roots, came from a tiny little marble of a seed? These are facts of nature you have to be taught. When presented with a bucket full of different kinds of seeds, you cannot guess (without a great deal of expert help) which is which. Which will produce trees and which bushes and which weeds? What kind of tree or bush or weed? How then can we guess what we will look like in the resurrection? "What is sown is perishable, what is raised is imperishable. It is sown in dishonor, it is raised in glory. It is sown in weakness, it is raised in power. It is sown a physical body, it is raised a spiritual body" (1 Cor 15:42-44). Paul gives a nod toward both the Greeks and the physicalists with his notion of the "spiritual body." In the resurrection we will be recognizably ourselves in "body," but the body will not be in the form to which we are accustomed, it will be "spiritual." How can we wrap our minds around the idea of a resurrection that is both spiritual and bodily? Paul admits that this is "a mystery," that "we will all be changed, in a moment, in a twinkling of an eye" (1 Cor 15:51-52).

There is at least one analogy for understanding this mystery given in Scripture: the resurrected Jesus. "Christ has been raised from the dead, the first fruits of those who have died" (1 Cor 15:20) and so has become "the pioneer and perfecter of our faith" (Heb 12:2). After his resurrection, Jesus appeared to his disciples in a real body, indeed he appeared to hundreds over a forty day period, eating a breakfast of fish with the disciples, inviting Thomas to touch his wounds. He showed them he was as real as he ever was. But something was different. In the garden Mary does not recognize him until he speaks her name; two disciples walk and talk with him all the way to Emmaus, and yet do not recognize him until he breaks bread with them. He appears and disappears at will, even within locked rooms. More mysteriously, he bears the marks of death, unbandaged gashes in his side and nail marks in his hands and feet, yet he lives. In the resurrected Lord we have our first glimpses of the spiritual bodies we are to become—recognizably ourselves and yet changed. So says Augustine, "we can justly hope that [resurrection and ascension] are going to happen to us because we have believed that they happened to him. So because what has originated in him has passed over into eternity, so too will what has originated in us pass over when faith arrives at truth."[18]

As tempting as it is, we should not allow Jesus' example or Paul's words bog us down in metaphysical speculations about the afterlife. The point of the Christian confession of resurrection is to say that even in death, God's Spirit remains with us. Resurrection is the final work of God's empowering presence. Although we will depart from our loved ones when life is extinguished, God will not depart from us. This is not a new insight, but the basic Christian message declared all along: God will not in the end abandon his creation. The journey of faith does not cease with death. Salvation means new life. The resurrection in the Spirit means new life. Creation is re-created. Our response should be one of joy and praise as is Paul's in 1 Corinthians 15:54-57:

> When this perishable body puts on imperishability, and this mortal body
> puts on immortality, then the saying that is written will be fulfilled:
>   'Death has been swallowed up in victory."

---

[18]Augustine, *Trinity* IV.4, Edmund Hill translation, p. 170.

"Where, O death, is your victory?
Where, O death, is your sting?'
The sting of death is sin, and the power of sin is the law. But thanks be to
God who gives us the victory through our Lord Jesus Christ.

* * *

Christian Theology Suggestions for Further Reading

Badham, Roger A., editor. *Introduction to Christian Theology: Contemporary North American Perspectives.* Louisville: Westminster/John Knox, 1998.

Clapp, Rodney. *A Peculiar People: The Church as Culture in a Post-Christian Society.* Downers Grove IL: InterVarsity Press, 1996.

McClendon, James Wm. Jr. *Systematic Theology.* Volume 2: *Doctrine.* Nashville: Abingdon Press, 1994.

Grenz, Stanley J., David Guretzki, and Cherith Fee Nordling. *Pocket Dictionary of Theological Terms.* Downers Grove IL: InterVarsity Press, 1999.

Hauerwas, Stanley M., and William H. Willimon. *The Truth about God: The Ten Commandments in Christian Life.* Nashville: Abingdon Press, 1999.

Jenson, Robert W. *Systematic Theology: The Triune God.* Volume 1. New York: Oxford University Press, 1997.

Jinkins, Michael. *Invitation to Theology.* Downers Grove IL: InterVarsity Press, 2001.

Lash, Nicholas. *Believing Three Ways In One God: A Reading of the Apostles' Creed.* Notre Dame IN: University of Notre Dame Press, 1993.

Laytham, D. Brent, editor. *God Is Not: Religious, Nice, "One of Us," An American, A Capitalist.* Grand Rapids MI: Brazos Press, 2004.

McGrath, Alister E. *Theology: The Basics.* Oxford UK: Blackwell, 2004.

Miles, Margaret R. *The Word Made Flesh: A History of Christian Thought.* Oxford UK: Blackwell, 2005.

Norris, Kathleen. *Amazing Grace: A Vocabulary of Faith.* New York: Riverhead Books, 1998.

O'Keefe, John J., and R. R. Reno. *Sanctified Vision: An Introduction to Early Christian Interpretation of the Bible.* Baltimore: John Hopkins University Press, 2005.

Olson, Roger E. *The Mosaic of Christian Belief: Twenty Centuries of Unity & Diversity.* Downers Grove IL: InterVarsity Press, 2002.

_____. *The Story of Christian Theology: Twenty Centuries of Tradition & Reform.* Downers Grove IL: InterVarsity Press, 1999.

Olson, Roger E., and Adam C. English. *Pocket History of Theology.* Downers Grove IL: InterVarsity Press, 2005.

Peterson, Eugene H. *Christ Plays in Ten Thousand Places: A Conversation in Spiritual Theology.* Grand Rapids MI: Eerdmans, 2005.

_____. *Eat This Book: A Conversation in the Art of Spiritual Reading*. Grand Rapids MI: Eerdmans, 2006.

Placher, William. *Jesus The Savior: The Meaning of Jesus Christ for Christian Faith*. Louisville: Westminster/John Knox, 2001.

_____. *The Triune God: An Essay in Postliberal Theology*. Louisville: Westminster/John Knox, 2007.

_____. *Narratives of a Vulnerable God: Christ, Theology, and Scripture*. Louisville: Westminster/John Knox Press, 1994.

Willis, David. *Clues to the Nicene Creed: A Brief Outline of the Faith*. Grand Rapids MI: Eerdmans, 2005.

Index